The farmer's tour through the East of England. Being the register of a journey through various counties of this Kingdom, to enquire into the state of agriculture, &c. ... By the author of the Farmer's letters, ... Volume 2 of 4

Arthur Young

ECCO
PRINT EDITIONS

Eighteenth Century
Collections Online
Print Editions

Gale ECCO Print Editions

Relive history with *Eighteenth Century Collections Online*, now available in print for the independent historian and collector. This series includes the most significant English-language and foreign-language works printed in Great Britain during the eighteenth century, and is organized in seven different subject areas including literature and language; medicine, science, and technology; and religion and philosophy. The collection also includes thousands of important works from the Americas.

The eighteenth century has been called "The Age of Enlightenment." It was a period of rapid advance in print culture and publishing, in world exploration, and in the rapid growth of science and technology – all of which had a profound impact on the political and cultural landscape. At the end of the century the American Revolution, French Revolution and Industrial Revolution, perhaps three of the most significant events in modern history, set in motion developments that eventually dominated world political, economic, and social life.

In a groundbreaking effort, Gale initiated a revolution of its own: digitization of epic proportions to preserve these invaluable works in the largest online archive of its kind. Contributions from major world libraries constitute over 175,000 original printed works. Scanned images of the actual pages, rather than transcriptions, recreate the works ***as they first appeared.***

Now for the first time, these high-quality digital scans of original works are available via print-on-demand, making them readily accessible to libraries, students, independent scholars, and readers of all ages.

For our initial release we have created seven robust collections to form one the world's most comprehensive catalogs of 18th century works.

Initial Gale ECCO Print Editions collections include:

History and Geography
Rich in titles on English life and social history, this collection spans the world as it was known to eighteenth-century historians and explorers. Titles include a wealth of travel accounts and diaries, histories of nations from throughout the world, and maps and charts of a world that was still being discovered. Students of the War of American Independence will find fascinating accounts from the British side of conflict.

Social Science

Delve into what it was like to live during the eighteenth century by reading the first-hand accounts of everyday people, including city dwellers and farmers, businessmen and bankers, artisans and merchants, artists and their patrons, politicians and their constituents. Original texts make the American, French, and Industrial revolutions vividly contemporary.

Medicine, Science and Technology

Medical theory and practice of the 1700s developed rapidly, as is evidenced by the extensive collection, which includes descriptions of diseases, their conditions, and treatments. Books on science and technology, agriculture, military technology, natural philosophy, even cookbooks, are all contained here.

Literature and Language

Western literary study flows out of eighteenth-century works by Alexander Pope, Daniel Defoe, Henry Fielding, Frances Burney, Denis Diderot, Johann Gottfried Herder, Johann Wolfgang von Goethe, and others. Experience the birth of the modern novel, or compare the development of language using dictionaries and grammar discourses.

Religion and Philosophy

The Age of Enlightenment profoundly enriched religious and philosophical understanding and continues to influence present-day thinking. Works collected here include masterpieces by David Hume, Immanuel Kant, and Jean-Jacques Rousseau, as well as religious sermons and moral debates on the issues of the day, such as the slave trade. The Age of Reason saw conflict between Protestantism and Catholicism transformed into one between faith and logic -- a debate that continues in the twenty-first century.

Law and Reference

This collection reveals the history of English common law and Empire law in a vastly changing world of British expansion. Dominating the legal field is the *Commentaries of the Law of England* by Sir William Blackstone, which first appeared in 1765. Reference works such as almanacs and catalogues continue to educate us by revealing the day-to-day workings of society.

Fine Arts

The eighteenth-century fascination with Greek and Roman antiquity followed the systematic excavation of the ruins at Pompeii and Herculaneum in southern Italy; and after 1750 a neoclassical style dominated all artistic fields. The titles here trace developments in mostly English-language works on painting, sculpture, architecture, music, theater, and other disciplines. Instructional works on musical instruments, catalogs of art objects, comic operas, and more are also included.

The BiblioLife Network

This project was made possible in part by the BiblioLife Network (BLN), a project aimed at addressing some of the huge challenges facing book preservationists around the world. The BLN includes libraries, library networks, archives, subject matter experts, online communities and library service providers. We believe every book ever published should be available as a high-quality print reproduction; printed on-demand anywhere in the world. This insures the ongoing accessibility of the content and helps generate sustainable revenue for the libraries and organizations that work to preserve these important materials.

The following book is in the "public domain" and represents an authentic reproduction of the text as printed by the original publisher. While we have attempted to accurately maintain the integrity of the original work, there are sometimes problems with the original work or the micro-film from which the books were digitized. This can result in minor errors in reproduction. Possible imperfections include missing and blurred pages, poor pictures, markings and other reproduction issues beyond our control. Because this work is culturally important, we have made it available as part of our commitment to protecting, preserving, and promoting the world's literature.

GUIDE TO FOLD-OUTS MAPS and OVERSIZED IMAGES

The book you are reading was digitized from microfilm captured over the past thirty to forty years. Years after the creation of the original microfilm, the book was converted to digital files and made available in an online database.

In an online database, page images do not need to conform to the size restrictions found in a printed book. When converting these images back into a printed bound book, the page sizes are standardized in ways that maintain the detail of the original. For large images, such as fold-out maps, the original page image is split into two or more pages

Guidelines used to determine how to split the page image follows:

• Some images are split vertically; large images require vertical and horizontal splits.
• For horizontal splits, the content is split left to right.
• For vertical splits, the content is split from top to bottom.
• For both vertical and horizontal splits, the image is processed from top left to bottom right.

THE

FARMER's TOUR

THROUGH THE

EAST of ENGLAND.

BEING

The Regifter of a Journey through various Counties
of this Kingdom, to enquire into the State
of AGRICULTURE, &c.

CONTAINING,

I The particular Methods of
cultivating the Soil

II The Conduct of live Stock,
and the modern Syftem of
Breeding.

III The State of Population, the
Poor, Labour, Provifions, &c.

IV The Rental and Value of

the Soil, and its Divifion into
Farms, with various Circumftances attending their Size
and State

V The Minutes of above five
hundred original Experiments,
communicated by feveral of
the Nobility, Gentry, &c

WITH

Other Subjects that tend to explain the prefent State of
ENGLISH HUSBANDRY

By the Author of the FARMER'S LETTERS, and the
TOURS through the North and South of England.

VOL. II

LONDON

Printed for W STRAHAN, W. NICOLL, No 51, St,
Paul's Church-Yard, B. COLLINS, at Salifbury,
and J BALFOUR, at Edinburgh,
MDCCLXXI.

CONTENTS

OF THE

SECOND VOLUME.

CONTENTS.

THE
FARMER's TOUR
THROUGH
ENGLAND.

AT *Maſſingham*, north of *Runcton*, have been practiſed many of the moſt conſiderable improvements that have been known in *Norfolk*. This country, before the great works done by incloſing and marling, was all a wild ſheep-walk; but through the uncommon ſpirit of many great farmers, has been advanced in value to an amazing degree.

The marle has been laid on in the proportion of 70 loads an acre, which has generally laſted 25 years; after that, many farmers have tried 30 loads more, but without ſucceſs.

Mr. *Carr* of this place, who has had long experience in the marle huſbandry, recommends laying on no more than 35 or 40 loads; and then as much more in three or four years, by which means it will far better incorporate with the foil. But the beft way of ufing it after the firft moderate marling, is to form compofts of it with dung; fo mixed, it works better in the foil. Mr. *Carr* thinks the beft criterion of marle is to try it in water; if it is good, it will fall at once and diffolve, and make the water white; but as to the effervefcence with acids, he has found the bad forts have that quality more than the good, which is very uncommon.— He is further of opinion, that marle fhould be laid on in autumn, that the weather may fhatter it.

Oil-cake, as a manure, is ufed by many farmers. Mr. *Carr*, in compliance with the general opinion, tried it in a large extent— he laid out 140 *l.* in oil-cake for one crop, but received very little benefit from it. On another occafion he fattened fome bullocks on oil-cake, and the dung he raifed from them, was twice as beneficial as the cakes themfelves fpread on the land: excellent manure!

Folding is here greatly depended on: they practife it throughout the year except juft at lambing time. Mr. *Carr*, from an attentive obfervation,

obfervation, prefers the winter folding much
to that of fummer : this muft be owing to
the fun exhaling the virtue of dung in the
latter feafon.

Six hundred fheep will fold 40 acres in
the year.

The foil here is a light fandy loam; and
lets in general at 8 s. an acre. The courfe
of crops is,

    1. Turnips, fed on the land.

    2. Barley or oats.

    3. Clover one year, without ray-grafs.

    4. Wheat.

The barley yields on an average 4 or $4\frac{1}{2}$
quarters *per* acre ; and wheat from $2\frac{1}{2}$ quarters to 5 : the average about 3. Turnips
are worth, one year with another, 27 s. an
acre : 400 fat fheep, Mr. *Carr* calculates,
will eat a good acre every day; but this feems
a very large allowance. They give an acre
at a time, and always pull them up with
cromes or hooks a day before the fheep are
let in : they do not pen the fheep, but move
on the hurdles, taking in an acre at a time,
and ufing but one row. They are fed off
fometimes with bullocks, but it is a bad way;
for they find that one acre drawn and car-

ried

ried off, will go as far as three on the land.
Their ftock fheep they put to turnips three
weeks before lambing time.

At the firft improvement, it was common
to take two crops of turnips running, for
cleaning the land, and it anfwered very greatly · the barley fown after the two crops was
much better than any ever known in the
common courfe. Mr. *Carr* has had 6½ quarters *per* acre in that manner.

They mow the firft crop of clover for hay,
get 1½ load an acre, and feed the fecond;
and they get better wheat after this management than after feeding through the whole
year. If the clover is fown as above for
mowing, they ufe but 10*lb.* of feed an acre:
but on that land defigned for fheep, they
fow a bufhel of ray-grafs with it. A fack
of ray-grafs fhould weigh 8 or 9 ftone.

The profit of ftock fheep is reckoned;

Lamb,	–	–	0 7 6
Wool,	–	–	0 1 0
			0 8 6

And to fhew from the inftance of fheep, the
amazing improvement of this country; it is
a fact, that as many fheep are now kept as
before

before the inclofure, while the whole country was fheep-walk. Mr. *Carr* keeps 500
ftock fheep, befides 340 fat ones ; and there
were but 600 before, of fo inferior a quality
that his 500 are much fuperior in product.
Upon Mrs. *Pigg*'s farm only 1700 were kept
while all was walk ; and her prefent flock
amounts to that number of much better
fheep.—If thefe inftances are not decifive in
favour of inclofing open lands, and do not
prove the abfurdity of the affertions that
arable improvements hurt our woollen manufactures, and therein prejudice the general
interefts of the ftate—Nothing can, nor is
there a plain fact in the whole circle of do-
meftic politics.

Land fells at 28 years purchafe. Some
tythes are gathered, but in general they are
compounded for in the great. Poor rates,
1 *s*. 3 *d*. in the pound.

In their tillage they ufe but two horfes in
a plough, all wheel ones ; and do two acres
on an average in a day. The price 2 *s*, 6 *d*,
an acre.

Mr. *Carr* has tried the cultivation of fpring
wheat ; he finds it to turn out as well as any
other crops he has had. The grain is equal

to the beſt in the country, fine ſoft corn, not hard or ſteely : his crop was 3 quarters *per* acre.   The particulars of Mr. *Carr*'s farm are as follow :

1000 Acres in all	30 Horſes
100 Wheat	2 Cows
200 Barley	20 Fatting beaſts
40 Oats	500 Stock ſheep
200 Turnips	300 Fatting ditto
250 Clover	in winter
60 Peaſe, &c.	40 Ditto in ſum-
150 Various	mer.

Being in the neighbourhood of *Weaſen-ham*, where Mr. *Billing* lives, the farmer who received ſeveral premiums from the *London* ſociety for the culture of carrots, I determined to requeſt a ſight of the fields in which he raiſed them ; and alſo to enquire into the truth of the report I had heard, that he had for ſome years totally done with car-rots.   I viewed the land, and tried the depth of it with a ſtrong ſtick ; it is a ſandy loam, moſt excellent turnip-land ; it was cropped with that root, and a finer appearance never was ſeen ; I could not thruſt the ſtick with all my force deeper than 6 inches, which ſurprized me.   Mr. *Billing* informed me that

he

he ploughed no deeper for the carrots than for common crops, but yet he had many roots 16 inches long, and 15 or 16 inches in circumference. He left off the culture after the crop of which he publifhed the account : this the world will doubtlefs think very extraordinary ; for nothing could be clearer or more decifive than the advantages there fet forth : the profit evidently beat that of turnips by many degrees. I afked him the reafon of his not continuing the culture : he faid, They did not anfwer. I defired to know why. He replied, that the expences were fo heavy that they could not do. Turnips are gained much eafier, and at a much lighter expence.—This I found his general opinion. I enquired more minutely into a comparifon of the two roots ; but Mr. *Billing* anfwered me only in generals.

This is a very critical circumftance in the hiftory of carrots. The enemies of the culture cry out, *See how finely this new hufbandry turns out, that has been fo praifed ! The only man that ever extended it over a large fpace of ground has given it up. Does not this fufficiently condemn it ?* This is the way in which many hereabouts, and doubtlefs elfe-

B 4　　　　　　　where

where, will reafon. To enter into a criticifm on any man's conduct while it is merely private, would be impertinent; but the general intereft of half the kingdom is concerned in the prefent cafe I fhall therefore offer a few remarks to fhew, that Mr. *Billing*'s conduct ought by no means to prevent the carrot culture from becoming common.

He condemned carrots in general, but it was only from general ideas: he praifed turnips in a rational manner; I plough fo often, at fuch an expence, hoe them for fo much, and they pay me fuch a fum, at the fame time that they clean the land; therefore I adhere to turnips. This was decifive; but now for carrots,—The medal was reverfed; he knew nothing of the matter; he had no idea of the expence; confequently it was magnified: he talked of 20*s* an acre; then of 30*s*. and at laft of 50*s*. and 3*l*. When I afked him the value of an acre; *he could not tell*. What fheep will it maintain? *He could not fay*. What beafts will it fat? *He did not know*. What *profit* will an acre pay in the grofs? *He was not certain*. And, after another query or two—*He knew nothing at all of the matter.*

The

The reader will naturally afk, *how can this be with a man who wrote fo clear an account of carrots?* In anfwer to which I would recommend to the fociety, to give their premiums to people who not only really perform the experiments required, but alfo give their own accounts of them; if a man cannot write, he fhould dictate—but the perfon who writes down his account ought not to fupply any thing but the mere pen. There is a general turn in Mr. *Billing's* pamphlet in favour of carrots, that fpeaks as ftrongly as the experiments themfelves : all which is directly contrary to his opinion. To fome of my queftions he told me there was a book publifhed about carrots; in the fame breath that he mentioned circumftances quite contrary to any in the pamphlet.

I take the real cafe to be this; he was advifed to try carrots, but againft his own opinion, and finding them better than he expected at firft, repeated the trials for fome time. When he came to enlarge the culture to whole fields, the attention they required in hoeing and the expence being much fuperior to turnips, gave him a difguft :— the largenefs of his bufinefs made more

compendious

compendious crops agreeable—his men went regularly to work with turnips almoſt without directions ; nor would he ſpare a ſufficiency of hands from the other crops to do juſtice to the carrots : and theſe circumſtances, I have little doubt, were the reaſon of his leaving off the practice. But as to drawing up an account of all the expences, with every diſadvantage of the crop, and then ſtriking a balance to diſcover its real merit—he never did it, and I will venture to pronounce he could not do it ; for he took not minutes ſufficient for the purpoſe—and thoſe which he did take he has now forgotten. Let us for a moment examine his account of his crop, in 1763, of 30½ acres, and calculate, as well as his *data* will allow, the expences and profit.

EXPENCES.

	£		
Ploughing 13½ acres thrice, at 2 s. 6 d. - -	£.5	1	3
Ditto 17 acres twice -	4	5	0
Dunging 3 acres, ſuppoſe we allow 12 load an acre, at 2 s. 6 d.	4	10	0
Seed, 30½ acres, at 4 lb. an acre	8	2	0
Sowing, ſuppoſe 6 d. an acre	0	15	3
Carry over,	22	13	6

Brought over,	£.22	13	6
Harrowing, fuppofe -	0	15	0
Firft hand-hoeing, at 11 s.	16	16	6
Harrowing - -	0	7	6
Second hand-hoeing, at 4 s. 6 d.	6	17	3
Harrowing - - -	0	7	6
Taking up, fuppofe 10 s. an acre	15	5	0
Rent, at 14 s. - -	21	7	0
Total expence,	84	9	3

Or 2 l. 16 s. 3 d. per acre.

The produce in the account is calculated various ways; firft it is by loads: the crop was 510 cart loads of carrots, equal to 300 loads of hay in the confumption.

300 Loads of hay, at 40 s.	600	0	0
Expences - -	84	9	3
Clear profit -	515	10	9

Or per acre 17 l. 5 s.

300 Loads of hay, at 35 s.	525	0	0
Expences - - -	84	9	3
Clear profit -	440	10	9

Or per acre 14 l. 13 s. 7 d.

300 Loads of hay, at 30s.	£.450	0	0
Expences - - -	84	9	3
Clear profit -	365	10	9

Or *per* acre 12 l. 3s.

I have given thefe various prices for the ufe of different places, where hay fells at different rates.

The calculation of the produce is by the ftock maintained.

By fattening 12 neat beafts; 49 fhearing wethers; 5 cows, an heifer, and 17 *Scotch* bullocks —yielded clear profit -	£.108	0	0
Feeding a dairy of 35 cows, and a flock of 21 fcore fheep, three weeks, in the month of *April**	20	0	0
Carry over,	128	0	0

---

* This is the calculation in the pamphlet, but the cows at 1s. 6d. and the fheep at 3d. a week, come to 23 l. 12s 6d. And turnips, it is faid, were gone; I leave the reader therefore to judge whether this is adequate.

Feeding

Brought over,   -   £.128   0   0

Feeding 16 cart-horfes from *November* to the latter end of *May*; 2 loads of carrots in this application faved 1 of hay *   35   0   0

Many fwine fed; but no account taken   ⸸   -   0   0   0

Total produce,	-	163	0 0
Total expence,	-	84	9 3
Clear profit,	⸗	78	10 9

Or *per* acre 2 *l*. 5 *s*. 1 *d*.

Add to this, that the barley fown after carrots undunged in the middle of turnips dunged, was better than after the turnips—which is a prodigious fuperiority.

According to the loweft of thefe accounts, the carrots pay more in CLEAR *profit* by at leaft 1 5 *s*. an acre, than any turnips in this country pay in TOTAL *produce*. If this is not decifive in their favour, I know not what can be.

In the preceding account, 10 *s*. an acre is allowed for taking up, whereas many were ploughed up · which I will venture to affert is a flovenly and lofing practice.

---

* No notice is taken of the faving of oats, which is the plain way of calculating

All thefe carrots, except what were given to the horfes, were fed on the ground like turnips: this is a deduction from their produce of at leaft two-thirds: it is every where known that one acre drawn and given in ftalls, or a warm yard, will go as far as three in the field. The objections at page 15 of the pamphlet, are trivial, and fuppofe bad management in the method difapproved. Beafts in a warm yard well littered with ftubble, and fheds around it, do not founder: nor need the ftale be loft; and as to the beef not being fo good, it is an abfurdity.

After thefe accounts drawn from Mr. *Billing*'s pamphlet, what are we to fay to his leaving off the culture, under the idea of *its not anfwering?* Is it not very evident, that he has declined the moft profitable crop that ever his farm produced? This is the effect of farmers not keeping accounts: they talk of experience; but written experience in thefe cafes alone deferves the name. Mr. *Billing*'s general notions (which are what farmers call experience) are diametrically contrary to the practice which he found excellent, and recommended as fuch to the public. He is

not

not peculiar in this, for the profit of crops to which they are not heartily inclined, will never have their experience an advocate.

About *Sandringham*, the feat of *Henry Cornish Henley*, Efq. are very confiderable tracts of fandy land, which are applied at prefent only to the feeding rabbits: it is a very barren foil, but not I apprehend incapable of cultivation; it lets from 1 *s.* 6 *d.* to 2 *s.* 6 *d.* an acre in warrens: Mr. *Henley* has tried fome experiments on it lately, with a view to difcover how far it will anfwer cultivating. The value of it is prodigioufly advanced by planting; that gentleman has formed feveral plantations, which thrive extremely: all the firs do well; and will pay a better rent for the land than any hufbandry.

Much of the country improves in foil about *Snettifham*. The better fort of lands there are generally thrown into what is properly called the *Norfolk* hufbandry.

Farms rife from 20 *l.* to 370 *l.* a year; but are in general from 70 *l.* to 90 *l.* The foil is either fand or fandy loam, on a chalky marle. The rent from 10 *s.* to 14 *s.* an acre: but the poor warren fands towards *Lynn* from 1 *s.* to 2 *s.* 6 *d.* an acre. The courfe moft common is,

1. Turnips	times one year
2. Barley	but by the beſt
3.Clover and ray-	farmers 2 years
graſs, ſome- 4. Wheat.	

For wheat they plough but once, ſow 3 buſhels, and gain on an average 3 quarters. Rye they ſubſtitute on ſome lands inſtead of wheat, ſow 3 buſhels, and get 3 ½ quarters For barley they plough 3 times, ſow 2 ½ or 3 buſhels, and get 3 quarters. For oats they plough but once, ſow 4 buſhels an acre, and get on a medium 4 quarters. For peaſe they give but one earth ; and reckon the average crop at 2 quarters.

Coleſeed they cultivate both for feeding ſheep and alſo for ſeed. They eat it off time enough to ſow wheat ; but the value of the food is not much. They feed thoſe crops they intend for ſeed, but do miſchief by it ; the crops vary from 3 ½ to 10 quarters. They always ſow wheat after it.

They plough four times for turnips, and hand-hoe twice. They draw ſome for fatting beaſts, but in general eat it off with ſheep. The average value 35 s. an acre.

Clover they often mow twice for hay the firſt year ; but always feed it the ſecond.

A few

A few tares are fown to foil horfes with in the ftable, green; but it is not common.

Some buck-wheat is fown, which they feed on the land with various cattle, and fow wheat after it. A little hemp is beginning to be cultivated on fpots of ftrong land; but not much.

They fold all their fheep, in winter as well as fummer. Salt has been tried as a manure by a few farmers, who have bought whole fhip-loads. It cofts 3 _l._ 5 _s._ a ton; and 10 _s._ more in expences, and a ton does for 3 acres. It was tried on a good loamy foil for wheat, this year, and the crop promifes fo greatly, that the farmer has bought a confiderable quantity more.

Oil cake is likewife much ufed; they break it to pieces not larger than walnuts by mills; one ton, at 3 _l._ 10 _s._ to 4 _l._ 10 _s._ does three acres. It is attended with very great benefit, but it lafts only one crop.

Lime they have tried, burnt from chalk: it does good; but is not comparable to marle. It does not laft.

Marle is their grand manure; they lay 80 loads an acre; it is a fine fat fort, white, and lafts from 14 to 20 years. They do not chop their ftubbles; but their hay they ftack at home.

The beft grafs lets at 20*s.* an acre : They ufe it for fattening fheep ; an acre will carry 5 or 6 fat wethers.

A cow will, in the beft part of the feafon, give 7 or 8*lb.* of butter a week : and the quantity of milk 3 or 4 gallons a day. The annual produce about 5*l.* 5*s.* a year. They underftand very well the ufe of a dairy in keeping fwine : they have much larger ftocks on account of their cows.— A dairy-maid can take care of 20. They keep them in winter in the yard, and give them many turnips. There are large tracts of frefh water marfhes . they buy beafts for them in the fpring, and after the fummer feeding give them turnips : they buy lean at from 7*l.* to 12*l.*; and fell at nearly double thofe prices. An ox-hide is worth from 15*s.* to 20 *s.*. it is now of double the value it was 25 years ago.

Breeding flocks rife to 7 or 800. The profit is,

Lamb,	-	-	£.0	7	0
Wool,	-	-	0	1	0
			0	8	0

The wether flocks they manage in the following manner; about *Lammas* they buy in wether lambs 6 or 7 months old; and keep them lean on ftubbles, and offal turnips, giving them the leavings of the old ftock of fat wethers; after which they are well kept through the fummer on graffes, and folded all the time. Soon after *Michaelmas*, they are put to turnips; and are fold fat from *Candlemas* to *May-day*, and fome even to *Midfummer:* they give them ray-grafs and clover in the fpring as foon as turnips are done. This conduct of fheep is reckoned much the moft profitable method of managing them. They ftock their graffes with 4 to an acre; and reckon that fpace of turnips will keep 10 from *Michaelmas* to *Candlemas.*

In their tillage, they reckon 16 horfes neceffary to 500 acres of arable land. They ufe 2 in a plough, do two acres a day; and in feed times 3, but it is with 4 horfes; 2 in the morning, and 2 in the afternoon. One man looks after 4 or 5 horfes, and every day ploughs 2 or 3 acres with 4 of them. They plough about 5 inches deep; and the price is 2 *s.* 6 *d.* an acre. The an-

nual

nual expence of a horfe they calculate at
5 *l.*; feed them much with ftraw cut into
chaff. They begin to break their ftubbles
for a fallow foon after winter corn fowing.
Wheel ploughs only are ufed; they find
that they can do more a day with them
than with fwing ones, and at the fame
time much truer.

The hire of a cart, 4 horfes, and a driver
per day, 10 *s.*

In the ftocking farms, they reckon 3000 *l.*
neceffary for one of 500 *l.* a year; with
which fum fome marling may be done.

Tythes are generally compounded; they
reckon 4 *s.* in the pound a fair compofition.
Poor rates 1 *s.* in the pound · 20 years
ago they were but 6 *d*; and 30 years ago
only 4 *d.*

LABOUR.

For the harveft of 5 weeks, 45 *s.* to 50 *s.*
and board.

In hay-time, 1 *s.* 6 *d.* to 2 *s.* and beer.

In winter, 1 *s.* 2 *d,*

Reaping, 5 *s.*

Mowing barley, 1 *s.*

———— grafs, 1 *s.* to 2 *s.*

Hoeing

Hoeing turnips, 4 *s.* and 2 *s.*

Hedging and ditching, 1 *s.* a rood of 7 yards.

Filling and spreading marle, 25 *s.* the 120 loads, of about 30 bushels. In general 5 or 6 horses and 2 carts with one driver will carry 40 loads a day; the expence 12 *s.* the 40 loads, besides the 8 *s.* 4 *d* filling, &c.

Thrashing wheat, 1 *s.* 2 *d.* to 1 *s.* 4 *d per* quarter.

———— barley and oats, 8 *d.* ditto.

———— pease, 1 *s.* 3 *d.*

Head-man's wages, 10 *l.* to 12 *l.*

Next ditto, 9 *l.*

Lad's, 4 *l* to 7 *l.*

Dairy-maid's, 5 *l.*

Other ditto, 3 *l.* to 4 *l.*

Women *per* day, in harvest, 1 *s.* and board.

———— in hay-time, 9 *d.* and beer.

———— in winter, 6 *d.*

Value of a man's board, washing, and lodging, 10 *l.* a year.

IMPLEMENTS.

A waggon, 24 *l.*

A cart, 10 *l.*

A plough, 3 *l.*

A pair of harrows, 1 *l.*

A roller,

A roller, 1 *l.* 5 *s.*
Harnefs *per* horfe, 2 *l.* 2 *s.*
Laying a fhare and coulter, 1 *s.*
Shoeing, 1 *s.* 4 *d.*

PROVISIONS.

Bread,   -   -   1 ½ *d. per lb.*
Cheefe,   -   -   4
Butter,   -   -   6
Beef,   -   -   3 ½
Mutton,   -   -   3 ½
Veal,   -   -   3
Pork,   -   -   3
Milk,   -   -   ½ *d. per* pint.
Potatoes,   -   -   4   *per* peck.
Candles,   -   -   7
Soap,   -   -   6
Labourer's houfe-rent, 40 *s.*
———— firing, 10 *s.*

BUILDING.

Bricks, 20 *s.* a 1000.
Tiles, 3 *l.*
Oak timber *per* foot, 1 *s.* 6 *d.*
Afh ditto, 1 *s.* 2 *d.*
Elm ditto, 1 *s.* 2 *d.*
Soft ditto, 6 *d.* to 8 *d.*
A carpenter a day, 1 *s* 9 *d.*
A mafon and thatcher, ditto.

The

The particulars of a farm are as follow.

300 Acres in all	14 Horfes
£.150 Rent	10 Cows
60 Acres Wheat	10 Young cattle
60 Turnips	10 Fatting beafts
60 Barley	100 Sheep
60 Clover 1 year old	3 Men
	1 Boy
60 Ditto 2 years old	4 Labourers.

Nicholas Styleman, Efq; of this place has effected a very important improvement by banking out the fea. which undertaking was by many thought very daring and hazardous. In 1750, he began to form a bank a mile long, and it was completed in a year. By means of fubftituting fingle horfe carts with 9 inch wheels, inftead of barrows, he made an immenfe faving in the labour of the work. A fquare of 7 yards, by 12 inches deep, was dug and thrown into the carts for 1 *s.* and only boys drove them. By this means he was enabled to be fo uncommonly expeditious. The marfhes were before let for only 4 *s.* an acre, but they were directly advanced to 20 *s.* In this manner 300 acres were at

once

once improved, at the fmall expence of
1500*l*. The advance of rent 240*l.* a year;
which from the above capital is a profit of
16 *per cent.* An inftance of fuccefsful
fpirit which does great honour to Mr.
Styleman.

This gentleman has been very active in
the inclofure of fome commons in the parifh of *Snettifham.* There were 41 houfes
that had a right of commonage over all the
open fields after harveft, which totally prevented the ufe of turnips and clover. This
great inconvenience induced Mr. *Styleman*
to give his confent to and promote an act
for inclofing the commons, and preventing
fo great an incumbrance on the hufbandry
of the open fields.

But in executing this idea he planned
the outline of it in fo candid and charitable
a manner, that he kept as ftrict an eye to
the intereft of the poor people, as to his
own. In lieu of rights of commonage, the
proprietors of a parifh inclofed, generally
divide it amongft themfelves, and give the
poor no indemnity: But Mr. *Styleman*
determined at firft that they fhould have
fomething valuable in exchange for their
right.

right. He allotted each of the 41 old common right houfes 3 acres contiguous to their dwellings, or their other property. 600 acres of old grafs common were left fo for thefe poor to turn their cattle on in a ftinted manner. It maintains 205 cows, 120 mares and foals till 10 months old; 80 yearling calves, and 80 fillies. In their little inclofures they grow turnips, barley, wheat, and a little hemp.

The poor of the whole parifh in general ufed to cut whins for firing over the whole extent of open fields : inftead of this practice, which was the deftruction of much land, he affigned them 100 acres of common in one inclofure for cutting turf: each houfe under 40 s. a year rent has a right to cut 3000 flag (turf) a quantity fufficient for the winter's firing.

This fyftem has been perfectly well adapted to the defign propofed of attending minutely to the intereft of the poor. Their little inclofures are of great ufe in maintaining their cows on a pinch in winter, on turnips or clover-hay ; and their tillage is executed by their brood-mares. And it is obfervable, that no inftance has been known

of

of any inhabitant of thefe 41 cottages ever being chargeable to the parifh. The poor rates are from 9 *d.* to 1 *s.* in the pound; before the inclofure they were 1 *s.* 6 *d.* This fall has been owing to the increafe of employment arifing from the inclofure and its confequences; and to the poor having been fo much favoured in the act.

At the fame time that fuch uncommon attention has been given to the poor; it has not deftroyed, through a falfe idea, the rife of the landlord's income, generally expected on fuch occafions. The rents of the parifh are in general raifed a third by the inclofure: one farm belonging to the corporation of *Lynn*, is raifed from 160*l.* to 360*l.* a year.

While thefe general good effects have taken place, an increafe of inhabitants has been fenfibly obferved—for the great increafe of employment, with the fuperior benefits attending a refidence here to what are elfewhere found, has tempted various people to fettle in the parifh. The number of fouls before the inclofure was 500; it is conjectured that they are now 600.

The comfort of living in this parifh induces many to come and refide in it. if 20

new

new cottages were built, they would be immediately filled. and Mr. *Styleman* is not clear, that was such an addition made, whether the rates would rife.

He farther informed me, that there is never any want of hands in this country to execute any the greateft works; had he miles of banking to do, the procuring hands for the execution would never be the leaft difficult.

There is a tract of country (it is fcarcely to be called *land)* in this place belonging to Mr. *Styleman*, which is not of any value at prefent, not producing 2 *d.* an acre. it is the fhore from which the fea has withdrawn, and confifts of nothing but fhingle; that is, ftones of various fizes, but none larger than a man's fift, of a great depth, and with a fmall mixture of fand among them. Here and there it yields a poor ftinted appearance of fomething like grafs—but bears a fprinkling of the eringo plant in tolerable luxuriance. it would be impoffible regularly to cultivate fuch a foil, but I apprehend it would yield fuftenance fufficient for feveral trees of the pine fort—fuch as firs, &c. &c. The experiment richly deferves the trial; for any

plantation

plantation would turn out wonderfully profitable on such an absolute waste as this. Mr. *Styleman* has 1500 acres of it.

On other soils this gentleman has formed large plantations; he has above 100 acres of thriving ones. He finds from particular observation on their growth, that *Scotch* firs planted at 2 years old are worth 1 *s.* 6 *d.* on an average in 14 years.

Rent of an acre of land 14 years,

	£		
at 10 *s.* - - -	£.7	0	0
Town charges, &c. -	1	0	0
Raising, fencing, planting, &c.	3	0	0
Expence *per* acre, -	11	0	0

Supposing the thinnings to pay the incidental expences; 5000 planted *per* acre at first, and thinned to 2000.

2000 trees, at 1 *s,* 6 *d.* cut down

at the end of 14 years -	150	0	0
Expences - - -	11	0	0
Clear profit, -	139	0	0
Upon 10 acres, this is £.1390		0	0
Upon 50 ditto, -	6950	0	0
Upon 100 ditto,	13900	0	0

I
                 What

What amazing profit is this to reap in 14 years! I have suppofed them all cut down at the end of the 14 years, to fhew the certain profit of a fpecies of farming never yet thought of, which is that of hiring land on a leafe of 14 years, under the covenant of liberty not only to plant, but alfo to cut down again :—What hufbandry will equal this? Suppofe the number of trees but a fourth of the above, ftill no common crops under great expences will equal this with none at all.

In my way from *Snett-fham* northwards, I paffed by *Sommerfield* and *Sunderland*, the two famous farms occupied by Mr. *Curtis*, and belonging to Mrs. *Henley* of *Docking*. I was miftaken upon another occafion in faying, that they confifted of 2500 acres: I was now informed that they amounted to no more than 1700. This farmer's fheep hufbandry is nearly executed on the plan above-mentioned of buying and felling wethers; he generally fats 1000 every year on turnips, giving fome the fpring grafs. So good a farmer's purfuing this conduct, gives one reafon to think it the moft profitable method.

The

The country is all under the best *Norfolk* culture from hence to *Wells*. About *Burnham*, land lets at 10 *s*. 6 *d*. an acre in large farms : the particulars of one are as follow:

1000 Acres in all	200 Turnips
£. 500 Rent	300 Clover
400 Corn	700 Sheep.

From *Burnham* to *Wells* I obferved the crops in general better than any I had feen fince I entered *Norfolk*. Rents are 14 *s*. an acre on an average. The produce of wheat from 4 to 5 quarters *per* acre. Of barley the fame.

Turnips worth 50 *s*. an acre.

Clover they leave two years on the land, but mix a peck of ray-grafs with it. They value clay more than marle ; lay 80 loads an acre, which lafts good 14 years ; after which they add a little more.

Oil-cake they alfo ufe; they lay about half a ton *per* acre.

About *Warnham*, the feat of Sir *John Turner*, Bart. the hufbandry is equal to any of the foregoing, with fome variations that render it fuperior.

Farms rife from 200 *l*. to 500 *l*. a year.

The

The foils are gravelly loams, and what they call here white corky land; which is a chalk foil without the qualities of marle. Lets at 8s. or 9s. an acre.

Rents on an average the whole way from *Snettisham* about 10s.—From hence to *Holt* 14s. Their courses are,

1. Fallow	5. Barley
2. Wheat	6. Clover, for 2
3. Barley	years
4. Turnips	7. Wheat.

And,

1. Fallow	5. Turnips
2. Wheat	6. Barley
3. Barley	7. Clover
4. Peafe	8. Wheat.

Alfo,

1. Turnips	3. Clover
2. Barley	4. Barley.

Likewise,

1. Turnips	3. Clover
2. Barley	4. Wheat.

Thefe are all good, except the crops of wheat and barley coming together, which is quite contrary to the principles of the beft *Norfolk* hufbandry.

For wheat, if not on clover, they plough four times; fow 3 or 3½ bufhels of feed, and

gain

gain 3 quarters in return. They ftir for
barley three or four times, fow 3 bufhels,
and reckon the average produce 4 ½ quarters.
They do not cultivate any oats; but buy
thofe they want for their own ufe. For
peafe they plough thrice, fow 3 bufhels, and
get on a medium 2 ½ quarters.

Their tillage for turnips confifts of four
earths: they always hoe twice; and feed
them off with beafts and fheep: they fat
beafts of 50 ftone upon turnips in this manner; they give them a little hay in the field,
but never fatten, in the yard, or in ftalls.
They are very attentive to follow a fat ftock
with a lean one.—Lean beafts or fheep come
after the ftock of fat beafts.

They often find the barley better after
beafts than after fheep alone: this I fhould
fuppofe could be owing to nothing but the
foil wanting heavier treading than fheep
give it.—The average price of turnips 30 s.
an acre.

They mow the firft growth of the firft
year's clover; but afterwards only feed it.

Some tares are fown, but they are chiefly
ufed for foiling horfes in the ftable.

In

In their manuring they are attentive to keep their land in great heart. The sheep-fold is used all winter through, except just at lambing time ; it is applied either for wheat or turnips.

Marling has been practised here these many years ; they lay 60 loads an acre, at the expence of near 30*s*. It lasts 15 or 16 years in perfection ; they then lay 25 or 30 loads more, which last 10 or 12 years longer ; and after that they will again repeat it ; being convinced from experience, that the benefit of these repetitions is very great, contrary to the idea in some parts, where it is imagined that after the first marling it will not answer.

Another excellent practice, which perpetuates marling, is the forming composts of that and dung, which mixed manure they find answers better than either separately. If they would use 10 loads an acre of dung alone, they will not substitute more than 12 of this compost, and find it more beneficial. In one circumstance, however, they are strangely deficient ; they form the heap in layers ; but all the mixing it gets is in loading, for they never turn the heaps over.

Oil-cake they ufe for wheat a ton and three quarters will do for 3 acres; the price from 3*l*. 3*s*. to 4*l*. a ton. They bring it both from *Ireland* and *Holland*, but they find the *Dutch* cakes beft, from their not preffing them fo much. It lafts ftrong only for one crop; but is a help to the following turnips.

They buy large quantities of dung at *Wells*, for which they pay 1*s*. a cart-load. Much of the dung which now brings crops of 8 quarters an acre in the inclofures round the town, Sir *John Turner* remembers being thrown into the haven; no man thought it worth the carriage.

Malt combs they fow on their barley lands; the price 3*d*. a bufhel.

One practice of which they are very tenacious, I cannot but condemn. They never chop their ftubbles, accounting them as good ploughed into the ground as a light coat of dung. I fhould not declare againft a maxim proved experimentally; but that is not the cafe here, they never chop—but are conducted by a general idea.

Good turnips are fometimes gained after wheat, fay they, without dung; to what

can

can that be owing but to the ftubble? I re-
ply, the fame thing is found in twenty places
where the ftubble is carried clean off. It
may be owing to the oil-cake, or to twenty
other reafons, not explained by them. But
they find their foil fo loofe, that beafts feeding off turnips are preferable to fheep—how
does this accord with leaving the land in fo
hollow and puffing a ftate as wheat ftubble
ploughed in, muft do? The ftubble is no
manure: it is too dry and fpread too thinly
to enrich the foil . common fenfe muft fpeak
this. But now to the only material comparifon : cut the ftubble of half a field, cart
it home, form it into a ftack without the
farm-yard, and where it fhall not be enriched by any of that dung which is preferved there, but let the drain, which carries off the urine from all the buildings,
and the wafh from the yard, be filled with
it from day to day, fo as to abforb the whole;
as faft as it is taken out, form it into a frefh
heap mixed with fome earth,, or marle; after the winter, turn the heap over twice,
and leave it till quite rotten . then cart it to
a part of that half of the field from whence
it was taken. Keep an exact account; charge

every

every expence of cutting, carting, re-carting,
mixing, &c. &c. and then fee which fide
of the field pays you beft in clear profit.
This cafe is not exactly neceffary, for if the
ftubble heap is formed by rain alone into a
mafs of *rotten* fubftance, the fuperiority of
the method will ftill be great. But I propofe a way of faving that, which in all the
farm-yards in *Norfolk*, and I may fay the
kingdom, runs to wafte.

With good management the fame fyftem
fhould be carried on within the yard—the
litter fhould be increafed by all the ftubble;
and the heap of dung receive all the urine
either by a pump or water-bowl.

The breed of cattle here is all the little
mongrel, *Norfolk* fort; but excellent for the
dairy : a good cow will give 12 to 15 *lb.* of
butter a week; they give 5 gallons of milk
a day, fome will give feven. Moft of the
dairies are let—the cow hirers give 3 *l.* 3 *s.*
a year, and 3 *l.* 10 *s.* for which the farmer
keeps up the ftock, and finds all food and
fuel. This is being paid little more than
1 *s.* 3 *d.* a week, befides the chance of loffes :
—it is aftonifhing how any perfon can think
fuch a fum an adequate value for a cow.

5   Many

Many fwine are here kept on account of cows; a dairy of ten will maintain 20 hogs, but in fummer all are kept on clover. A dairy-maid will take care of twelve. The winter food is turnips alone; no hay, except a little at calving.

Their fyftem of fatting beafts is to buy in in *November*; they choofe thofe that are forward in flefh; put them directly to turnips, and fell fat from clover and ray-grafs in *June*. Buy at about 7 *l.* and fell from 11 *l.* to 12 *l.*

The hide of a *Scotch* beaft of 30 ftone, is worth 15 *s.*

Swine generally fat to 16 or 18 ftone.

Flocks of fheep from 500 to 700: the profit the lamb and wool; which they reckon,

Lamb	-	-	-	0	9	0
Wool	-	-	-	0	1	3
Total profit,	-	-	0	10	3

The winter food is turnips alone; no hay, unlefs the fnow is fo deep that they cannot get at the crop.

In their tillage they reckon 12 horfes neceffary to 200 acres of arable land. They ufe 2 in a plough; do 2 acres or 2 ½ a day,

at

at 2 journeys with 4 horses. Stir 4 inches deep the price *per* acre 2*s*. 6*d*. The annual expence of a horse they calculate at 6*l*. 6*s*. The summer joist 2*s*. a week. They cut much straw into chaff.

They do not break up their stubbles for a fallow till *February* or *March*. Use only wheel ploughs; have tried swing ones, but find the former much lighter to the horses.

In the stocking farms, they reckon 2000*l*. necessary for one of 550 acres, the rent 300*l*. a year; and they divide that sum in the following manner:

30 Horses,	-	-	£.300	0	0
20 Cows,	-	-	120	0	0
15 Beasts,	-	-	105	0	0
500 Sheep,	-	-	270	0	0
Swine,	-	-	-	10	0	0
3 Waggons,	-	-	60	0	0
4 Carts,	-	-	56	0	0
5 Ploughs,	-	-	16	0	0
5 Pair harrows,	-	-	7	0	0
2 Rollers,	-	-	2	0	0
Harness,	-	-	60	0	0
Sundries,	-	-	40	0	0
Furniture,	-	-	100	0	0
Rent,	-	-	-	150	0	0
Carry over,	-	-	1356	0	0

Brought over,			£.1356	0	0
Town charges,	-		25	0	0
Tythe,	-	-	50	0	0
Housekeeping,		-	120	0	0
4 Men,	-	-	29	0	0
2 Boys,	-	-	-	7	0	0
3 Maids,	-	-	11	0	0
2 Labourers,	-	-	35	0	0
Extra labour,	-	-	50	0	0
Seed, 60 acres wheat,	-	45	0	0
—— 130 Barley,	-	52	0	0
—— 130 Clover,	-	30	0	0
—— 80 Turnips,	-	3	0	0
Cash in hand,	-	200	0	0
Total,	-	-	2013	0	0

Land fells at 27 or 28 years purchafe.

Tythe 2 s. an acre in general.

Poor rates 8 d. in the pound · 20 years ago they were but 4 d The employment fpinning; all drink tea twice a day; and many a third time for dinner.

All the farmers have leafes.

LABOUR.

In harveft, 2 l. 2 s. or 2 l. 5 s. and board for the harveft.

D 4

In

In hay-time, 1 s. 6 d. a day and beer.

In winter, 1 s. and beer.

Mowing grafs, 1 s. 6 d. and beer.

Hoeing turnips, 4 s. and 2 s.

Filling marle cart, 25 s. *per* 120, fill and fpread.

Thrafhing wheat, 1 s. 6 d. to 1 s 8 d. *per* quarter.

———— barley and oats, 10 d. *per* quarter.

———— peafe, 11 d. ditto.

Head-man's wages, 10 l.

Next ditto, 8 l.

Next ditto, 5 l. to 6 l.

Lad's, 3 l. 10 s.

Maid's, 3 l. to 3 l. 10 s.

Value of a man's board, wafhing and lodging. 10 l.

The rife of labour, a fifth in three months of the year; and an eighth during the other nine.

PROVISIONS.

Bread,	- -	1 ½ d. *per lb*.
Cheefe,	- -	3
Butter,	- -	6
Beef,	- -	3 ¼
Mutton,	- -	3 ¼
Veal,	- -	3

Pork,

Pork,   - - $3\frac{1}{2}$

Bacon,   - -   7

Milk,   - - $\frac{1}{2}$ *d per* pint.

Potatoes,   - -   3   *per* peck.

Candles and foap,   7   *per lb.*

Labourer's houfe-rent, 33*s.*

————— firing, 20*s.*

————— wear of tools, 10*s.*

BUILDING.

Bricks, 1*l per* 1000.

Oak timber *per* foot, 1*s.* 6*d.*

Afh ditto, 1*s.* 2*d.*

Elm ditto, 1*s.*

Soft woods, 9*d.*

A carpenter and mafon a day, 1*s.* 8*d.* and beer.

A thatcher, 1*s.* 8*d.* and beer, or 1*s.* a fquare yard.

    The particulars of a farm.

500 Acres in all	130 Spring corn
£. 260 Rent	130 Clover
30 Horfes	60 Turnips
20 Cows	4 Men
12 Beafts	2 Boys
500 Sheep	2 Labourers.
60 Acres wheat	

Sir *John Turner* has for feveral years

given much attention to hufbandry; he has in fome inftances improved on the management of his neighbours, good as that is—and in others, introduced practices unknown here before.

Experiment, No. 1.

As the lord of the manor of *Wells*, he enjoyed a large tract of fea coaft, and had a confiderable fpace of low land cut by a creek and flooded every tide, which he thought would make good marfh-land if fecured from the fea by a bank. He immediately executed it · and the fuccefs has anfwered his utmoft wifhes. the bank was made at the expence of 650*l*; and 130 acres gained by it, which let at 25*s*. an acre.

As foon as the firft work was done, he ftopt all the fprings, and little water-courfes from the higher grounds, by large and deep drains on the edge of the marfh; and then cut a great carrier drain 10 feet wide, along the middle of it; into which fmaller drains were cut; and all the water let into the fea by a fluice in the bank, the doors opening to let out the frefh water, and fhutting by the fuperior weight of the tides.

A very

A very fortunate circumſtance in this drainage is the ſurprizing plenty of freſh water:
the ſea was no ſooner ſhut out, than the
old creek was at once full of very fine fieſh
water, and has ſince been a winding freſh
water of 4 acres · Such plenty of good
water is of vaſt conſequence in grazing
lands.

As ſoon as the drains were made, the
next buſineſs was to level the old creek,
which ran very irregular, and in many
places formed miſhapen ſwamps and holes;
all theſe were filled up · then the ſurface
was pared and burnt an inch deep, and the
land ſowed with coleſeed . the produce half
a laſt an acre, ſold at 18 l. a laſt. After
the coleſeed a crop of oats was taken of 3
quarters an acre, and then another of 4
quarters. After which it was ſummer
fallowed; then oats again; the crop 4 ½
quarters an acre, and with them all ſorts of
graſs ſeeds were ſown, particularly white
clover, red clover, trefoile, hay ſeeds, ray-
graſs, &c. In ſome places, all failed except the ray-graſs · but white clover came
amongſt that the following year.

The graſs has been extremely good ever
ſince,

fince, as may eafily be fuppofed from much
of it being let at 2 5 s. an acre; though the
rent before the banking was only 6 d. One
acre fats an ox of 50 ftone, and a wether,
fufficiently to put them to turnips; or
would fatten 5 large *Lincolnfhire* fheep.
The grafs is fo fweet, that it will completely
fatten beafts of 40 or 50 ftone in 7 months.
—Much of it has fattened 2 beafts of 40
ftone, *per* acre.

After the drainage, Sir *John* affigned a
piece of ten acres for the poor of the parifh,
which maintains a very great number of
ftock: nothing was done to this piece, and
yet it is extreme good and rich grafs; from
which hint he determines, in cafe of a future undertaking of this fort, not to pare or
plough it at all; only to level the fmall
holes, and make the cuts for draining;
which would render the improvement much
lefs complex.

Sir *John Turner* has another tract of
marfhes of 1800 acres, let at prefent at
only 4 d. an acre; it is capable of being
fecured from the fea: The bank for
that purpofe fhould be 100 feet bafe, regularly floped to 6 feet at the top; the
height

height of it in the centre 10 feet. The expence of such a bank 3 miles long would be 5148 *l.*; the interest of which sum, at 5 *per cent.* amounts to 257 *l.*; and the product of the improvement the two first years, at

10 *s.* an acre,	-	-	£.900
The third year,	-	-	-	1350
The fourth,	-	-	-	1800
And afterwards,	-	-	2250

a year. The undertaking upon the whole, would be uncommonly profitable; far more advantageous than any other expenditure of such a sum in any part of the kingdom.

In forming a bank, the price of the work is 2 *s.* 6 *d.* to 4 *s.* a floor of 400 cubical feet, for filling and barrowing the earth a single run; which is such a length, that men who run the barrows need not be relieved . planks to run on, to be found them , but they find their own barrows.

Experiment, No. 2.

Sainfoine, Sir *John Turner* has cultivated with great success. He has several pieces of it, which have answered better than the common husbandry on the same soil would have done. The soil is a light turnip loam

on

on chalk. The firſt year the produce was very inconſiderable: The ſecond, it was a pretty good crop: from that time to the preſent (18 years ago) it has produced at an average 1½ load an acre, worth 4*l.* on a moderate computation. and the after-graſs 15*s.* an acre. For 7 years in the height of the crop, it yielded 2 loads an acre   Let us calculate the common huſbandry according to the particulars given above.

Expences.

Firſt; Turnips.

	£		
4 Earths and harrowings, -	£.0	12	0
Manuring, -	1	10	0
Seed and ſowing, -	0	0	9
Hoeing, - -	0	6	0
Rent, &c. -	0	12	0
			3 0 9

Second; Barley.

3 Earths and harrowing, - -	0	9	0
Seed and ſowing,	0	8	0
Mowing and harveſting,	0	6	0
Thraſhing, -	0	3	9
Carrying out, -	0	4	6
Rent, - -	0	12	0
			2 3 3

Carry over,	5 4 0

Brought over,   -   £.5   4   0

Third; *Clover*, &c. two years.

	£	s	d
Seed and fowing,	£.0	6	0
Mowing, carting, and			
ftacking, -	0	6	0
	0	12	0

Fourth; *Wheat.*

	£	s	d
1 Earth, -	0	3	0
Seed and fowing,	0	16	0
Manuring, -	1	5	0
Reaping and harvefting,	0	7	6
Thrafhing, -	0	5	0
Carrying, -	0	3	0
Rent, - -	0	12	0
	3	11	6
Total, - -	9	7	6

Produce.

	£	s	d
Turnips, - - -	1	10	0
Barley, 4 ½ quarters, -	4	1	0
Clover, firft year, -	3	0	0
———— fecond, - -	1	5	0
Wheat, 3 quarters, -	6	0	0
Total produce, -	15	16	0
Total expences, -	9	7	6
Profit in 5 years, -	6	8	6
Or *per* acre *per annum*,	1	5	8

SAINFOINE.

Expences.

	£.	s.	d.
Mowing, making, carting and stacking, - -	0	7	6
Rent, - - -	0	12	0
	0	19	6

Produce.

1 ½ Load hay, - -	4	0	0
After-grafs, - - -	0	15	0
Total produce, -	4	15	0
Total expences, -	0	19	6
Profit, - -	3	15	6
Ditto by common hufbandry,	1	5	8
Superiority, - -	2	9	10

I have formed this calculation as an anfwer to thofe who infift that money is loft
by this experiment. I have on both fides
taken the particulars from the fame autho-
rity—and from a perfon (Sir *John*'s fteward)
who feemed to be of opinion, that the
tillage courfe was moft profitable. It is
evident from hence, that fainfoine is the
moft advantageous. It would appear yet

more fo if the intereſt of the firſt ſtock was on both ſides carried to account : Indeed the rents on poor foils, that are in many parts of the kingdom paid for this graſs, are twice over what the *Norfolk* farmers pay for their beſt land; which ſhould give one ſome idea of its real value. The ſuperiority of the ſainfoine is ſo great, that it will admit the expenditure of 20 *s. per* acre *per annum* in ſoot or aſhes,—without any correſponding increaſe of crop, and yet remain much more beneficial than the other.

Experiment, No. 3.

Lucerne he has cultivated with as much ſucceſs as ſainfoine. The foil on which it is ſown is a good turnip land ; ſuch as lets here at 7 *s.* 6 *d.* an acre. There is an acre and half of it ; half ſown three years, and half four years ago it was on a turnip fallow in the ſpring without corn · the weeds did not riſe much, as the land was clean ; and thoſe that came were cut down with the lucerne at the firſt mowing before they ſeeded. After which the growth of the crop was always quicker than that of the grafs, confequently they were deftroyed by the fcythe.

Every fpring it is harrowed until it carries the appearance of a fine fallow. It has been regularly cut every five weeks; and is found, from an accurate obfervation, to grow from 22 to 26 inches every 28 days. Every fpring it is manured after the harrowing, at the rate of 6 loads an acre of rotten dung.

As to the produce, it is very great: Six coach, and fix other horfes are chiefly fed with it through the fummer, but if horfes were to be confined folely to it, it would maintain at the rate of five *per* acre from the middle of *April* to *Michaelmas*, at 2 s. *per* horfe *per* week. Laft year's five cuttings, had they been made into hay, would have amounted to 6 tons *per* acre; which cannot be calculated at lefs than 12 *l.* 12 *s.*

One part of the crop, for a trial, was fet out with hand-hoes in the fame manner as turnips: I remarked that part of the piece to be about 2 inches higher growth than the reft, and was fomething of a deeper green.

Sir *John Turner* has, upon the whole,

found

found it fo extremely profitable, that he recommends it to every one; and has endeavoured, though in vain, to perfuade his tenants to try it

That the profit is very great, will appear from ftating the expences and produce.

	£		
Rent, &c. &c. - -	0	10	0
Harrowing, - - -	0	2	6
Cutting five times, -	0	7	0
Raking together, loading and carting home, -	0	15	0
	1	14	6

Produce.

Keeping 5 horfes 26 weeks, at 2 s.	13	0	0
Expences, - -	1	14	6
Clear profit, -	11	5	6
The common hufbandry of this country was found to pay *per* acre profit, - -	1	5	8
Superiority of the lucerne,	9	19	10

Sir *John*'s common hufbandry is very perfect; and remarkably adapted for keeping his land as clean as a garden. The foil of his farm is of two forts, one a very

E 2

light loam naturally poor, and is unprofitable if not very attentively managed.
When he took it into his own hands he
found it in miserable order; the courfe of
crops he followed to bring it into good
heart, is,

1. Turnips
2. Barley
3. Clover 12 *lb.* and half a peck of ray-
   grafs an acre, left on the land 2 years.

And then turnips again. So that only one
crop of corn is taken in four years. The
firft growth of the clover is mown; and
then fed for a year and half. Was a crop of
wheat to be taken on the clover in the farmer's method, it would be a very poor one;
and that of barley be as 6 to 10 at prefent.

Upon his better foil he takes,

1. Turnips   3. Clover
2. Barley   4. Wheat.

And a proof of the goodnefs of the
former, is the crops of turnips, barley and
clover on the poor foil, being equal to thofe
in this courfe on the rich one.

His turnips are worth 1 *l.* 15 *s.* on an
average. The barley produces 5 quarters
an acre; he has fometimes on weak land
had

had 6 quarters. The clover gives a load and half of hay at one mowing · and the wheat 3 quarters *per* acre.

His farm is a very well diftributed one. It in general is,

236 Acres in all	1 ½ Lucerne
24 Acres Turnips	24 Meadow
24 Barley	16 Rich marfh
24 Clover for	15 Pafture
mowing	50 Plantation
24 Ditto fed	14 Water.
16 Sainfoine	

Experiment, No. 4.

Ofiers he tried for an experiment in his marfh land · three roods were planted, and let without difficulty for five guineas a year.—So vaft a rent has determined him to apply more land to fo profitable an ufe.

Experiment, No. 5.

In the preparation of a piece of very ftiff, clung, marfh land for wheat, forefeeing that a great many ploughings would be neceffary to reduce it, he determined to fow it with buck-wheat, with intention to plough it in in time for fowing the wheat.

It

It was accordingly done; and it anfwered greatly in mellowing this harfh foil—much more than feveral extra ploughings would have done.

Experiment, No. 6.

The neighbourhood of the fea in this country, fuggefted to this gentleman the thought of a manure which had totally efcaped the farmers: it was that of fea ouze. Some of his tenants occupied a confiderable tract of arable land that joins to the marfhes by the fhore; he directed one of them to ouze a fmall field at the rate of 50 loads an acre, in the fame manner as if it was marle, and to fow it with turnips. No effect appeared in that crop; but in the barley which followed, the richnefs of the manure fhewed itfelf ftrongly, it yielded four loads and an half an acre in the ftraw; the crop 6 or 7 quarters. The clover was uncommonly fine, and the wheat which followed the fame—and the land ever fince has difplayed in the cleareft manner, the vaft fertility it has gained by this manure.

A proof no ways equivocal, is the practice of the tenant; for on feeing the firft crop of barley he immediately went to work

again,

again, and ouzed a larger field; and since
that has been as regularly at it, as any one
can be at marling : he has thus manured a
large space of land, and continues the improvement. I rode over several of his fields
thus managed, let at only 4 *s.* an acre, and
others at 6 or 8, which were covered with
as fine crops of turnips, clover, and barley,
as can be seen in *Norfolk*; he has no barley
on ouzed land that will yield less than 5 or
6 quarters an acre; and he gets 3 quarters
an acre of wheat on 4 *s.* land.—There are
marle pits in these fields, but the farmer
prefers the ouze.

Experiment, No. 7.

Sir *John Turner* has not only planted
many acres as an addition to the beauty of
his situation, but has also attended to the
growth of the trees, for discovering the
profit of planting on his soils. In one
plantation, *Scotch* firs, at 12 years growth,
are worth 1 *s.* each.

Experiment, No. 8.

In a plantation of 50 years growth, the
land 8 *s.* an acre, the trees are various, and
the value as follows.

E 4

Oak,

Oak, worth 10 _s._ each.

Aſh, 12 _s._ 6 _d._ ditto.

Elm, 10 _s._ ditto.

Scotch fir, 7 _s._ 6 _d._ ditto.

Lime, 5 _s._ ditto.

Suppoſe the number of each equal, the average value is 9 _s._ The number about 5000 on an acre.

500 trees, at 9 _s._ are 225 _l._ or 4 _l._ 10 _s._ _per_ acre _per annum_, from the firſt planting; but the thinnings have produced very conſiderable ſums. and the graſs under the trees would now let at 5 _s._ an acre.

Experiment, No. 9.

In another plantation of 50 years growth, on land of 8 _s._ an acre, the trees, 250 _per_ acre, are worth—

The oak, 16 _s._ each.

Aſh, 10 _s._ ditto.

Lime, 9 _s._ ditto.

Scotch fir, 16 _s._ ditto.

Average, 12 _s._ 9 _d._

250 at that price, come to 154 _l._ 7 _s._ 6 _d._ _per_ acre _per annum_, beſides the thinnings. this is above 3 _l. per_ acre _per annum_ from the firſt planting.

Had all been oak or fir, the total would have been 200 _l. per_ acre; or 4 _l. per_ acre _per annum_ from the firſt planting.

Experiment, No. 10.

In another plantation, elms of 40 years growth (300 on an acre) are worth 22 *s.* each · this is 330 *l. per* acre; or more than 8 *l. per* acre *per annum*; and the land now would let as well as before the planting

Experiment, No. 11.

A plantation of *Scotch* firs of 15 years growth, 300 on an acre, are worth 1 *s.* 6 *d.* each. This is 22 *l.* 10 *s.* an acre, or 1 *l.* 10 *s*, *per* acre *per annum*, besides thinnings.

The great profit of planting is obvious from these trials, but the whole state of the case by no means appears here; for the product of the thinnings is confiderable. Sir *John* calculates, that he never receives lefs than a guinea an acre in thinnings throughout his plantations; which is eafily to be conceived, as they are at firft planted only 4 feet afunder.—The loweft profit here mentioned, is 1 *l.* 10 *s.* an acre; add 1 *l.* 1 *s.* for thinnings, it is 2 *l.* 11 *s. per* acre; deduct 11 *s.* rent and expences, there remains 40 *s.* an acre clear profit, which is more than the farmers make by all their trouble, induftry and hazard.

I I cannot

I cannot but add to thefe trials in hufbandry and planting, that Sir *John Turner*
has proved himfelf to be not only a true
friend to his country, in profecuting thefe
undertakings with fpirit, but has alfo fhewn
himfelf a fuperior farmer in the midft of a
country cultivated better than moft in *England* *.

From

---

* The fituation of *Warbam* is the moft beautiful in *Norfolk*, and as much worth viewing as
half the houfes to which travellers are fo eager
to run. The houfe ftands on the brow of a
gently rifing hill, backed to the north with very
fine plantations of 50 years growth   They have
fomewhat the appearance of a crefcent form,
fheltering from the north, eaft, and weft, and
opening to the fouth, down over a beautiful
winding vale, and then commanding a rich varied
profpect of diftant enclofures.   Some villages
and churches, fcattered about the view, and a
large, tho' regular water in the valley, all tend
to make it chearful   While the thick woods
which crown the tops of feveral hills, and the
groves that fink into the vale, throw a picturefque
beauty over the fcene that cannot fail to ftrike
the fpectator
The view that breaks at once upon you on
coming through the dark fir wood in the ap-
proach from *London*, is very beautiful   You
look at once upon a range of lofty plantations
around the houfe, whofe dark fhade forms a

contraft

From *Warham* I took the coaft road to *Sherringham*, making that the way to *Holt*. The crops, I obferved, were not fo good as about *Warham*, tho' much of the country is very well cultivated. I paffed through *Stukey*,

---

contraft to the brilliancy of the landfhip that fets it off in the fineft colours —In front, you look upon various clumps, rifing boldly from the water, united in fome places with thick hedges, and in others broken by inclofures, that fpreading over the hill to the left, the water is loft under a dark grove · the fields rife fo thick above it, as to unite with a diftant plantation which crowns the hill , a church is happily fituated on the point of it, and beyond is feen a more diftant rich wood-land Full to the left, is a large *Danifh* camp of three entrenchments, which are quite perfect * Turning to the right, you look upon an incl fure which breaks into the plantations, it is fringed with open wood-that half obfcures the village, fcattered thickly with trees , and *Warham* fteeples, one peeping over the thick plantation near the houfe, and the other more open, complete the view

As you advance through the vale in the way to the houfe, the fcenes change, but all are beautiful The varied lawns, and hanging flopes, crowned in fome places with woods, and in others broken by rich inclofures, are all truly picturefque and beautiful

---

* An encampment of *Sweno* the *Dane*. One of the meadows is called *Sweno*'s mead.

Stukey*, and near to *Blakeney*, about *Sher-ringham*, land lets at 15 *s.* an acre. Their course,

1. Turnips
2. Barley
3. Clover
4. Wheat.

The turnips are generally as fine as any; the barley produces 3 ½ quarters *per* acre

on

---

* The ride from *Warham* by *Stukey*, is thro' a much more picturesque country than is commonly met with in *Norfolk*, the road runs on the brow of the hill looking down on *Stukey* vale, and commanding, for some distance, a very complete landscape. The vale, which is composed of meadows of the finest verdure, winds in a very beautiful manner from out a thicket of woody inclosures, and retires, at the other, behind a projecting hill: an humble stream glides through it, and adds a chearfulness, which water can alone confer. The hills rise in a bold manner: they are bare of wood, but that is compensated by the thick inclosures in which the village is scattered; forming with its church in a dip of the hill, and that of *Blakeney* above it, in a prouder situation, a most complete and pleasing picture.

Between *Stukey* and *Cley* is the little village of *Cockthorp*, which contains but three houses, and yet has furnished *Britain* with three famous admirals; Sir *Cloudsley Shovel*, Sir *John Narborough*, and Sir *Christopher Mims*

Near *Blakeney* is another uncommon view, quite

different

on an average; their clover is bad; not often more than a load of hay an acre: wheat 3, or 3 ½ quarters.

From *Sherringham* to *Holt*, is across a
flat

---

different from that at *Stukey* the road winds into a sequestered valley shut out from the sea, by a bold, uncultivated hill. To the right, the grounds shelve from the road into a narrow vale In this little woody hollow, is a village half seen among straggling trees the steeple is uncommonly picturesque, half of it is hid by a rising slope, and the church three fourths obscured by a thicket of trees. The opposite hill rises very boldly, it presents a large inclosure, under the thick shade of a noble spreading wood, which hangs to the right into another valley, but is lost behind a regular bare hill of a conic form; which rises from the junction of the vales, in a very remarkable manner, and almost screens a distant range of rising inclosures. Immediately to the right, is a sloping tract of fields, and above them wild ground, with a white tower rising from behind it The whole forms one of those half gloomy, and yet not unpleasing scenes, in which *Poussin* delighted, it is a spot worthy of such a pencil

Sherringham Cliff is a very high steep shore; it looks on one side full upon the sea, and on the other over a various country abounding with inequalities of ground many hills scattered wildly about, numerous cultivated inclosures, and six or seven villages are seen *Sherringham* is prettily overlooked, backed by a rising hill

flat difagreeable country : nine tenths of it a black ling heath, or a whin cover, but all greatly capable of cultivation.

About *Melton* *, land lets at 14 s. an acre on a medium ; barley yields 4 quarters ; wheat, 3 ½ ; turnips very fine ; but the clover, like that at *Sherringham*, is but middling. Large dairies are kept about here; they feed the cows in the paftures and meadows, but are wretched managers (like the generality of the *Norfolk* farmers) of their grafs lands ; they are all over-run with rufhes and other rubbifh ; very wet, but no drains made.

From *Holt* towards † *Aylfham*, the country is in general rich and well cultivated; but

---

* Sir Edward Ashley, at this place, has a large park which has lately been ornamented judicioufly ; and a water made with uncommon difficulty; which, when properly united with wood, will have a good effect From a windmill near the park is a prodigious view of a rich woodland country, finely intermixed with cornfields, and wanting nothing but a river to be complete

† At Wolterton Lord *Walpole* has a feat well environed with wood. The *Hall*, 30 by 27 —A *Dining-room*, 30 by 27 A good picture
of

but improves as you advance. In the neighbourhood of the latter place for fome miles
around, particularly towards the coaft, the
hufbandry is very good.

Farms are rather fmall; in general from
50 *l.* a year to 100 and 150 *l.* The foil a
mixed one; gravelly, and fandy loams;
excellent for turnips; lets from 7 *s.* 6 *d.* to
20 *s.*; average about 14 *s.* The whole way
to

---

of King *Charles* —A *Dreffing-room,* 21 by 18,
hung with tapeftry of lively and fpirited colours.
—A *Bed-chamber,* 25 by 22, the tapeftry here
alfo is very fine, the chimney-piece handfome.
The *Saloon,* 36 by 30, the tapeftry, fophas,
and chairs, reprefent *Æfop*'s fables, done in a
natural, and pleafing manner. The windows
look on fome very fine woods.—A *Drawing-
room,* 25 by 21, the tapeftry fine —A *Bed-
chamber,* 22 by 21.—A *Dreffing-room,* 21 by 18.
The pier glaffes throughout the houfe are large
and very handfome

Adjoining to *Wolterton* park is *Blickling,* the
feat of the Earl of *Buckinghamfhire,* the park is
large, and the water (in the form of a great
winding river) one of the fineft in the kingdom:
It is near a mile long, and in general from 2 to
4 or 500 yards over, the colour is very bright.
But what renders it uncommonly beautiful, is
the noble accompanyment of wood. The hills
rife from the edge in a various manner in fome
places

to *Norwich*, it runs at about 12 *s.* Their
courses of husbandry have variations.

1. Turnips·   4. Wheat
2. Barley   5. Barley.
3. Clover

This last crop of barley is bad.—Another
course they have, is to leave it out, and
take turnips again.

1. Turnips

---

places they are steep and bold, in others they
hang in waving lawns, and so crowned and spread
with wood, that the whole scene is environed with
a dark shade, finely contrasting the brightness of
the water.—Some woods of majestic oaks and
beech, dip in the very water, while others
gently retire from it, and only shade the distant
hills. Sometimes they open in large breaks, and
let in the view of others darker than themselves,
or rise so boldly from the water's edge, as to ex-
clude every other view.—About the center of the
water, on the right of it, is a projecting hill,
thickly covered with beech : their stems are free
from leaves, but their heads unite and form so
deep a gloom, that not a ray of the sun can find
admittance, while it illumines the water, on
which you look both ways. This partial view of
the lake (for the branches of the beech hang
over the water, and form an horizon for the
scene) is strikingly beautiful You will dwell
on it with uncommon pleasure.

The house is unfortunately situated close upon
one

1. Turnips   4. Wheat
2. Barley   5. Peafe.
3. Clover

Alfo,

1. Turnips   4. Barley
2. Barley   5. Peafe.
3. Clover 2 years

This

---

one end of the water, but it is a large and good one. The following are the principal rooms.

The *New-room*, 27 by 26.

The *Study*, 33 by 21. Here is a very fine portrait of Sir *John Maynard*: and another of Sir *H Hobart*, by *Lely*.

Dreffing-room, 21 fquare.

Bed-chamber, 27 by 21.

Dreffing-room, 25 by 21.

Breakfaff ditto, 28 by 22. Here is a good copy of a portrait of Sir *James Hobart*.

On the principal floor, firft,

An *Anti-room*, 25 by 24

Drawing-room, 45 by 24. Here are the King and Queen, by *Ramfay*, both well done. Portrait of Sir *John Maynard*, a good one. And another of Lord Chief Juftice *Hobard*, in which both the face and hands are fine.

Dreffing-room, 25 by 22.

Bed-chamber, 25 by 16. Ditto, 27 by 22.

Library, 120 by 22, and 22 high. The bookcafe arranged on both fides. It is an excellent collection, and an admirable rendezvous room,

This is a good courfe for many foils. Another they find extremely beneficial, is,

1. Turnips
2. Barley
3. Clover 2 years
4. Buckwheat
5. Wheat.

They plough once for wheat, fow 2 ½ bufhels if they get it into the land early, but 3 bufhels if later; 3 quarters or 3 ½ are the average produce, but 5 quarters are often gained. For barley they plough three or four times; fow 4 bufhels, and get 4 quarters in return; feldom more than 5. They give the fame tillage for oats as for barley, which is an uncommon inftance of good hufbandry; fow 4 ½ or 5 bufhels, and get 5 ¼ or 6 quarters on an average. For peafe they ftir but once, fow 4 bufhels; never hoe, but get 3 ½ quarters an acre.

They give four or five earths for turnips, hand-hoe twice; and feed off with cattle and fheep: if the crop is large, they have a method of expending them, which I believe is peculiar to themfelves. They firft feed one piece, fuppofe an acre, by running a row of hurdles acrofs the field: then, before they move the hurdles, they draw another acre; and cart them on to the

acre

acre eaten off for the cattle; and fo on throughout the field · always carting the crop from the land where it grows to the part cleared. Their motive for putting themfelves to this expence, is to make the turnips go fo much the further, and at the fame time preferve the benefit of the cattle to the barley crop · if the produce is large, and cattle are turned in, they fpoil as much as they eat; but when the turnips are laid clear above the foil, and the earth partly fhaken off, they eat them up clean.—The price *per* acre, to draw and cart them in this manner, is from 50 *s.* to 3 *l.*

Of clover they mow the firft crop, and feed the fecond: the crop of hay generally 2 loads an acre, fometimes 3. They fow 10 *lb.* of clover, and a peck of ray-grafs, which they here call by its proper name Darnel; but if for their lambs in fpring, they fow a peck of the latter.

No tares cultivated.

For buck-wheat they plough three or four times, fow 5 pecks to an acre; the average crop 4 quarters, fometimes 6. It is as good as oats for horfes; fells gene-rally 2 *s.* a quarter under the price of barley

F 2 —but

—but its being an ameliorating crop like peafe, the inferiority of price is abundantly made up. They always fow wheat after it; and on cold fpringy land fometimes plough it in for that crop, by ufing a bufh faggot before the ploughs to level it: and this management anfwers prodigioufly for two crops; better than dung. They never fow buck-wheat till the beginning of *June:* and they reckon that is more beneficial to the land than any other crop. Wheat very feldom fails of great crops after it.

In their manuring they are pretty attentive. They fold all the year through, for wheat or turnips. Marle they depend much on; the fort they ufe moft is a grey marle, it is foft and foapy: they do not lay above 12 large loads an acre, as much as five horfes can draw, and this quantity will laft 20 years; after which they repeat it. But then I fhould add, as an explanation of the fmallnefs of this quantity, that they regularly cart out their farm-yard dung on to layers of marle, mix them up together, and then fpread them on their land; this is a regular addition to it, and they have long experienced the practice to be excellent.

lent. They harrow their ftubbles by way of chopping them, and cart them home to the yard.

They apply their meadow and pafture lands to keeping young ftock and cows; the former they bring into them for water, but keep them on the uplands of nights: 2 acres will carry a cow through the fum- mer: A good one will give 6 gallons of milk a day: as to the product, they are generally let at 3 *l.* 10 *s.* to 4 *l.* a head.—— To 20 cows they keep from 25 to 30 fhots; that is, $\frac{1}{2}$ and $\frac{1}{4}$ grown hogs. A dairy- maid will take care of 20 cows. The winter food is ftraw or turnips; no hay: and a calf is worth 30 *s.* in 7 or 8 weeks. They keep them in winter in the yard.

They fatten their fwine to 28 ftone, but the average is not above 16. They have no regular flocks of fheep; but they fold thofe they keep. In *Auguft* they buy old crones, and alfo lambs of that year; like- wife fhearling wethers; all which forts they turn into their ftubbles at *Chriftmas*, when they put them to turnips, and after that to clover and ray-grafs. If they buy in at

10 *s.*

10 _s._ they will fell them fat in _April_ or _May_ at 18 _s._; which, for the time, is great profit.

Sometimes they buy lean wethers, and get them flefhy enough by _Chriflmas_ to put to turnips, and will fell them fat from that food—fhearling ewe lambs will clip 3 or 3 ½ _lb._ of wool.

In refpect to the rot, they apprehend that it is owing in a great meafure to fpringy land in low meadows. thofe fields in which heavy fogs are apt to hang are bad, but no land, whatever may be its quality, will rot if the fheep are never turned on it until the fun has exhaled all the dew. Floods they reckon not at all prejudicial.—Thefe ideas appear to me not to be fo clear as I could wifh.

In their tillage, they reckon 5 horfes neceffary for 100 acres of ploughed ground; ufe 2 in a plough, and do 2 acres a day. The ploughman goes out at 6 in the morning, and does an acre by 11 o'clock; he then comes home and baits till 2, and goes out again till 7 at night; in which time he does an acre more: all this is done with a pair of horfes, befides taking care of 5 in all; this is great work, and much exceed-

ing

ing what is done in moſt other countries. But they aſſert, that it can only be done with wheel ploughs; they have tried ſwing ones, but they do not equal the wheeled. They ſtir from 3 to 5 inches deep; the price 2 s. 6 d. an acre.——The annual expence of a horſe they reckon at 5 l. 10 s. They feed much with ſtraw cut into chaff.——— They do not break up their ſtubbles for a fallow till after *Chriſtmas*.

In the hiring and ſtocking farms, they reckon 700 l. neceſſary for 300 acres.

Tythes are compounded; they pay 3 s. in the pound.

Poor rates 2 s. in the pound; they have riſen a fourth in 20 years.—The employment of the women and children ſpinning; all drink tea.

Many leaſes are granted, but not ſo many as formerly.

The farmers carry their corn from 6 to 10 miles.

LABOUR.

In harveſt, 36 s. and board for the harveſt.
In hay-time, 1 s. 2 d. and beer.
In winter, 1 s. and beer.

Reap-

Reaping, 5 *s.*

Mowing spring corn, 1 *s.* to 1 *s.* 2 *d.*

——— grass, 1 *s.*

Hoeing turnips, 4 *s.* and 2 *s.*

Filling marle cart, 2 ½ *d.* a load; and 1 *s.* an acre spreading.

Thrashing wheat, 2 *s.* a quarter.

——— barley and oats, 1 *s.*

——— pease, 1 *s.* 4 *d.*

First man's wages, 7 *l.* 7 *s.* and 8 *l.*

Second ditto, 6 *l.* and 5 *l.* 5 *s.*

Lad's, 3 *l.*

Dairy-maid, 3 *l.* 10 *s.*

Other ditto, 2 *l.* 10 *s.* to 2 *l.* 15 *s.*

Women *per* day, in harvest, 6 *d.* and board.

——— in hay-time, ditto.

——— in winter, 6 *d.*

The rise of labour a fourth in 20 years.

PROVISIONS.

Bread,	- -	1 ½ *d. per* pound.
Cheese,		4
Butter,	- -	6 ½
Beef,	- -	3 ½
Mutton,		3 ½
Veal,	- -	3
Pork,	- -	3 ½
Bacon,	- -	6 ½

Labourer's

Labourer's houfe-rent, 40 s.

———————— firing, from the commons.

The particulars of a farm as follow.

300 Acres in all	12 Horfes
250 Arable	20 Cows
50 Grafs	20 Fatting beafts
£. 200 Rent	30 Young cattle
42 Acres of Tur- nips	100 Sheep
	2 Men
60 Barley	1 Boy
24 Wheat	2 Maids
84 Clover	4 Labourers.
42 Peafe	

LETTER XII.

THE city of *Norwich* is one of the moſt conſiderable in *England* after *London*; it ſtands on more ground than any other: But in number of inhabitants, ſome others aſſert an equality. By an accurate account taken a few years ago, the number reckoned by the houſes amounted to 40000; but by the bills of mortality only to 36000; the average therefore of theſe (38000) may be taken as more probable than either,

The ſtaple manufactures are crapes and camblets; beſides which they make in great abundance damaſks, ſattins, alopeens, &c. &c. &c. They work up the *Leiceſter-ſhire* and *Lincolnſhire* wool chiefly, which is brought here for combing and ſpinning, while the *Norfolk* wool goes to *Yorkſhire* for carding and cloths. And what is a remarkable circumſtance, not diſcovered many years, is, that the *Norfolk* ſheep yield a wool about their necks equal to the

beſt

beſt from *Spain*; and is in price to the reſt as 20 to 7.

The earnings of the manufacturers are various, but in general high.

Men on an average do not exceed 5 ſ. a week; but then many women earn as much: and boys of 15 or 16 likewiſe the ſame.

Draw-boys, from 10 to 13, 2 ſ. 6 d. a week.

Pipe-boys and girls, from 5 to 9 years old, 9 d.

Combers, on an average, 7 ſ.

Dyers, 15 ſ.

Hot-preſſers, 13 ſ.

Women by doubling yarn, 2 ſ.

Ditto ſilk, 8 ſ.

Ditto by ſpinning, 2 ſ. 6 d to 3 ſ.

The weaving man and his boy, who now earn in general 7 ſ. a week, could earn with eaſe 11 ſ. if induſtrious.—But it is remarkable, that thoſe men and their families who earn but 6 ſ. a week, are much happier and better off than thoſe who earn 2 ſ. or 3 ſ. extraordinary; for ſuch extra earnings are moſtly ſpent at the alehouſe, or in idleneſs, which prejudice their following work. This is preciſely the ſame effect

effect as they have found when the prices of provisions have been very cheap; it results from the same cause. And this city has been very often pestered with mobs and insurrections under the pretence of an high price of provisions, merely because such dearness would not allow the men that portion of idleness and other indulgence which low rates throw them into.

- In the management of the poor, there was once a circumstance that deserves noting. Previous to the year 1727, the rates throughout the city were immoderately burthened with weekly allowances to the poor, of 1 s. 6 d. 2 s. 2 s. 6 d. or 3 s. a family, in which manner 1200 l. a year was given. A resolution was taken in that year to strike them all off: it was accordingly done; and nothing ensued but murmuring; no ill consequence at all.—

7 or 800 souls are kept in the workhouse of this city for 7 or 8000 l. a year in all expences.

In respect to the present state of the manufacture, it is neither brisk, nor very dull They could execute more orders than they have; and some among them complain because caufe they have not fo great a trade as during the war; for then they could not anfwer the demand, it was fo uncommonly great (from 1743 to 1763 was their famous æra). This was however owing in fome meafure to many manufacturers exporting fo largely on fpeculation, that the markets have been overftocked ever fince;—and have occafioned that falling off which has been perceived fince.—Indeed the unfortunate difference fubfifting between *Great Britain* and the colonies is a great injury to them.

They now do not fend any thing to *North America*; but much to the *Weft-Indies*. Their foreign export is, to

Rotterdam	*Cadiz*
Oftend	*Lifbon*
Middleburgh	*Barcelona*
All *Flanders*	*Hambro'*
Leghorn	All the *Baltic* ex-
Trieft	cept *Sweden*,
Naples	where they are
Genoa	prohibited.

In 70 years laft paft, the manufacture is increafed as from 4 to 12.

During the laft war, *Norwich* fupplied

4   the

the army and navy with 4000 recruits; but her manufactures did not suffer in the least: for they carried on more trade than ever.—The truly induftrious do not enlift; and as to the idle, the greateft favour to be done to any place is to fweep them all away.

They are in this city curious in building with flint; they cut it in regular fquares, and form as neat joints as with the beft bricks. The Bridewell is thus built, and fo well executed, that it is worth a traveller's notice.

The general amount of the *Norwich* manufacture may be calculated thus.

A regular export to *Rotterdam* by fhipping, every 6 weeks, of goods to the amount of *per annum*, - - £.480,000

26 tons of goods fent by broad- wheeled waggons weekly to *London*, at 500*l.* a ton on an average, 13000 tons *per an- num*: Value, - - 676,000

By occafional fhips and waggons to various places; calcu- lated at, - - - 200,000
_____

£.1,356,000

Upon a reconfideration of this table, it was thought that the 676,000*l.* by waggons, was rather too high : fuppofe therefore only 10,000 tons, it is then 520,000*l.*, and the total 1,200,000 *l.*

Another method taken to calculate the amount was, by adding up the total fum fuppofed to be returned annually by every houfe in *Norwich*; and this method made it 1,150,000 *l.* This fum coming fo near the other, is a ftrong confirmation of it.

A third method taken, was by various ways to calculate the number of looms : thefe were made 12,000; and it is a common idea in *Norwich* to fuppofe each with all its attendants works 100 *l. per ann.* :— this alfo makes the total 1,200,000 *l.*; which fum, upon the whole, appears to be very near the real truth.

Refpecting the proportion between the original material, and the labour employed upon it, they have a very fure and eafy method of difcovering it. The average value of a piece of ftuff is 50 *s.*: it weighs 6 *lb.* at 10 *d.* a *lb.* which is 5 *s.*: fo the material is a tenth of the total manufacture.

Total,	- - -	£. 1,200,000
A tenth,	- - -	120,000
Amount of labour	-	1,080,000

In which is included the profit of the master manufacturer.—There is no occasion to separate that from the grofs fum, as it is in fact *labour* as much as the manual part. All the people maintained and employed by a manufacture are the same in a publick view, whether they earn 10,000 *l.* a year, or but 10 *l.*

The material point remaining is to discover how many people are employed to earn the publick one million *per annum*; and for this calculation I have one *datum* which is to the purpose. They generally imagine in *Norwich*, that each loom employs 6 perfons in the whole; and as the number is 12,000, there are confequently 72,000 people employed by this manufacture. And this is a frefh confirmation of the preceding accounts; for I was in general told that more hands worked out of *Norwich*, for many miles around, than in it. 1,200,000 *l.* divided by 72,000, gives 16 *l.* each for the earnings of every perfon.

This,

This, I muft confefs, appears to me a very large fum; for I have no conception of all the perfons employed earning 16*l.* a year, which is 1*s.* a day; if therefore any miftake is in the preceding account, it muft be in the number of looms.—The total amount of the manufacture is taken from clear facts (not fuppofitions) there muft confequently be looms fufficient to work to that amount. 16*l.* a year may not be *much* above the truth, though probably *fomething*, for we fhould confider that women and boys of 15 or 16, earn as much as moft of the men: whereas in various other manufactures with which I am acquainted, they do not nearly equal them: and we fhould further confider, that we include in this 16 *l.* a year, the whole profit of the mafter manufacturer.—The deviation therefore from fact, cannot be very confiderable. For if the mafter manufacturer's profit is calculated at 14 *per cent.* and deducted accordingly, this 16 *l.* a year is thereby reduced to about 11 *l.* 11 *s.* a year.—

It may therefore be taken as no contemptible fact, that 70 or 80 thoufand people employed in a manufacture, whatever it

may be, will earn 1,000,000*l.* a year. I
say *whatever it may be*; becaufe I conceive
that the variations of earnings in the general number not to be very great.—Provifions are pretty much on a par; and few
of them more than work to live.

LETTER XIII.

THE hufbandry near *Norwich* is generally good. About *Earlham*
farms rife from 50 *l*. to 200 *l*. a year, the
foil a loamy fand with both marle and chalk
under it. Lets from 14 *s*. to 20 *s*. an acre;
average 16 *s*.

The rent from *Norwich* to *Yarmouth* is
about 14 *s*.

The courfe of crops,

1. Turnips   only 8 *lb*. and ½
2. Barley or oats   a peck ray-grafs
3. Clover, 9 or 10 *lb*.   4. Wheat
    of feed; but if   5. Bailey.
    with ray-grafs,

This latter crop of barley is unworthy a
Norfolk man. Another courfe is,

1. Turnips   4 Peafe
2. Barley   5. Wheat,
3. Clover

They plough once for wheat, fow 3 bufhels,
and reap 2 quarters. For barley they
plough thrice, fow 3 bufhels, and reckon
the average crop at 3 ½ quarters. For oats

after

after turnips they ftir as often as for barley, but if they fow them after wheat only once, which is a diftinction I do not comprehend; why the land, when it is fo run, fhould not be favoured as well as when clover is to be fown. They fow 4 bufhels; the crop 4 quarters. For peafe they give but one earth; of the white fort they fow 4 bufhels, but of the grey only 2—never hoe them; the crop 3 quarters.

They give 4 earths for turnips, hand-hoe twice. They have a particular method of ufing them, they draw the lands alter-nately; draw one and cart the turnips on to a clover lay, then leave one, then draw another; and fo on. Thofe they carry off they give to beafts for fatting, or to milch cows, with a crib of ftraw in the field; and the remainder of the crop they feed on the land with fheep, and fometimes with beafts.—The crops are in value, from 21 s. to 4 l. 10 s.; average about 40 s. fed off.

They mow the firft and fecond growths of clover for hay; which they do not only on account of the hay, but under the ex-perimental certainty of the wheat that fuc-ceeds being much better than after feeding

I repeated

I repeated my enquiries on this head, to know if it was only a private opinion, or a general obfervation and practice; and I was anfwered the latter.

Buck-wheat they plough twice for, and always mow it for feed; then they dung the ftubble, and fow wheat on one earth, in which method they never fail of good crops of that grain.

Carrots are not an uncommon crop here. They plough up the ftubble defigned for them in autumn, and on that ploughing manure with long yard dung, 10 loads an acre; which they turn in by a trench ploughing, with two ploughs, one a pair of horfes, and the other following in the fame furrow with 4. In *February* the feed is harrowed in. It is generally 2 months before the carrots come to the hoe; they have three hoeings given, at the expence of a guinea an acre. They take up the crop with a three pronged fork, as it is wanted, never ftowing them for fecurity in a houfe. I could find no clear idea of the quantity produced on an acre, nor of any other value than that of 1 s. 2 d. *per* bunch of 120, as large as a man's wrift; which

is

is the price of *Norwich* market.   Barley is always sown after them.

The best farmers chop their stubbles for manure; but it is not general.   All stack their hay at home.

They have good marle all over the country, but not much used.   But Mr. *Henry Raven* of *Brammerton*, has introduced claying; he lays 70 loads an acre with great success.—The only use made here of marle is however a very good one; they form composts of it with earth, farm-yard dung, &c. and mixing them well together, spread it for turnips, and find very great benefit from the practice.

Ashes they use sometimes on strong wet land.

They do not fold their sheep.

Soot they lay on grass lands, and also on wheat in the spring; 30 bushels an acre, at 6 *d.* : It does great service for one crop, and is sometimes of benefit to the succeeding one.

Malt-dust they use in the same manner; 40 bushels an acre, at 4 *d.*

Norwich manure of all sorts they have for 1 *s.* a four horse cart load; they use much of it, and find it answers greatly.

Grass

Grafs land lets from 40*s.* to 3*l.* an acre; but about *Brammerton* at only 20*s.* An acre will, about *Norwich,* carry a cow through the fummer; but at *Brammerton* it takes 1 ¼. Dairies let at 3*l.* 5*s.* to 3*l.* 10*s.* a cow. At *Brammerton* they keep about a hog to every cow.

A dairy-maid will take care of 20 cows; fome will undertake 30. The winter food of cows turnips, and ftraw in the yard chiefly.

Swine fatten to 16 ftone.

Flocks of fheep at *Earlham* are from 300 to 600; but few at *Brammerton.*

The profit,

				£.		
Lamb,	-	-		0	7	6
Wool,	-	-	-	0	1	0
				0	8	6

The winter food turnips.

In their tillage, they reckon 6 horfes neceffary for 100 acres of arable land; ufe 2 in a plough, and do 2 acres a day, 5 inches deep. The price 2*s.* 6*d.* an acre. They cut much ftraw into chaff.

The time of ploughing ftubbles for a fallow, autumn.

They

They reckon, on hiring farms, that three rents will ftock.

Freehold eftates fell at 27 years purchafe; copyhold 22.

Tythes are generally compounded.

Poor rates at *Brammerton* 2 *s.* in the pound. At *Earlham* 1 *s.* 9 *d.* They are in both places doubled in twenty years.

Particulars of a farm at *Brammerton.*

100 Acres in all	36 Barley
90 Arable	18 Turnips
10 Grafs	18 Clover
£.65 Rent	1 Man
5 Horfes	1 Boy
8 Cows	1 Maid
18 Acres Wheat	1 Labourer.

LABOUR.

For the harveft, 2 *l.* 2 *s.* and board.

In hay-time, 1 *s.* 6 *d.* and beer.

In winter, 1 *s.* and beer at *Brammerton*; 1 *s.* 2 *d.* at *Earlham.*

Mowing-grafs, 1 *s.* 6 *d.* an acre and beer.

Hoeing turnips, 4 *s.* and 2 *s.*

Filling cart, 25 *s. per* 120 loads.

Firft man's wages, 10 *l.* 10 *s.*

Second ditto, 6 *l.* 6 *s.*

Lad's,

Lad's, 3 *l.*
Dairy-maid's, 4 *l.* 4 *s.*
Other ditto, 3 *l.*
Rise of labour in 20 years a sixth.

PROVISIONS.

Bread,	-	-	1 ¼ *d. per lb.*
Cheese,	-	-	2 ½
Butter,	-	-	7
Beef,	-	-	3 ½
Mutton,	-	-	3 ¼
Veal,	-	-	3
Bacon,	-	-	6
Milk,	-	-	1 *d. per* pint.
Potatoes,	-	-	6 *per* peck.
Candles,	-	-	7 *per lb.*

House-rent, 4 *l.* out of *Norwich.*
———— in ditto, 2 *l.* 10 *s.*
Firing in ditto, 40 *s.*
——— in the country, 20 *s.*

Nockold Thompson, Esq; of *Norwich,* has executed some experiments at *Earlham,* which will prove sufficiently how capable the country is of improvement.

When this gentleman began farming, his land yielded very poor crops, being all in extreme bad order. None of the fields produced

produced more than 2 or 2 ½ quarters of barley; no wheat was grown, only rye, and that indifferent: nor did the clover or turnips amount in weight to half what he now gains. The following is the register of his fields.

No. I. *Five acres.*
1768.

Manured, 12 loads an acre, with a compost made of *Norwich* dung, marle, and earth, in equal quantities, and sown with barley; the crop very good.

1769.

This year it yielded colefeed; was hand-hoed like turnips, and weeded; the produce 4 ½ quarters *per* acre; sold for 10 *l.* This practice of hand-hoeing colefeed cannot be too much commended; it is no where common.

1770.

Manuring for wheat.

No. II. *Nine acres.*
1768.

Yielded barley after wheat, 3 ½ quarters *per* acre.

1769.

Manured with compost as above: sown

3

with

with turnips; carted half off, and the other half fed on the land: the crop would have fold, from the great fcarcity, for from 5*l.* to 7*l.* an acre.

1770.

Buckwheat.

No. III. *Nine acres.*
1768.

Manured with the compoft for turnips; half fed off as above; the value 2*l.* 10*s.* Some of them came to 14*lb.* weight.

1769.

Barley, 3 quarters an acre.

1770.

Clover mown; 3 loads of hay an acre at one cutting, 46*s.* a load.

No. IV. *Eleven acres.*
1768.

Manured as above with compoft; and fown with barley: the produce 2 ¼ quarters an acre.

1769.

Again manured with ditto.——Clover, mown for hay, a load an acre.

1770.

Wheat, will be 3 ¼ quarters.

No. V. *Twelve acres.*

1768.

Manured as above with the compoft for wheat, on a clover lay. The produce 4 quarters an acre.

1769.

Barley, 2 ½ quarters an acre.

1770.

Manured again with the compoft, and fown with turnips; the crop very fine.

No. VI. *Eleven acres.*

1768.

Barley after clover, the crop 3 ½ quarters.

1769.

Manured with the compoft, and fown with turnips; the crop very good.

1770.

Oats; at leaft 5 quarters.

No. VII. *Eleven acres.*

1768.

A corky foil; manured with the compoft for clover.

1769.

Peafe, 2 quarters.

1770.

Manured for carrots and turnips; fine.

No. VIII. *Nine acres.*

1768.

A clover lay in 1767, manured with the compoft for wheat; the produce 4 quarters *per* acre.

1769.

Barley, 2 ½ quarters.

1770.

Manured with compoft for cabbages and turnips, the ciops extremely fine.

No. IX. *Seven acres and an half.*

1768.

Manured with the compoft for turnips; the value 3 *l.* an acre.

1769.

Barley, 2 ½ quarters.

1770.

Clover, 3 loads an acre.

No. X. *Eleven acres.*

1768.

An old meadow broken up in 1766 for oats, and oats again in 1767; clover with them; marled the clover lay, 70 loads an acre; fed the crop with horfes, cows and fheep.

1769.

Manured with the compoft for wheat; the crop 4 ¼ quarters *per* acre.

1770.

Barley; a good crop.

No. XI. *Three acres and an half.*

1768.

Manured with compoft for turnips; the crop very fine.

1769.

Lucerne in drills.

1770.

Ditto, manured with compoft.

No. XII. *Seventeen acres,*

1768.

Barley, 3 ½ quarters.

1769.

Clover; manured with the compoft; the crop a load and half of hay.

1770.

Wheat; promifes fair for 4 quarters.

No. XIII. *Seven acres and an half,*

1768.

Barley, 3 ½ quarters.

1769.

Clover, 1 ½ load. Manured with compoſt.

1770.

Charlton peaſe, and white ditto—the latter the beſt.

No. XIV. *Seven acres.*
1768.

Turnips, manured with compoſt; worth 3*l.* an acre.

1769.
Barley, 3 quarters.

1770.
Clover, 3 loads hay.

No. XV. *Eleven acres.*
1768.

Peaſe; white and grey: the white 3 ½ quarters: the grey, 1 ½.

1769.
Manured with compoſt for turnips; the crop a fine one.

1770.
Oats, very good.

No. XVI. *Four acres and an half.*
1768.

Clover, 1 ½ load.

1769.

Manured with the compost for wheat;
the crop 4 quarters.

1770.

Barley.

No. XVII. *Two acres and an half.*
The fame as No. 16.

No. XVIII. *Eight acres and an half.*

1768.

Old pasture, marled; 50 loads an acre.

1769.

Peafe, 3 ½ quarters.

1770.

Wheat; will be 4 ½ quarters.

No. XIX. *Five acres and an half.*

1768.

Pasture.

1769.

Ditto.

1770.

Peafe——good.

All the preceding crops of wheat were
manured with a dreffing of malt combs
or foot, in *February*, about 30 bufhels an
acre.—The fmallnefs of the crops of barley
must

muft be ftriking; the wheat exceeds it.
This is owing to following wheat, and alfo
to half the benefit which barley ufually receives from turnips, being transferred to the
wheat, by the turnips being drawn and
fed on the clover lays; and the wheat has
alfo the fuperior advantage of the fpring
top dreffing. It feems to appear from this
regifter, that all the turnips ought to be
fed on the land for the barley. But Mr.
Thompfon's marling and compoft manuring
has brought his farm into excellent order;
and made it yield far-different crops from
what it did before.

CARROTS.

Experiment, No. I.

Three acres of gravelly and fandy loam
on chalk, and marle, were ploughed in
autumn 1769, and again in *February*,
upon which earth 10 loads an acre of long
ftable dung were fpread, and turned in by
a trench ploughing, and the feed harrowed
in; but it proved bad, and the feafon was
very cold and unfavourable. They were
long in the ground before fprouting;—but
by two good hand-hoeings have gained a

VOL. II.   H   fine

fine appearance. I found them a very promising crop; they are to be hoed again

CABBAGES.

Four acres of a good light mixed loamy soil were ploughed at *Michaelmas*; again in *February*, and a third time in *March*. Upon this earth it was manured with the compost, 12 loads an acre, and turned in in *June*. The seed, 3 *lb.* was sown in a garden the middle of *April*. The sort, the great *Scotch* cabbage. The plants were pricked out when in 2 leaves, 6 inches square. The 20th of *June* they were transplanted into the field in rows 3 feet asunder, and the plants 18 inches distant. It was done by the slight mark left by the plough in striking every fourth furrow; and the rows are quite straight. This is a very easy way of planting, in saving the complex and troublesome exactness of a line, which is otherwise necessary on flat land. The appearance of the crop is very fine, and promises to yield at least 30 tons an acre, and the whole plantation is perfectly clean.

LUCERNE

Experiment, No. 3.

Three acres of a loamy fand with ouzing fprings under it at the depth of 6 or 7 feet (unknown at the time of fowing) were cropped with turnips in 1768, well manured for. It was ploughed the beginning of *February*, and had two earths more before *April*, in the middle of which month it was drilled with lucerne in equally diftant rows, 18 inches afunder, it was kept quite clean by hand-hoeing; and cut once, in *Auguft*, which cutting was given to horfes in the ftable.

1770.

In *March* it was cleaned by hand-hoeing, at a very heavy expence. The latter end of *May* it was cut in portions for horfes as before, but the crop not large—not near equal to clover at the firft cutting. Had it been made into hay, the produce would have been about a load an acre.

The beginning of *July* cut it a fecond time; the produce the fame as before; and after cutting it was again hand-hoed.

Began to cut it the third time the firft of

Auguft,

August, at about a foot high. But I did not find it clean.

The produce may therefore be calculated at three cuttings, each giving a load of hay an acre, the quantity of which three loads eaten green by horses, will not be of less value than five loads of common hay: this is no trifling produce. But lucerne, unless it is kept as clean as a garden, never yields its full product: As Mr. *Thompson* cleaned it only by hand, he found the expences to over-balance the produce; I recommended the shim for the intervals, and to harrow it across to extirpate the weeds that come up in the rows; and he is determined to try that method.

IMPROVEMENT OF MEADOWS.

Experiment, No. 4.

Mr. *Thompson* found several of his lower grounds, called meadows, quite boggy; and yielded nothing but a cold sower grass, and rushes; the utmost they were worth was 10*s.* an acre. In the spring of 1768, he mowed the rushes twice, and then drained the whole by deep and wide cuts: after which, he manured the whole with

the

the uncovering of a marle pit, called here the *callow*, 30 loads an acre. Upon this manuring he fowed *Dutch* clover and *Suffolk* hay feeds, and harrowed and rolled them in · they fprung well; and the effect was very advantageous.

1769.

This year the rufhes were again mown twice, and the drains opened. The improvement greater ftill.

1770.

This year above half the breadth was broken up, and there has been a very exact rule for deciding the value of the improvement. The whole piece was 45 acres; now only 20, and this 20 has fed· exactly the fame cattle that the whole did before · It could now be let for 30*s* an acre.

CLEARING AWAY WEEDS.

I mention this part of good hufbandry to obferve, that Mr. *Thompfon* makes it a· regular practice to mow all the weeds in his hedges, borders, ditches, &c. and alfo in the adjoining lanes, before they feed; and he finds his account in this excellent practice by keeping his farm clean.

MARLE.

The marle dug at *Earlham* is rather hard, and like chalk on the firſt digging; but it breaks in pieces eaſily, and on being thrown into water will diſſolve in a quarter of an hour and be ſoapy if powdered, it effervefces immediately with vinegar. the colour is white, with a tinge of a reddiſh yellow. He finds that the deeper it is dug, the better it is. It deſtroys weeds almoſt at once, particularly ketlocks and poppies. Theſe were common in his fields, but have diſappeared ſince the marling. He lays from 40 to 70 loads an acre when alone, but generally mixes it with dung.

NORWICH MANURES.

Mr. *Thompſon* buys 400 loads of dung, &c. from *Norwich* every year, at the price of 1*s.* and he reckons the carriage 2*s* 6*d.* more: he always forms it into a compoſt with marle, &c. Lays a bottom of marle; then a layer of virgin earth, then dung, both the *Norwich* ſort and the farm-yard; and then covers the whole heap completely
with

with marle. After laying fome time, it is turned over and mixed well together.

He brings from *Norwich* ftable-dung, and fweepings of ftreets; alfo the riddance of privies mixed with coal afhes; likewife hops from a brewhoufe · and large quantities of foot and malt-duft for top dreffings of wheat.

COURSE OF CROPS.

This is particularly fet forth in the table of fields given above: but Mr. *Thompfon* has made one remark which fhould be mentioned. He finds that the barley after the turnips eaten laft is always very poor, owing to being fown late. This has determined him to fow buck-wheat on fuch lands in future; and wheat after it. This obfervation I do not remember hearing fo particularly remarked before; but it is certainly an evil attending a crop of late turnips; and the remedy here propofed will in all probability anfwer well on many foils: but clover muft be harrowed in upon the wheat in fpring, or that neceffary crop is left out of the courfe.

H 4

SWINE.

This gentleman obferved that the meadows which he fed with his horfes and cows, were eaten very uneven; much grafs remaining untouched. this induced him to try fwine in grazing them, and it has anfwered; they affift fo well, as to keep the grafs fed level. and he eats it in general with them clofe at *Michaelmas*, for the young crop in the fpring to come the better. He likewife has fed them entirely on clover, but does not make it a conftant practice, as it anfwers much better to mow that crop, where hay fells from 2 *s.* 6 *d.* to 3 *s.* 4 *d per* C. *wt.* He keeps the lean ones in winter on turnips and malt grains. Propofes to fat on carrots and buck-wheat.

The following are the particulars of Mr. *Thompfon*'s farm when got in perfect order,

200 Acres in all	50 Swine
170 Arable	3 Men
30 Grafs	3 Boys
14 Horfes	2 Maids
27 Cows	8 Labourers
12 Young cattle	30 Acres wheat
60 Sheep	40 Barley

10 Oats   4 Cabbages
10 Peafe   3 Lucerne
30 Turnips   7 Sainfoine
30 Clover   5 Colefeed.
 6 Carrots

It cannot be doubted but this farm will do excellently well for carrots—cabbages—lucerne——and fainfoine.——I have little doubt but Mr *Thomfon* will find thofe crops uncommonly profitable, and efpecially as he is in fo good a fyftem of manuring; fufficient to keep any farm in great heart.

The foil changes between *Earlham* and *Bracon Afh*; the farther this way you move, the heavier the land grows—there being much more clay in this country than about *Norwich*. But they have various tracts of gravelly and fandy loams; and alfo loofe wood-cock brick earths. It lets on an average at 15*s*. an acre. Farms rife from 16*l*. to 200*l*. a year, general average 120*l*. The courfes,

1. Turnips   6. Barley
2. Barley   7 Trefoile and
3. Clover and   ray-grafs
    ray-grafs   8. Wheat
4. Wheat   9, Oats,
5. Turnips

The oats come in very badly, and muſt do miſchief: the change from the clover to trefoile, is on account of the clover hav-ing of late years failed very much, but by introducing trefoile alternately, this evil is quite prevented.

For wheat they plough but once, ſow 2 or 3 buſhels an acre, and gain 3 ½ quarters. For barley they plough thrice; ſow 3 buſhels, and get 4 quarters an acre For oats they vary their tillage from once to three times; ſow 4 buſhels, and reap 5 quarters on an average. They give but one earth for peaſe; ſow 3 buſhels; ſome-times dibble them in on a clover or trefoile ſtubble, in which way only 2 buſhels are uſed; the crop on a general average 3 quarters.—They never hoe.

They ſtir four or five times for turnips, hoe them twice, and uſe them all ways; the value about 40 s. an acre. They mow their clover twice; the firſt cutting yields about 2 loads of hay an acre, the ſecond one: ſome leave the latter for ſeed.

Buck-wheat they ſow as a preparation for wheat, 6 pecks *per* acre; the crop 3 ½ quarters. The price varies, it is often higher

higher than barley; but the rate of that grain is the common rule.

Marle is not regularly found in this country; when they can get it, they lay from 80 to 100 loads an acre, and find it a very great improvement of light lands.

The best farmers chop their stubbles for manure; but many neglect it · all stack their hay at home, and most of them bring dung from *Norwich*, though 7, 8, or 10 miles off.

Plashing hedges quite unknown here; they cut off *all* the live wood, when they repair

Good grafs land will let at 20*s.* an acre: they apply it both for grazing and the dairy. An acre and quarter will carry a cow through the fummer. they give 6 ¼ *lb.* of butter each *per* week; and a good one 6 gallons of milk a day. The total produce 4*l.* 15*s* a year. The winter food straw and turnips, and a little hay in spring. In the nights they keep them in the yard, but in the field by day.

The graziers buy *Scotch* beafts chiefly; though fome home-bred ones: If they give 5*l.* and keep them a year on grafs and tur-

nips,

nips, they do not more than double their money.

Their fwine fatten to 16 ftone. Flocks of fheep rife only to 100. In autumn, they buy in lambs; and fell them in fpring. They turn them firft into the ftubbles; after which they put them to turnips; they buy at 7*s.* and fell at 11*s.*

In their tillage, they reckon 8 horfes neceffary to 100 acres of arable land; ufe 2 in a plough, and do an acre a day: which quantity is a great falling off from that performed fo little a way from them. They plough 3 inches deep: the price 2*s.* 6*d.* an acre; which is as low, as where they do 2 acres a day. They very feldom cut any ftraw into chaff. Their ftubbles they plough up for a fallow in autumn: ufe only wheel ploughs.

In the hiring and ftocking farms, they reckon 300*l.* neceffary for a farm of 100*l.* a year: for thofe who have cafh enough for 60*l.* a year, are fure to hire an hundred —a miftake much complained of by land-lords.

Land fells at 32 years purchafe. Tythes

are compounded; they pay 2*s*. 6*d*. or 3*s*.
in the pound.

Poor rates, 2*s*. to 3*s*. in the pound;
they are doubled in 20 years. The employment of the poor women and children,
spinning wool. All drink tea twice or
thrice a day

Most of the farmers' have leases.

Rev. Mr. *Howman*, of *Bracon Ash*, to
whom I am obliged for the preceding particulars, has tried *Reynold's* cabbage turnip
on strong clay land: It came to as great a
size as common turnips on the best land,
but grew so forky, and entwined its roots
about so much earth, that half the crop
was lost. Cows eat them after a little difficulty.

Turnip cabbages he also cultivated on a
strong clay soil; the seed was sown the beginning of *April*: the latter end of *May*
the strongest plants were drawn out to
plant half a rood. The beginning of *July*
they were again pricked for another rood.
The seed bed itself was also half a rood—
and what is remarkable, proved the finest
of the three. This experiment is very
curious, for it seems to prove a point never

recom-

recommended by any of the cultivators of cabbages, *viz.* that it is more advantageous to sow where the plants are to remain, than to transplant them from a bed. This might easily be tried, and probably would be found a very good way of cultivating them.

Horses, cows, and sheep were turned in, who fell at once on them, and eat the crop clean up; they all seemed to like them exceedingly. Some were left to the spring, to discover how long they would last. The beginning of *January* was a week's sharp frost without snow, which left the plants a mere rotten pulp. They did not come to a larger size than common turnips, but were much heavier than those of an equal size.

This gentleman, on a strong clay soil of 16s. an acre, gained the following crops:

Wheat, 3 ½ quarters.

Oats, 6 quarters.

Peafe, 3 quarters.

Mowed from 2 to 3 loads of hay from his pastures. But his management was very perfect, for he kept his fields under a con-stant manuring, from compost heaps,

4   made

made in layers of dung and earth, and well mixed together.

He attributes his good fuccefs with his grafs lands, in fome meafure to mowing off all the weeds and leavings of his cattle, when they were fed.

Thomas Bevor Efq; of *Ethel* in this neighbourhood, has for fome years kept part of his eftate in his own hands, and culti-vated it in a very complete manner; pur-fuing feveral practices not common in this country, which he has found of particular utility.

The courfe which he adheres to in pre-ference to all others, is,

1. Turnips   3. Clover
2. Barley   4 Wheat.

For his turnips he ploughs 4 to 6 times; they are worth on an average 3*l.* 3*s.* an acre; when he draws them he has gene-rally 40 great cart loads an acre. feeds his horfes on them to great advantage. $\frac{1}{2}$ an acre will winter a cow. His barley yields 5 $\frac{1}{2}$ quarters an acre: he ploughs 5 times for it; fows 3 bufhels an acre. The clover produces 3 loads of hay, at 40*s.* a load; and wheat upon an average, 4 $\frac{1}{2}$ quarters:

he

he sows 2 bushels; once tried 6 pecks, but it was the worst crop he had. These crops are all great, and could not be gained unless the management was excellent.

Turnips,	-	-	£. 3	3	0
Barley,	-	-	5	10	0
Clover,	-	-	6	0	0
Wheat,	-	-	9	0	0
Total,	-	-	23	13	0

Or *per* acre *per ann.*   5   18   3

I do not think that common husbandry admits any thing more profitable than this. We ought to attend particularly to the management that ensures such noble crops · it consists chiefly in a very spirited conduct respecting manures.

He is principally solicitous to raise large quantities of farm-yard dung, as the cheapest and readiest method of improving a farm. For this purpose he stacks all his hay at home, ready to be consumed in the yard—he chops his stubbles, 25 acres, and carts them in for litter—he clears the lanes, &c. of fern, rushes, &c. getting 7 or 8 waggon loads yearly; all which he applies to the same use as his stubble. And one

point,

point, in which he is quite peculiar, is the raking together all the leaves that fall in his park; he employs women in this bufi-nefs, they load the carts with large fans; the whole expence of raking, loading, carting, &c. is 6 d. a load. He annually collects 200 loads; they are fpread about the yard, and the cattle tread them into one general hard cake, which, receiving the dung and urine all winter, converts into as rich a manure as any in the world. By thefe exertions of excellent management he raifes annually 1400 large loads of dung; made by

20 Cows	11 Horfes
14 Young cattle	40 Swine.

Thefe confined the winter through, alfo 20 horfes joifted on hay, with liberty of run-ning in and out to the park at pleafure, in all 105 head of cattle—but fwine reckoned, we fhould not call them more than 85, which is 16 ½ loads *per* head. A great quantity, confidering that 20 horfes run out at pleafure. Mr *Bevor* carts thefe 1400 loads from his yard on to heaps, pre-paring layers of pond mud, ditch earth, ant-hills, wafh fand, &c. &c. the dung is thrown on them, and then more layers of earth, &c. In this work, he is attentive to keep the carts off the heaps; they shoot down their loads by the side, and men are ready to throw them up with spades. He follows this method to prevent the carts driving on to the heaps, which he thinks press them too much, and thereby prevent the fermentation which rots the compost. He has tried the dung alone; and has found from long experience, that this mixture will do more benefit upon a given quantity of land, than the dung alone; and be superior to a much greater degree, than the amount of the expences. He mixes the 1400 loads of dung with 600 of earth, &c &c.—using annually 2000 loads. The quantity of the compost, after being well mixed together, that he spreads on an acre, is 12 loads, every other year.—

Besides this general system, which is undoubtedly excellent, he attends to other ways of improving his land.

Experiment, No. 1.

Buck-wheat he has sown on a strong clay land as a preparation for wheat, after

four

four ploughings . it was partly fed off by
cattle, and what remained ploughed in the
end of *July*, and after two ſtirrings more,
wheat ſown : 'the crop was 5 quarters an
acre.

Experiment, No. 2.

An ordinary paſture was broken up and
dibbled with peaſe , the crop 5 quarters an
acre ; the old turf was ſo rotten that Mr.
Bevor intended wheat ; but being prevented,
he ſowed it with buck-wheat, 1 buſhel an
acre ; after which he ſowed wheat, and had
6 quarters an acre. This was ſucceeded by
turnips ; and it was laid down with graſſes
among the following barley.

Experiment, No. 3.

Soap aſhes he has uſed on graſs land,
with ſuch ſucceſs, that land let at 5 s.
manured with 20 loads an acre, was improved by them to a guinea an acre rent.

Experiment, No. 4.

Ant-hills he tried once for manure,
mixing them with dung. A large quantity
was formed into a heap, which he turned
over ſeveral times, till the whole was one

uniform

uniform mafs of putrid mould it was quite black and moift. this he fpread on grafs, and found the benefit of it fully equal to that of dung alone: and it has lafted longer than he apprehended that manure would have done.

Experiment, No. 5

Mr. *Bevor* tried the burning of clay · it was of a hard ftrong kind he formed a heap with whins, rufhes, ftubble, and fome turf; the clay calcined into bricks, which were broken and fpread on the land; few afhes But the benefit has been very little.

In preferving all the urine which runs from the farm-yards, &c. this gentleman is very attentive, he has a fmall well to which it is conducted, with a pump fixed. as faft as it fills, it is carted away in fuch a machine as they water the roads about *London* with. He fprinkles the worft grafs with it, and finds it the means of prefently converting it into the beft. This is an excellent practice, and cannot be too much recommended.

Experiment, No. 6

Hearing it afferted that young fwine would not do well on clover, he ordered fome fows and pigs to be turned all day long into the clover field with his other hogs; they were fo, and no ill effect arofe; they were as well, and throve as faft as before He has fince adhered to the practice, and whenever a clover field, or part of one, is fed, *all* his fwine, without diftinction, have it.

This gentleman's farm confifts of

530 Acres in all	32 Wheat
400 Grafs	22 Cows
130 Arable	20 Oxen
£.400 Rent	20 Young cattle
40 Acres of grafs mown	180 Sheep
	100 Horfes
32 Turnips	10 Colts and foals
32 Barley	40 Swine.
32 Clover	

The number of horfes is owing to his taking many joift ones from *Norwich*, at 2 *s* 6 *d.* a week, the year through, giving them hay in winter, for them to go to at pleafure

He keeps none but polled cows, that is,

with-

without horns, on account of his plantations and hedges; and he finds they give
more milk than others.

His sheep are the *Lincolnshire* breed, of
which he finds he can keep in proportion
to the *Norfolk* ones, as 3 to 5. If 500 of
the latter, he can keep 300 of *Lincolnshire*,
and the latter will pay him much better
than the 500 *Norfolks*, He clips 6 s. worth
of wool from each.

Experiment, No. 7.

In planting, Mr. *Bevor* finds that *Scotch*
firs, in 18 years, are worth 2 s. 6 d. A
plantation of his taken through are of that
value.

Experiment, No. 8.

A whole plantation of 50 years growth,
worth 50 s. on an average: they stand 20
feet square—which is 108 to an acre.

Experiment, No. 9.

In another plantation on a moist sandy
loam, larches of 18 years growth, are
worth 3 s. 6 d.: Spruce firs among them
not half so good, which Mr. *Bevor* attributes

butes to their being trimmed up; others on same soil and growth, not served so, are almost double the size.

—— *Rogers*, Esq, of *Ethel*, has taken a farm, which he is improving, particularly by claying, and other manuring. He has three acres of cabbages. He ploughed for them five times, transplanted from the seed bed (sown in *March)* in *June*, in rows 4 feet by 2 from plant to plant, and he has observed that the larger the plants at setting out, so much the better the crop; which is a matter of importance. I observed a great difference in the field; but it was owing alone to the plants being larger: they promise well, and are kept perfectly clean.—The following are the particulars of Mr. *Rogers*'s farm.

175 Acres in all	10 Horses
150 Arable	2 Men
20 Grass	12 Labourers.

£. 105 Rent

—— *Berney*, Esq; at *Bracon Ash*, has made great improvements by planting land of 20 s. an acre.

Oak, of 50 years growth, are worth

15 s.

15 s each they stand 15 feet square, this is 180 on an acre.

Larch, in 18 years, (20 from the feed) are worth 6 s each. they grow out of underwood that pays 20 s. an acre. Some few of 20 years, worth 15 s. each. Silver firs in the fame wood not quite fo large, but they beat both the fpruce and *Scotch* They all stand 15 feet square in the underwood

In another plantation without underwood, *Scotch* firs, of 18 years, are 2 s. 6 d. each. they stand 8 feet square; which is 680 on an acre, or 85 *l*.; that is, 4 *l*. 14 s. *per* acre *per annum*, exclufive of thinnings.

An adjoining plantation of fpruce, of the fame age and diftance, are worth 4 s. each, which is 136 *l per* acre, or 7 *l* 6 s. *per* acre *per ann*. from firft planting, and exclufive of thinnings. No hufbandry will equal this. A man who would plant for profit muft not regret land of 20 s. an acre

Weymouth pines, in 18 years, much larger than *Scotch* firs of 22 years.

Mr. *Berney* has found it beft to trim up the firs,

Plate

Plate VII & XII part.

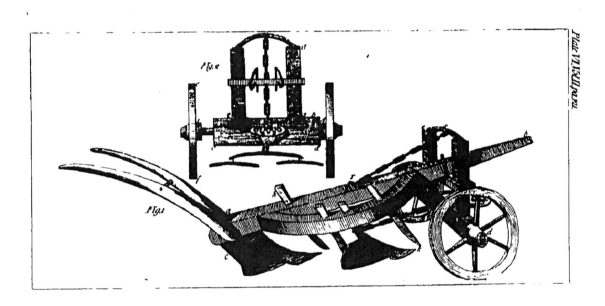

Fig. 2

Fig. 1

Plate VI. Fig. 1. repiefents an improvement made by Mr. *Berney* in the double plough, of which I gave a plate in Vol. 3. of my *Six Months Tour through the North of England.*

From   a to b. —— 7 feet 6 inches.

         c to d. —— 6 feet.

         b to d —— 3 feet 6.

         h to 1. —— 3 feet.

         f to g. ——   6 inches.

         e to b. —— 2 feet.

         c to k. —— 4 feet 8.

         r to s. ——   31 inches.

Fig 2 the carriage in front. From 1. to 2 is four inches wider than from 3. to 4.

From   a to b. —— 20 inches.

         c to d. —— 28 ditto.

         e to f —— 26 ditto.

Two horfes only are ufed in it, by this means of raifing the front carriage fo much higher than in the old one, and alfo by fhortening the beam fo much. It worked againft the common *Norfolk* wheeled ploughs; and did with 2 horfes, three acres in the time they did two.

Several very important trials in hufbandry and planting have been executed by *William Fellowes,* Efq; of *Shottefham.*

Experiment, No 1.

To difcover which was the beft manure for turnips, yard dung or earth mixed with lime, a field was divided into two parts: one half dunged with 12 loads an acre, directly from the yard to the land; the other half, 30 loads an acre of earth mixed with 3 chaldron of lime The former part turned out much the beft.

Experiment, No. 2.

Wheat Mr. *Fellowes* drills in equally diftant rows, 18 inches afunder, and hand-hoes it twice, at 2 *s.* 6 *d.* an acre each time. I viewed it with great pleafure, for not a weed was to be feen; it is calculated at 3 ½ quarters *per* acre; which is a better crop than moft broadcaft hereabouts.

There was likewife fome wheat drilled with 4 feet intervals. I examined the ears, and found them not at all larger or heavier than thofe of the 18 inch rows.

Experiment, No. 3.

Some feed of the great *Scotch* cabbage was fown the 10th of *March*; and in *May* tranfplanted into the experiment field, in

fquares

fquares of 2 feet 6 inches, upon a well tilled turnip loam, manured with 20 loads of dung an acre. I found them very fine, and perfectly clean; turnips were on one fide of them, fo that Mr. *Fellowes* will be able to fee which will laft longeft good— and yield the beft crop.

Experiment, No. 4.

In 1765, two acres of a light loamy foil, manured with 12 loads an acre yard dung, were fown with carrots the beginning of *April*, 4^{lb} of feed *per* acre. They were hand-hoed thrice, at the expence of a guinea an acre.

They were taken up with forks as wanted; the product 20 loads an acre, 30 bufhels each, or 600 bufhels; which, at 1s. a bufhel, is 30l. *per* acre They were all ufed for horfes, kept all winter in a fmall dry grafs clofe: the carrots were thrown about the field. No horfes could do better, or be freer from diftempers.

Experiment, No. 5.

In 1766, four acres of the fame foil were ploughed four times, the third time

in the trenching manner, one plough following another in the fame furrow, gaining a depth of 10 inches; after which it
was ploughed in the common manner, and
4 *lb.* *per* acre of feed harrowed in they
were hoed thrice, at a guinea an acre
The crop was ufed in the fame manner as
that of 1765; and was as good a one.
Some cows being turned in with the horfes,
the butter received an higher colour, but
was improved in flavour : none could be
finer.

Experiment, No 5

In 1767, four acres in the fame field
were fown, upon the fame preparation as
the preceding year. They were given to
cows and horfes in the former manner, and
turned of incomparable ufe. Numbers of
the carrots weighed 3 or 4 *lb.* but the general average was not more than 1 *lb.* They
were fet out at 8 inches diftance from each
other in general; but fmall fpots failing,
that diftance, Mr. *Fellowes* apprehends,
was encreafed in the whole field to 10 or
11; but I fhall fuppofe to 12. There would
then be 43560 carrots on an acre, which,

at

at 1 *lb* each, amounts to 19 tons 9 C. *wt.* and fuppofing a bufhel to weigh 56 *lb* it is 778 bufhels on an acre, which at 1 *s.* comes to 38 *l.* 18 *s* ; at 6 *d* only, they come to 19 *l.* 9 *s per* acre. And to fhew the undoubted greatnefs of the value of a carrot crop ; allow 2 fquare feet to each carrot, which would make them all far greater than 1 *lb* weight; the crop in fuch cafe, at 6 *d.* a bufhel, would be 9 *l.* 14 *s.* 6 *d.* an acre. But I know from various experiments of my own, that they will pay in feeding cattle 1 *s* a bufhel

Experiment, No 6

In 1768, four acres more of the fame foil were fown with carrots, the culture, produce, and expenditure, the fame as the year 1767.

Experiment, No. 7.

In 1769, Six acres were fown; the fuccefs the fame.

Experiment, No. 8.

This year, 1770, the crop is four acres, in the fame experiment field ; *6 lb per* acre

4 of

of feed were fown; the crop is regular, clean, and very fine. Mr. *Fellowes* is clear that they will come to 1 *lb.* each on an average; of which I have not any doubt.

Barley has been conftantly fown after the carrots; and refpecting their value as a preparation for that grain, he is very clear in his account: the crop is always much fuperior to that which follows turnips drawn; but fomething inferior to fuch as fucceed turnips fed on the land.

Obfervations.

Thefe experiments on carrots are very valuable; the facts to be drawn from them are perfectly fatisfactory, in being the refult, not of a fingle vague trial or two, but a regular profecution of an eftablifhed hufbandry. The carrot crop, though fmall, is as certain a one as any other on Mr. *Fellowes*'s farm. It evidently appears that they yield a very confiderable quantity of produce, and that produce of uncommon ufe in feeding both horfes and cows.

But the idea of the value of a crop is throughout this country extremely indeterminate, and below the truth. From

four

four to fix or feven guineas an acre, have been thought high prices. This ftrange circumftance has been owing to two caufes; firft, the price at *Norwich*, which is not half what I experimentally know them to be worth in feeding cattle; and, fecondly, to a want of keeping minutes of the confumption.

Carrots are worth 1 s. a bufhel of 56 *lb.* in feeding horfes or oxen, or in rearing, feeding, or fattening fwine But the clear method of knowing their value is to buy a lot of hogs or oxen, fat them with fo many hundred bufhels of carrots, then fell them: the value of the carrots is decided at once.

Let us calculate the profit of the preceding crops.

Expences.

Rent, tythe, and town charges, £.1	1	0
Five ploughings and harrowings,	0	16	0
6 *lb.* of Seed, - -	0	8	0
Sowing, - - -	0	1	0
12 Loads dung, directly from yard,			
fuppofe - - -	1	10	0
Hoeing, - - -	1	1	0
Taking up, fuppofe -	0	12	0
Carting from field, fuppofe	0	5	0
	5	14	0

Produce.

778 Bufhels, at 1 *s.* -	£.38	18	0
Expences, - -	5	14	0
Profit, - - -	33	4	0

If each carrot is only ½ *lb* it is

389 bufhels, which, at 1 *s.* is	19	9	0
Expences, - -	5	14	0
Profit, - -	13	15	0

And lower than this it cannot reafonably be eftimated. This profit on a crop which keeps fo much ftock, and confequently raifes a prodigious quantity of dung, at the fame time that it prepares the land for barley, ought to induce the farmers to cultivate it upon a large fcale: they would affuredly find it the moft beneficial article in *Britifh* hufbandry.

Rents about *Shottefham* rife from 8 *s.* to 20 *s.* an acre; the average about 14 *s.* The general courfe is,

1. Turnips, worth 2 *l.* 2 *s.*

2. Barley, 3 ½ quarters *per* acre.

3. Clover, worth 3 *l.* 3 *s.* an acre.

4. Wheat, 2 ½ quarters.

But it is found pretty generally that clover fails much more than formerly: it comes up very thick and fine, but

dies,

dies away in the winter—Mr *Fellowes*, by means of more fpirited management, gets better crops, his wheat 3 ½ quarters, his barley 4, and has up to 6; and his turnips 2*l*. 10*s*. No farm can be neater, or carry greater marks of its being in the hands of a gentleman. He has grafs borders 15 feet wide around all his fields, which are mown for hay and kept level, and free from ruts: and either fingle or double rows of elms run along many of them, for the pleafure of walking in the fhade, befides the beauty of the object. I obferved alfo, that the fences throughout his farm were in excellent order, regular, and free from gaps and rank weeds.

Mr. *Fellowes* has given yet greater attention to planting than to hufbandry, and has tried various trees, fome years ago, fo that he is now able clearly to judge which is the moft profitable.

Experiment, No. 9.

A plantation of *Scotch* firs of 45 years growth, 20 feet fquare, on land of 15*s*. an acre, are now worth 20*s*. each on an average. At that diftance there are 108 trees on an acre, or 108*l*, which is 2*l*. 9*s*.

VOL. II. K *per*

per acre *per ann.* from the firſt planting, excluſive of thinnings, which would more than double it. But the graſs under the trees would have let, for many years paſt at 7*s.* an acre.

Experiment, No. 10.

Another plantation of *Scotch* firs, 38 years growth, ſtanding in rows 14 feet wide and 10 in the rows, are now worth 12*s.* on an average. This diſtance gives 300 on an acre; and at 12*s.* come to 180*l.* or 4*l.* 14*s. per* acre *per annum*, beſides thinnings. The rent of the land 15*s.*; poor rates 1*s.* 3*d.* in the pound; and tythe, till 20 years old, 5*s.* an acre; the graſs under them now 5*s.* an acre. It is ſufficiently evident that no huſbandry can equal this.

Experiment, No. 11.

Cheſnuts in 38 years *, on the ſame land, ſtanding 14 feet by 10, are worth 15*s.* each. This is 225*l. per* acre; or 5*l.* 16*s. per* acre *per annum*, beſides thinnings.

Experiment, No. 12.

Scotch firs in 38 years, on the ſame land, meaſure 17 feet of timber on an average,

for

---

* Note that all theſe ages are from the ſeed, not the planting

for which Mr. *Fellowes* has been offered
11*d.* a foot, that is 15 *s.* 7 *d.* a tree. They
ſtand 14 feet by 10. An acre would therefore be 233 *l* 15*s.*; or 6*l* 3 *s. per* acre *per
annum*, beſides thinnings. Theſe trees are
60 feet high.

Experiment, No. 13.

On the ſame land larch trees, of only 31
years growth, are as large as the firs of
Experiment, No. 12. which ſhews that the
larch is a much quicker grower. Spruce
by them, not ſo laige as either. The pinaſter of 38 years, larger than the *Scotch:*
The cedar of *Lebanon*, of the ſame age,
would now cut into planks 12 inches wide.

Experiment, No. 14.

A very ſtriking compariſon between the
larch and the ſpruce fir, was tried by planting an old gravel pit levelled, ſurrounded
by a plantation of *Scotch* fir, with thoſe
two ſorts in alternate rows. The larch is
from 6 to 12 feet high; whereas the ſpruce
is but 2 feet on an average.

Experiment, No. 15.

A large plantation of many acres of a
poor gravelly land, at 8*s.* an acre, contain-
ing *Scotch* and ſpruce firs and larches, is

now 16 years old, they are in squares of 10 feet, and are worth,

> The *Scotch*, 2 s. 6 d each.
> The spruce, 3 s. 6 d
> The larches, 4 s. 6 d.

At ten feet, there are 435 trees on an acre.

The *Scotch*, at 2 s. 6 d. come to 54 l. 7 s. 6 d.; or *per* acre *per annum*, 3 l. 7 s.

The spruce, at 3 s. 6 d to 76 l. 2 s. 6 d.; or *per* acre *per annum*, to 4 l. 15 s.

The larch, at 4 s. 6 d to 97 l. 17 s. 6 d.; or *per annum*, 6 l. 2 s.

All three exclusive of thinnings —Suppose we calculate these at no more than paying the rent, tythe, and town charges; and that the larch, in 20 years, come only to 100 l. which is however under the truth; let any one calculate the profit of hiring land on a 21 (or more) years leafe, and immediately planting. In what other application of the land can such great profit be made, as gaining 6 l. an acre without any rifque, and almost without any expence? It is true, such a conduct cannot, like the culture of corn and grafs, be general, for reasons obvious to every one—but as far as the whole demand of any neighbourhood extends, it is profitable to execute

it.

it. Such a demand is every where very great, for the use of rails, spars, beams, board, planks, &c. &c. according to the age of the trees, and great quantities of these are perpetually importing from the *Baltic.* So far, therefore, as the demand extends, it is highly advifeable to plant these trees.

Suppofe 5 acres of larch planted every year; at the end of 16 or 17 years, five acres will every year be cut down, of the value of 500*l* from that day a regular product of 500*l* a year is gained from the application of 100 acres of land Let to a tenant, thefe 100 acres produce 40*l*. a year; but planted, they produce 500*l* a year. What an amazing difference!

Suppofe a fingle acre planted every year. after the expiration of 18 or 20, to cut annually 100*l* a year from only 20 acres, which let, would yield but 8*l*. a year. How beneficial a conduct.

It fhould here be obferved, that the larch is valued the fame as the *Scotch* fir; but the beft authorities tell us, the timber is one of the moft ufeful known; probably, there-fore, the value of it would turn out greater than the fuppofition in thefe experiments.

Experiment, No 16.

Sixteen *Scotch* firs and two pinasters raised from feed, fown between *Michaelmas* 1732, and *Lady Day* 1733, were meafured *June* 7, 1768. The meafure is exclufive of the bark, for which 6 feet *per* load was allowed; the bark being very thick they were valued at 9*d*. a foot. They being full of fap. The 306 feet come to 11*l* 9*s*. 6*d*. The trees ftand in a row at unequal diftances; but are on an average at 15 feet.

No. 1. *Scotch* fir ——— 22 feet.
2. Ditto. ——— 13
3. Ditto. ——— 21
4. Ditto. ——— 26
5. Ditto. ——— 9
6. Ditto. ——— 22
7. Ditto. ——— 16
8. Ditto. ——— 10
9. Ditto. ——— 22
10. Ditto. ——— 18
11. Ditto. ——— 15
12. Ditto. ——— 22
13. Ditto ——— 22
14. Ditto. ——— 8
15. Ditto. ——— 18
16. Ditto. ——— 16
——
280

Brought over,   280 feet.

17. Pinaſter ———— 11

18. Ditto. ———— 15
————
306

A beech ſown at the ſame time, mea-
ſured in *January* 21, 1769, 19 feet 7 inches.

Mr *Fellowes* has had both the boughs
and feed of the red deal from *Norway*, and
he finds that it is the *Scotch* fir.

In a regular planting and cutting down
a given quantity of land, it would be ad-
viſable, I ſhould apprehend, to plant the
old land again, which would ſave grubbing
up the ſtumps and roots, which in rotting
would turn to a rich manure for the new trees.

Plane trees Mr. *Fellowes* has planted;
and he finds them to thrive amazingly in
low moiſt ſituations. It will in ſuch, grow
much faſter than the poplar. One he has
of 30 years growth that will cut into planks
20 inches broad; but ſo vaſt a ſize he
attributes in ſome meaſure to its ſtanding
on the edge of a ditch through which the
drainings of a farmer's pigſties run. Poplars, in ſome parts of the kingdom, are
planted in low ſituations to the excluſion of
every thing elſe: it is of conſequence there-

         fore

fore to know that the plane will do better;
and in beauty it infinitely exceeds that rag-
ged, crooked, unsightly tree, the poplar.

Mr. *Fellowes* in general recommends the
larch as preferable to every other tree that
he has tried; and which will pay a planter
much greater profit than any of the rest.
As to the method of cultivating them, or
any firs, he is of opinion that the land
should be cropped with turnips, and the
trees set about the 10th of *April* following.
but if that season is omitted, late in *August*
will do. They should be 2 years old, and
set at 4 feet square. For four years it will
be advisable to hand-hoe the land about
them twice a year, which will cost 3 *s.* each
hoeing: after that there will be no further
expence *.

—— *Gooch*, Esq; of *Shottesham*, has
cultivated lucerne with success: He has
kept two horses through a summer on the
produce of only a rood of good land.

---

* Mr. *Fellowes* in the corner of one of his
fields has a rustic temple of a design which cannot but please It is the imitation of a round
hay-stack, thatched from the ground I do not
remember seeing one before. It is a stroke of
pure taste

Suppofe the fummer 26 weeks,

    and the horfes at 2 _s._ 6 _d._;

    this amounts to _per_ acre   £ 26 0 0

Lucerne is a plant that will ever be found to anfwer in an uncommon manner on good foils.

From this part of _Norfolk_ I took the road to _Yarmouth_ through the hundred of _Flegg_; which I had been told was cultivated in a moft complete manner.

Farms in this country rife fiom 50 _l._ to 500 _l._ a year; but are in general about 120 _l._ The foil is various, but chiefly a fine, mixed, dark good loam, lets at 15 _s._ an acre. Their courfes of crops moft common, aie,

1. Turnips   4. Wheat

2 Barley   5. Barley.

3. Clover

              Alfo,

1. Turnips   4. Buck-wheat or

2. Barley   peafe

3. Clover and ray- 5. Wheat.
    grafs for 2 years

This is an excellent courfe. They plough but once for wheat; fow 3 bufhels, and gain 3 ¼ quarters an acre. For barley they ftir thrice, fow 3 bufhels, and reckon the average produce 4 quarters. They get 5 quarters of oats, and 10 have been known. For peafe they plough but once; fow 3 bufhels, and get 2 ½ quarters *per* acre.

They give four or five earths for turnips; hoe them always twice. Many are drawn for the fattening of beafts, fome in fheds, fome in bings in the farm yards, and fome on dry grafs fields; but they reckon them to fatten beft and quickeft in fheds; but one evil is, they wont drive fo well in this method. They buy at the *Michaelma* fairs both home bred and *Scotch* beafts, almoft lean; they put them to turnips, and fell in *April*. If they buy at 5 *l.* they wil fell at 8 *l.* 8 *s.* or 9 *l.* They give no hay with the turnips; or a very trifle, but they have ftraw at command. Three rood of turnips will fatten a beaft of 45 ftone, or 6 *Norfolk* wether fheep.

The clover crop is both mown once—twice—and alfo fed wholly. Thefe variations depend on the wants of the farmer; but it is generally agreed among them, that the wheat which follows the crops cut for hay, are better than thofe which fucceed the crops fed. Tares are cultivated by

fome

fome farmers for foiling their horfes with green in the ftable, alfo for feed; and they fow wheat after them.

In their manuring they are very good and attentive farmers. They chop their ftubbles for littering; and their hay they ftack all at home. Marle is ufed at a very great expence. It is brought from *Norwich* by water to *Yarmouth*, and from thence, by many farmers, to *Ormfby*, &c. from 4 to 7 and 8 miles by land. The expence is 3*l.* for a keel load of 18 cart loads, each 1 ½ tons, and the land carriage is 4*s.* a load more; fo that the whole price is 7*s.* 4*d. per* cart-load. The greatnefs of this expence prevents their laying on fuch large quantities as in other parts of *Norfolk.* Clay they likewife ufe; lay 40 loads an acre, and find it lafts 20 years. They make compofts of clay or mould, farm-yard dung, and fea fand; covering the whole heap with the latter; but in one circumftance they are very deficient, they never mix them by turning over.

Malt-duft they fow on clover, and find great benefit; about 4 quarters an acre.— *Yarmouth* dung they buy at 2 *s.* a load

They

They have scarcely any meadow or pasture in the country, their cows they feed on clover and ray-grafs; an acre of which they reckon sufficient for the summer food of one. Good cows give 5 gallons of milk a day. They let their dairies at 4 *l.* 4 *s.*; and reckon that the hirers make 1 *l.* 1 *s.* to 1 *l.* 11 *s.* 6 *d.* a head profit.

Swine fatten to 15 stone a head.

The number of sheep kept is very small; many farmers none at all; but those that do, buy chiefly wethers and year old lambs, and sell them fat within the year.

In their tillage, they reckon that 6 horses are necessary to 100 acres of arable land: they use 2 in a plough; and do an acre and half a day in general, but 2 acres in barley sowing; do not cut deeper than 4 inches on account of a poor barren sand below the surface, which is pernicious to their land. The price *per* acre 2 *s.* 6 *d.* The annual expence *per* horse they reckon at 6 *l.* Their stubbles they begin to break up for a fallow about *Chriftmas.* They use none but wheel ploughs; which they reckon much the easiest and most expeditious:

ous · but if they want to plough up a very ftubborn piece of land—or to cut deeper than ordinary, they ufe fwing ploughs.

In the ftocking farms they reckon 1500*l.* neceffary for one of 300*l* a year.

Land fells at 26 or 27 years purchafe.—

Tythes are compounded in all forts of ways, but the general rule is 3 *s.* an acre.

Poor rates 1 *s.*: Twenty years ago they were but 3 *d.*: the employment of the women and children fpinning wool: all drink tea; and fome thrice a day.

The following are the particulars of a farm.

350 Acres in all	4 Men
300 Arable	1 Boy
50 Marfh	2 Maids
£.260 Rent	5 Labourers
17 Horfes	60 Acres turnips
20 Cows	60 Wheat
40 Young	120 Barley
50 Fatting beafts	60 Clover.
on turnips	

They have throughout this country a machine which I have not feen any where elfe, which is a cart convertible into a waggon by adding at pleafure two fore wheels.

The

The farmers very fenfibly remarked the danger that the filler horfe is always in when a two wheeled cart is heavy loaded, either of being lifted up by loading too heavy behind, or having his back broken by a load too heavy before:—carts in harveft are of but little ufe from the danger of loading them freely on this account. Thefe motives induced them to contrive this addition, which they have to many of their carts in harveft, rendering them as ufeful as waggons: They alfo ufe them on the road for carrying corn to market; they load them with 10 or 12 quarters of barley with the utmoft eafe, which is near as much as a waggon will carry: on the other hand, the fore carriage takes off with the greateft eafe, and then the cart is ready for marle, dung, earth, &c.

Plate VII. Fig. 1. and 2. is a reprefentation of one of them.

John Ramey, Efq; of *Ormfby* near *Yarmouth*, has executed fome experiments in hufbandry which deferve being known. Lucerne he tried in comparifon with common hufbandry. In 1763, he threw a clofe of 7 acres and an half of fine rich

light

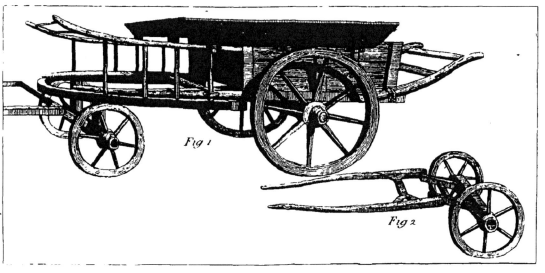

Plate VII pa. 142 Vol.II

Fig 1

Fig 2

light land into three divisions; one of 3 acres of lucerne transplanted; one of half an acre of lucerne broad-cast; and one of three acres for common husbandry. The whole piece turnips in 1762, manured for. The three acres designed for transplanted lucerne were cropped in 1763, with *Charlton* pease, which were off the land time enough to give it three ploughings, and harrowings sufficient to make it perfectly fine; and the lucerne was in *August* set in rows 3 feet asunder, by 1 foot from plant to plant in the rows. It was kept clean of weeds by hand-hoeing, but came that autumn to nothing.

At the same time that the pease were sown on that piece, barley was sown on the other 3 ½ acres, broad-cast lucerne on the half acre, and clover on the 3. The barley yielded 5 quarters *per* acre, which quite destroyed the lucerne, but did no damage to the clover.

1764.

This year the transplanted lucerne was cut three times; it was horse-hoed four times, and hand-hoed thrice, at a great expence. But the product was small, not

I

more

more than the three acres keeping two horfes through the fummer.

The clover was cut twice ; the firft time it yielded 35 C. wt. per acre of hay ; the fecond 20 C. wt.

1765.

This year the lucerne was horfe-hoed three times, and hand-hoed as often ; it was cut thrice, and given to the horfes in the ftable : the product was fomething better than the preceding year, but not to the amount of keeping another horfe.

The clover land was ploughed up, and yielded 3 ½ quarters of wheat per acre.

1766.

This year the lucerne declined ; which Mr. *Ramey* perceiving, he did not attend to keeping it clean, fo the weeds got the better of it.

The clover land, wheat ftubble, was fown with barley ; the produce 4 quarters per acre.

In this trial the common hufbandry was beyond comparifon more advantageous than lucerne ; but in extenuation of the ill fuccefs of the latter, I muft be allowed to obferve

that

that it was given up just when it was coming to perfection For 3 acres of tranfplanted lucerne to keep 2 horfes the *firft
year*, is extraordinary, and bid fair for
great things. The fecond year it improved There cannot be a moment's doubt
of that improvement going on till it maintained 3 horfes *per* acre at leaft: but all this
depends on its being kept as clean as a
garden. Mr. *Ramey*, difgufted at the vaft
fuperiority of the common hufbandry during two years, might not fufficiently confider that the 2 firft of tranfplanted lucerne
are but preparatory · Certainly, if a comparifon is not conducted for fome time
after a plant arrives at maturity, the conclufions drawn from it will not be decifive

Mr. *Ramey* has this year a crop of the
great *Scotch* cabbage. The field was under
barley laft year ; it was winter fallowed,
and the plants fet the laft week in *May* in
rows 3 feet afunder, by 2 from plant to
plant. The feed was fown the third week
in *March*. The tranfplantation was performed by women only; 2 ½ acres took
one day of 6 women, and one day of 4,
all at 8 *d.* a day ; the coft therefore 6 *s.* 8 *d.*

which is 2 s. 8 d. an acre. This is doing it very cheap, for 3 feet rows are clofer than ufual; from whence it is very evident, that the tranfplanting fhould always be done by women. None of the plants were watered. they have been horfe-hoed twice, and hand-hoed as often. Mr. *Ramey* defigns them for late fpring feed, and has very judicioufly fown an adjoining 2 ½ acres with turnips; the whole field equally manured. This will enable him to judge which plant is the moft profitable.

The following is Mr. *Ramey*'s common hufbandry.

1. Turnips, worth 3 l. an acre,
2. Barley, yields 4 quarters.
3. Clover, 3 loads of hay at 2 mowings.
4. Wheat, 3 ½ quarters.
5. Barley, 4 quarters.

This barley being as good as the crop after turnips is furprizing. He always manures for his turnips; the firft hoeing he gives with a machine, in which 7 fhares cut up the turnips in ftripes; this he finds cuts the land deeper than the hand-hoe and though irregularly, yet the fecond hoe-

ing

ing in the common manner, leaves the crop perfectly even.

In the application of his clover crop, this gentleman puts it to one use that deserves great ' attention   He begins the second week in *May* to soil 20 horses with clover in the stable, and continues it till the wheat stubbles are ready to turn into: 7 acres feed 20 horses and 7 cows, the latter in a house, or rack yard, but drove twice a day to water :—also 5 calves—and as many pigs. The horses have neither corn nor hay.

Respecting the value of the crop, Mr. *Ramey* could not have his horses so kept under 8 *d.* a day; but as the joisting price of the country is 2 *s.* 6 *d.* a week, I shall calculate from that.

20 Horses 17 weeks,
  at 2 *s.* 6 *d.*   -   -   £.42 10 0
7 Cows ditto, at 2 *s.* 6 *d.*   -   14 17 6
5 Calves ditto, at 1 *s.* 6 *d.*   -   6 7 6
5 Pigs ditto,   -   -   0 0 0
                    ——————————
                    63 15 0
                    ——————————
Or *per* acre,   -   -   9 2 1

This is one of the most curious experiments I have met with ; for though it is a

L 2   practice

practice that has been often recommended, yet I never met with an accurate account of what a given quantity would do. It is from hence clearly evident, that this method of ufing clover is by far the moft beneficial. the quantity of dung raifed, where there is litter at command, is immenfe; much more than in winter, from the cattle making fo much more urine when fed on green food. I fhould value this article at 4 or 500 loads of manure from the above cattle, at 2 s. 6 d. a load.

But a ftrong confirmation of the preceding valuation, is the confumption of clover by a tenant of Mr. *Ramey*'s, who fed the very fame ftock (in number) in the field. Mr. *Ramey* watched it minutely, and when he had eaten 5 acres, this man's ftock had confumed 30 acres, and his horfes were not in fuch good condition Thus does one acre of clover *mown*, go exactly as far as 6 *fed* *.

---

* In Mr *Ramey*'s houfe on *Yarmouth Quay*, he has furnifhed a parlour with drawings of Mrs. *Ramey*'s execution with a hot poker. there are feveral pieces of ruins after *Panini*, *Gifolphi*, &c. a *Dutch* fkating piece, and fome landfcapes
The

The neatnefs and minute accuracy with which they are done are wonderful There is fre-quently a fpirit in the ftrokes fuperior to the original prints After you have viewed *Yar-mouth Quay*, which is one of the fineft in *England*, you will find nothing in the place fo much worth feeing as thefe very elegant performances.

LETTER XIV.

AS I shall presently leave *Norfolk*, it will not be improper to give a slight review of the husbandry which has rendered the name of this county so famous in the farming world. Pointing out the practices which have succeeded so nobly here, may perhaps be of some use to other countries possessed of the same advantages, but unknowing in the art to use them.

From 40 to 60 years ago, all the northern and western, and a part of the eastern tracts of the county, were sheep-walks, let so low as from 6*d.* to 1*s.* 6*d* and 2*s.* an acre. Much of it was in this condition only 30 years ago. The great improvements have been made by means of the following circumstances.

First. By inclosing without assistance of parliament.

Second. By a spirited use of marle and clay.

Third. By the introduction of an excellent course of crops.

FOURTH   By the culture of turnips well hand-hoed.

FIFTH.   By the culture of clover and ray-grafs

SIXTH.   By landlords granting long leafes.

SEVENTH   By the country being divided chiefly into large farms.

In this recapitulation, I have inferted no article that is included in another. Take any one from the feven, and the improvement of *Norfolk* would never have exifted. The importance of them all will appear fufficiently evident from a fhort examination.

THE INCLOSURE.

Provided open lands are inclofed, it is not of very great confequence by what means it was effected; but the fact is, that parliamentary inclofures are fcarcely ever fo complete and general as in *Norfolk*; and how fhould they, when numbers are to agree to the fame meafure? Had the inclofure of this county been by acts of parliament, much *might have been* done, but on no comparifon with what *is* done. The great difficulty and attention *then* would

have

have been to inclofe. *Now* the works of improvement enjoy the immediate attention. And undoubtedly many of the fineft loams on the richeft marles would at this day have been fheep-walks, had there been any right of commonage on them. A parliamentary inclofure is alfo (through the knavery of commiffioners and attorneys) fo very expenfive, compared with a private one, that it would have damped the fucceeding undertakings; in taking too large a portion of the money requifite for the great work, in a mere preparation for it.

These circumftances are to be feen more or lefs in moft of the countries inclofed by parliament.

MARLING

It is the great felicity of the fandy part of this county, that dig where you will, you find an exceeding fine marle, or clay. The marle is generally white, with veins of yellow, and red; fometimes only tinged with thofe colours. If dropped in fair water, it falls, and bubbles to the top; if it is very good, it has an effervefcence. All effervefce ftrongly in vinegar, if dropt in it in a lump, and fome will at once make the glafs, though but half full, boil over in a froth. But moft will do this if the marle is powdered before it is put in. The clay has none of thefe qualities. The beft marle is that which falls the quickeft in water, for fuch will always have the greateft effervefcence in acids.

It is common in this county to hear of the *falts* of marle. As well as they under-ftand the ufe of it, they know little of its nature; no falts are to be extracted from marle: though a little oil is to be gained. It may produce falt when fpread on the land, by its abforbent and alkaline quality, attracting the vitriolic acid, and converting it into a neutral falt; and this quality is probably one of its greateft advantages. It likewife not only attracts oil from the air, but diffolves, and fits it for the purpofes of vegetation.

I have not met with any perfons that have been curious enough to form a feries of fmall experiments on marle, for the dif-covery of the proper *quantities* for ufe, in proportion to the given *qualities* of it.

The farmers, on the firft ufe of marle,

I   fpread

spread it in larger quantities than others have done since: 100 loads were common, and few used less than 80. But land is now marled for the first time in some places with not more than from 40 to 60 loads. The reason given me for this change was principally a view to future marlings: if 80 or 100 are laid on at first, they do not think a repetition of 20 or 30, at the end of 20 or 25 years, will answer so well as if the first quantity had been smaller

It is yet an opinion among some farmers that their land will not pay for a second marling. But the best husbandmen in the county are clearly of a different way of thinking. When the first manuring is wearing out pretty fast, which generally happens in about 20 years, they (on the renewal of their lease) replenish the ground with an addition of from 20 to 35 loads an acre more. And several tracts of country have been marled with success for the third time.

But it is not the marle or clay alone that has worked the great effects we have seen in *Norfolk*. It must be spread on a suitable soil: this is a light *sandy loam*, or *loamy sand*;

fand; not a fand. In fome places a *gravelly loam*, but not a gravel. What they
call their *woodcock* loams are free from
gravel, and rather fo from fand; they are
more inclinable to a dry friable clay, but at
the fame time found and dry enough for
turnips.

Thefe are their beft foils.

Some tracts of pure fand have been
marled, and with fuccefs, though not fo
great but clay, from its fuperior tenacity,
is reckoned better for them than marle.

The reader is not to fuppofe that the
Norfolk men have depended on thefe manures alone; on the contrary, they have
been very attentive to others. Folding
fheep, through both winter and fummer,
is no where more practifed, or better underftood. Winter fatting beafts on turnips
in the farm-yards, confining the cows to
thofe yards; and keeping in them very
large ftocks of fwine, convert their plenty
of ftraw into manure; which they make
good ufe of. Oil cake they lay on their
wheat, at an expence of 40 s. or two guineas an acre. All thefe manures they ufe
to far greater profit than if their land had
not

not been marled.—That foundation of their hufbandry is a preparative for all fucceffive manurings ; they take the greater effect from following an abforbent earth, and laft (it is afferted) the longer : but that I fhould doubt.

THE COURSE OF CROPS.

After the beft managed inclofure, and the moft fpirited conduct in marling, ftill the whole fuccefs of the undertaking depends on this point. No fortune will be made in *Norfolk* by farming, unlefs a judicious courfe of crops be purfued. That which has been chiefly adopted by the *Norfolk* farmers is,

1. Turnips
2. Barley
3. Clover ; or clover and ray-grafs
4. Wheat.

Some of them, depending on their foils being richer than their neighbours (for inftance, all the way from *Holt* by *Aylfham* down through the *Flegg* hundreds) will fteal a crop of peafe or barley after the wheat; but it is bad hufbandry, and has not been followed by thofe men who have made fortunes. In the above courfe, the

turnips

turnips are (if poffible) manured for; and much of the wheat the fame. This is a noble fyftem, which keeps the foil rich; only one exhaufting crop is taken to a cleanfing and ameliorating one. The land cannot poffibly in fuch management be either poor or foul

The only variations are in the duration of the clover; which extends from one year to three or four. On the firft improvement, ray-grafs was generally fown with it, and it was left on the ground 3 or four years. but latterly they fow no more ray-grafs than merely fufficient for their flocks, and leave it 2 years on the ground. The reft of their clover crop is fown alone, and left but one year. Opinions are not clear on thefe variations. Some think the modern method an improvement, others, that the old one was better.

If I may be allowed to hazard an idea on this point, I fhould venture to condemn the ploughing up the clover the firft year; and for thefe reafons. It is exhaufting the land more: Two crops of corn in four years, exhauft much more than two in five years: hence appears to me the *modern* neceffity

ceffity of buying oil cake at two guineas an acre. The marle is loft fooner in this method, for that fubfides in exact proportion to the quantity of tillage in a given time. It does not fink while the land is at reft; but while it is pulverizing by the plough. Laftly, the ftock of cattle is lefs, confequently the quantity of dung inferior, inftead of folding 25 acres, only 20 are done. They do not pretend that the wheat after a lay of *two* years is worfe than after that of *one*—but they fay it is not fo clean. I admit that there will be more trouble in clearing the turnip fallow of twitch; but let that trouble be carried to account, and it will not balance the counter advantages.

Befides, the beft farmers agree, that if the turnip fallow is well executed; the plants twice well hoed, and the land ftirred thrice for barley; that, then the clover lying 2 years, will not give a foul crop of wheat. Twitch generally comes from fome neglect.

TURNIPS.

Every link of the chain of *Norfolk* hufbandry has fo intimate a connection and depend-

dependance, that the deſtruction of a ſingle one, ruins the whole. Every thing depends not only on turnips, but on turnips well hoed; an aſſertion that will receive but little credit in various parts of the kingdom. Turnips on well manured land, thoroughly hoed, are the only fallow in the *Norfolk* courſe; it is therefore abſolutely neceſſary to make it as complete as poſſible. They cannot be changed for a mere fallow, becauſe the ſtock of ſheep kept for folding, and eating of the clover and ray-graſs; and farm-yard cattle would then all ſtarve; and add to this, that the tillage during the latter part of the ſummer, &c. which muſt be ſubſtituted inſtead of them, would pulverize the ſands too much, which are greatly improved by the treading of the cattle that eat the crop off. In a word, the improved culture of this plant is ſo important to the *Norfolk* huſbandry, that no other vegetable could be ſubſtituted that a common farmer would cultivate.

CLOVER AND RAY-GRASS.

This alſo is another article that could not poſſibly be diſpenſed with. The light parts of the county have neither meadows nor paftures; their flocks of fheep, dairies of cows, their fatting beafts in the fpring, and their horfes all depend on thefe graffes, and could fubfift by nothing elfe; nor could they raife any wheat without this affiftance. Their foil is too light for that grain before it is well bound and matted together by the roots of the clover, which are at the fame time a rich manure for the wheat: a fallow inftead of clover would be worfe than nothing, it would render the land much too light. For thefe reafons, which certainly are decifive, nothing could be done here without clover.

LEASES.

It is a cuftom growing pretty common in feveral parts of the kingdom, to grant no leafes: this will do very well where no improvements are carried on; where a tenant can never lofe any thing by being turned out of his farm · but it is abfurdity itfelf to expect that a man will begin his hufbandry on your land by expending 3, 4, or 5 *l*. an acre, while he is liable to be turned out at a year's notice. I fhall not

take

take up more of your time on a point which is felf-evident. Had the *Norfolk* landlords conducted themfelves on fuch narrow principles, their eftates, which are raifed five, fix, and tenfold, would yet have been fheep-walks.

LARGE FARMS.

If the preceding articles are properly reviewed, it will at once be apparent that no fmall farmers could effect fuch great things as have been done in *Norfolk*. Inclofing, marling, 'and keeping a flock of fheep large enough for folding, belong abfolutely and exclufively to great farmers. None of them could be effected by fmall ones—or fuch as are called middling ones in other countries. —Nor fhould it be forgotten, that the beft hufbandry in *Norfolk* is that of the largeft farmers. You muft go to a *Curtis*, a *Mallet*, a *Barton*, a *Glover*, a *Carr*, to fee *Norfolk* hufbandry. You will not among them find the ftolen crops that are too often met with among the little occupiers of an hundred a year, in the eaftern part of the county. Great farms have been the foul of the *Norfolk* culture. fplit them into tenures of an hundred pounds a year, you will find nothing but beggars and weeds in the whole county. The rich man keeps his land rich and clean.

These are the principles of *Norfolk* husbandry, which have advanced the agriculture of the greatest part of that county to a much greater height than is any where to be met with over an equal extent of country. I shall in the next place venture slightly to mention a few particulars in which the *Norfolk* farmers are deficient.

1. Pease are never hand-hoed.
2. Wheat, though weedy, the same.
3. Beans, the same every where, except in marshland.
4. No regular chopping of stubbles for littering the farm-yards: it is very incompletely practised.
5. Meadows and natural pastures managed in as slovenly a manner as in any part of the kingdom.
6. The breed of sheep contemptible.
7. That of horses very indifferent.
8. Vast tracts of land admirably fit for

carrots;

carrots, but none cultivated except a very few near *Norwich*.

9. All their hedges managed on the old sad syftem of cutting off live wood, and supplying the place with dead. no plashing

Thefe circumstances, however, are by no means a balance to the merit of the good hufbandry before stated; I hint them only as matters deserving the attention of farmers, who have shewn in general such enlightened views.

I am, Sir, &c.

M 2

LETTER XV.

FROM *Yarmouth* to *Beccles* the country is various, but in general cultivated pretty well; rents rise from 9*s.* to
16*s.*—The latter mentioned town is clean,
well built, paved, and prettily situated
by a river. Four miles south of it, land
lets on an average at 12*s.* an acre. I observed several fields that seemed new laid
to grass, and extremely well done; and
having several times heard of *Suffolk* being
famous for grass seeds, I made enquiries
concerning them. They lay down with
3*lb.* of trefoile *per* acre, 1 ½*lb.* of white
clover, and 5 sacks of hay seeds, which
they gain by shaking the hay off clean
upland meadows of a rich soil, with forks
in winter before they use it. And then
they dress them with great care. They
assured me, that they get the seeds quite
clean and free from weeds. An acre of
hay yields 3 or 4 sacks of 3 bushels; and
they sell in proportion to the goodness,

from

from 2 *s.* 6 *d.* to 4 *s.* a fack. Very fine feeds they reckon to grow about *Laxfield*, *Baddingham*, *Freffingfield*, *Ottley*, and *Helmingham*. When they lay down, they always fow with fpring corn: mow it the firft year, and get a load and half of hay an acre.

Their products of corn are as follow.

Wheat, 2 quarters.

Barley, 2 $\frac{1}{2}$ quarters.

Oats, 4 quarters.

Beans, 4 quarters.

Turnips, worth 30 *s.*

Clover, 2 loads of hay, at 2 mowings. But they infift that the land is tired of clover; it comes up thick and fine, but is all eaten off in *February* by a red worm, which did not ufe to happen to them.

They ufe only wheel ploughs, and but 2 horfes.

In feveral parts of this country, particularly towards *Hoxton*, and *Rumburgh*, there are very great dairies kept; up to 40, 60, and 70 cows, which they ufe all for butter and cheefe; their cows give from 2 to 8 gallons of milk a day; the breed, all the little *Suffolk* mongrel. One of them will

M 3

will eat 2 acres of grass in summer, and if she has nothing else, a ton and half of hay in winter. They calculate the product from 4 *l.* to 5 *l.* each; but many dairies are let at 3 *l.* 5 *s.* a head. They reckon that each cow maintains a hog. The attendance upon them is in proportion to 3 dairy-maids and one boy to 40 cows.

On a farm of 250 *l.* a year, they often keep 60 cows. And they reckon 3000 *l.* necessary to stock a dairy one of 300 *l.* a year.

Farms in general, rise from 100 *l.* to 300 *l.* a year.

From *Beccles* to *Yoxford*, I observed little patches of hemp in the gardens of most of the cottagers, which is an instance of industry much to their honour.

At *Yoxford* I observed, for the first time, swing ploughs chiefly used. The farmers here think quite contrary to those throughout *Norfolk*.

Towards *Saxmundham*, and about that place, the soil is all sandy. Two miles on the other side of it, towards *Woodbridge*, I remarked exceeding good crops. Rents rise from 6 *s.* to 17 *s.* but on an average are

14s. Farms, from 100l. to 500l. a year.

Their crops, Wheat, 2¼ or 3 quarters; Barley, 4; Oats, 4; Peafe 3 quarters, all hand-hoed, Beans, 4 or 5 quarters, all hand-hoed twice, and many in drills. Let me here remark, that I have no where elfe found very light fands fo rich as to be commonly cropped with beans, as thefe are; an inftance of richnefs that is great. It proves that the opinion of beans requiring a great tenacity in the foil is quite falfe; for I ran a cane 2 feet deep in many fields here with eafe.

They cultivate fome carrots, but not fo many as nearer to *Woodbridge*; but they are greatly to blame, for when they do fow that root, they get 5 bufhels *per* fquare rod, which are 800 *per* acre; and at 1s. come to 40l. They give them to their horfes inftead of oats, and alfo fatten hogs on them.

For fome miles further the land continued the fame, a rich fand; the courfe,

1. Turnips 3. Clover, one year
2. Barley 4. Wheat.

Their turnips are worth about 30s. on an average, and the clover yields from 1

M 4 to

to 2 loads of hay at a cutting. But they have fome tracts of poor fands which are not good enough for the above courfe; they will not yield turnips without dung; fo are fallowed for oats, with the oats, clover, and ray-grafs for 3 years, as a fheep-walk, then break it up for oats again; and after them fallow as before: where turnips *cannot be had*, this it muft be confeffed is not a bad courfe.

But the famous hufbandry of this country is near *Woodbridge*; particularly in the fpace of country comprehended in the parifhes of *Eyke*, *Wantefden*, *Bromefwell*, *Sutton*, *Shattifham*, *Ramfholt*, *Alderton*, and *Bawdfey*: through which country I have paffed with pleafure; the fands about *Capel St. Andrews* are poorer—they form one farm of near 4000 acres. The former places lie pretty much together, forming a retired corner of the world, fcarcely ever vifited by travellers, and yet abounding in feveral inftances with the beft hufbandry in *Britain*. In many particulars, it will furprize a ftranger more than any thing to be feen in *Norfolk*.

Farms are of various fizes, from 100 *l.*

to 500*l.* a year; and the rents of two forts:
the poor fheep-walk fands, run at 4*s.*
or 5*s.* an acre; but the better kind from
14*s.* to 20*s.*; in general about 16*s.*

Their courfes on the good fands, are,

1.	Carrots	4.	Beans
2.	Turnips	5.	Wheat.
3.	Barley		

This is an excellent one.

1.	Turnips	4.	Wheat
2.	Barley	5.	Beans
3.	Clover	6.	Barley.

Another admirable courfe.

At other times, they drop the 5th and 6th
crops; ftopping at the fourth. Peafe are
fometimes ufed inftead of the beans; and
at others added after the barley as a 7th
crop. It is an univerfal rule with them
never to let wheat, barley, or oats, come
twice together, and they adhere to it very
ftrictly.

They plough the clover land but once
for wheat; but the bean ftubbles twice or
thrice, if wanting. If the crop happens to
be weedy, they hand-hoe it. The average
crop 4 quarters *per* acre.

They plough three times for barley, and

reckon the mean crop at 5 ¼ quarters; it rises very often to 6 or 7. When they fow oats, they never get lefs than 5 quarters.

Of peafe, their culture is extremely perfect; they plough from once to 3 times for them; generally drill them, and never omit keeping them clean by hand-hoeing; from one to 3 hoeings, as the weeds happen to arife: the average crop about 3 ¼ quarters. Beans they are equally attentive to; they generally dibble them in rows equally diftant, 16 or 18 inches afunder. The fetting cofts 3s. 6d. an acre. they never fail hand-hoeing twice, at the expence of 8s. an acre. They ufe the horfe-bean, and alfo many *Windfor* ticks: Of the former fort their crops rife from 5 quarters to 7 ½ quarters; and this upon fand!— Such are the effects of good culture! They get 4 or 5 quarters of the *Windfor* bean; and fell them from 40s. to 3l. a quarter.— This hufbandry of peafe and beans is no where exceeded.

They always hand-hoe their turnips twice, and feed them on the land with fheep and cattle.

Carrots are a crop that do them honour.

2   They

They fow them to choofe on their rich
deep fand; I examined it particularly, and
brought away about half a peck of it.—It
is almoft a running fand, of a dark red colour, but has a principle of adhefion in it
fufficient to produce any thing; it cakes
together without the leaft baking or plaif-
tering, fo that a flight touch crumbles it.
They plough the ftubble but once for carrots, holding that better than giving any
previous tillage.

About old *Lady Day* they trench plough
with two ploughs in the fame furrow, the
firft with three horfes, and the laft with
two, getting a foot depth, they then immediately harrow in the feed, without any
manuring I enquired particularly into
the failures of the crop; they faid that if
the feed was good, carrots never failed:
when once they came up they were fure.
They never omit hand-hoeing them thrice,
at the expence (the three times) of from
16 s. to a guinea an acre. The hoe they
ufe at firft is not above 4 inches wide; but
they leave them at laft a foot afunder.

They begin to take up about *Michaelmas*,
with three pronged forks; and except
having

having a small store before hand, in case of hard frosts, always take up as they are wanted. The carrot tops wither, and rot upon the land; but no frosts affect the roots. Leaving them in the ground renders it necessary to sow turnips after.

As to the produce, I had in different places three accounts · First, that they yielded from 3 to 6 bushels on a square rod; the average is 4½; or 720 bushels on an acre. Secondly, that a crop generally gave 12 loads an acre, each 40 bushels, besides what is used at home; this was indefinite: the 12 loads come to 480 bushels:—one man thought the crop was 15 loads, or 600 bushels. Thirdly, I was informed that they came on an average to 1 *lb.* each, and stood over a whole field on a medium at 1 foot square; this quantity, at 56 *lb.* the bushel, is 776 bushels. The fairest way will be to take the average of the three accounts.

			Bushels.
By the rod,	-	-	720
By the load,	-	-	600
By weight,	-	-	776

Average 698 bushels.

They

They fell at 6*d*. a bufhel: the crop therefore pays 17*l*. 9*s*. an acre. But I have already remarked that they are worth 1*s* for fattening cattle.

They give large quantities to their horfes; after wafhing clean, they are cut into the chaff. They allow a bufhel *per* horfe *per* day, and give no corn at all—yet their horfes are conftantly worked; but on carrots they will do as much work as on any food.

They likewife feed their hogs on them; and fatten many completely. No food does better for fwine in general.

In their tillage they plough with but two horfes, and break up their ftubbles at *Michaelmas*; at firft ploughing they do only an acre a day, but afterwards 1½ or 2. They never keep their horfes in the ftable of nights, but turn them loofe into the farm-yards. The breed of horfes peculiar to this country is one of the greateft curiofities in it: I never yet faw any that are comparable to them in fhape, or the amazing power they have in drawing. They are called the forrel breed; the colour a bay forrel. The form, that of a true round
barrel,

barrel, remarkably short, and the legs the
same; and lower over the forehand than in
any part of the back; which they reckon
here a point of confequence. They fell at
furprizing rates; the good geldings or
mares, at from 35 to 60 guineas each; and
fmaller ones, of 8, 9, or 10 years old, at
20*l*. But none of them are very large.
The work they will do is extraordinary,
being beyond comparifon ftronger and
hardier than any of the great black breeds
of *Flanders, Northamptonfhire*, or *Yorkfhire*.
They are all taught with very great care to
draw in concert; and many farmers are fo ·
attentive to this point, that they have teams,
every horfe of which will fall on his knees
at the word of command twenty times
running, in the full drawing attitude, and
all at the fame moment, but without exerting any ftrength, till a variation in the
word orders them to give all their ftrength
—and then they will carry out amazing
weights.

It is common to draw team againft team
for high wagers.

I was affured by many people here, that
four good horfes in a narrow wheeled waggon

gon would, without any hurt or mifchief from over working, carry 30 facks of wheat, each 4 bufhels, (near 9 gallon meafure) 30 miles, if proper fair time was given them. A waggon weighs about 25 C. wt. this weight therefore is very near 5 tons. And let me add, that they have not a turnpike near them. One might venture to affert, that there are not 4 great black horfes in *England* that would do this

Another moft uncommon circumftance in the hufbandry of this country, is the ufe of a manure peculiar to them, which they call *crag*. It is found in almoft all the hills and higher lands in the country, at various depths, fometimes only 2 or 3 feet from the furface; and it lies in a deeper ftratum than they find neceffary to dig. It appears to be totally compofed of fhells crumbled into powder, many are found in it of their entire form, particularly mufcles. The colour of it, a mixture of white and red. I brought away half a bufhel; and have fince tried it in ftrong vinegar, but it has not the leaft effervefcence—nor any ebulition. And yet it undoubtedly enriches the foil far more than any marle;

for

for the farmers here lay on but 10 or 12 cart-loads an acre, and the effect is amazingly great, with this uncommon circumstance, the soil is ever after greatly the better for it; nor do they, in 12 or 15 years, as is common with such small quantities of marle, find the benefit declining fast. But there is a strong notion among them, that the land can be cragged but once; if it is afterwards repeated, no advantage is found from it. This part of my intelligence I doubt very much; and especially as they find it very advantageous to form composts of crag and dung; which they practise much: carting the dung to the crag pits, and there making the compost heaps, turning it over twice, and sometimes thrice.

The redder the crag is, the better they reckon it.

The effect of it is so great, that in breaking up the poor heaths of this country, they have had a succession of exceeding fine crops of all sorts from such parts as they have manured with it; while at the same time, other parts unmanured have scarcely

yielded

yielded the feed again.—All the rich inclofures of this country have been cragged.

The farmers here are very attentive to
all forts of manures They raife large
quantities of farm-yard dung, and cart it
all on to heaps, and mix it either with crag
or virgin mold; and this univerfally.
They turn over and mix thefe heaps well
together before they fpread them on theii
land. They chop their ftubbles; ftack
their hay at home, and fold their fheep
conftantly.

Upon the whole, this corner of *Suffolk*
is to be recommended for practifing much
better hufbandry, all things confidered,
than any other tract of country with which
I am acquainted.

Their crag hufbandry, their culture of
cariots, their breed of horfes, are circumftances peculiar, no where elfe to be
feen. Their management of the pea and
bean crops, is much more mafterly than
any thing met with in moft parts of
the kingdom. Their courfes of crops are
unexceptionable:—in a word, they exert
every effort of good hufbandry to command
fuccefs.—They enjoy it and well deferve

the fruit of their labours.—That of *Norfolk* is juſtly famous; but every thing conſidered, it muſt undoubtedly yield to the more garden-like culture of this country:—their crops are far ſuperior to any thing in the neighbouring county.

Flanders has long been mentioned as the moſt perfectly cultivated country in *Europe*. What the ſoil is I know not; but I will venture to aſſert that,—ſoil equal, no *Flanders* huſbandry can exceed the above deſcribed.

From *Woodbridge* to *Ipſwich* the country is various; but much of it not cultivated ſo well as what I had paſſed. It lets from 10 s. to 16 s. *per* acre. I went from the latter named place to *Nacton*, purpoſely to view the houſe of Induſtry there. It is a large irregular building; the diſpoſition of the apartments does not ſeem very well contrived for convenience. The original ſum raiſed for the building and furniſhing it was 4800 l.; the average of the laſt ſeven years rates over the hundred was taken, and produced 1475 l. a year. They have generally from 120 to 200 poor in the houſe; at preſent 144. They earn upon an average 250 l. a year, which makes
the

the income of the houfe 1725*l.* a year This has been confiderable enough to enable the truftees to pay off 1200*l.* of the debt; and it has been erected but 12 years.

It ftands in an high airy fituation a healthy fpot, and the whole appears to be kept in a very clean and wholfome manner. There are various apartments for men with their wives—for fingle men and lads—and alfo for fingle women and girls. For the fick, &c. and a furgery. There are likewife proper rooms for the different manufactures carried on; fuch as fpinning, weaving, making twine, making facks, &c. &c. alfo offices for baking, brewing, &c. with proper ftore rooms; and an apartment for the governor of the houfe, and for the truftees to meet in · the whole open to the view of any perfon that comes to fee them; and alfo all the provifion with which the poor are fed. They are undoubtedly taken excellent care of, both fick and well. The following is a table of their diet.

SUNDAY.

Breakfaft. Bread, and cheefe, and butter, and milk.

Dinner. Beef and dumplings. Pudding and mutton for the fick.

Supper. Bread, and cheefe, and butter, and milk are the fupper every day in the week

MONDAY.

Breakfaft Beef broth.

Dinner. Baked fuet pudding.

TUESDAY.

Breakfaft. Milk broth in winter; milk in fummer.

Dinner. Beef and dumplings.

WEDNESDAY.

Breakfaft. Beef broth.

Dinner. Rice-milk or broth, &c

THURSDAY.

Breakfaft. Milk in fummer; milk broth in winter.

Dinner. Beef and dumplings.

FRIDAY and SATURDAY.

Breakfaft. Meat broth.

Dinner. Bread and butter.

Peafe porridge ufed to be the dinner on the two laft days, but they petitioned for bread and butter inftead of it, which

found

found their favourite dinner, becaufe they have tea to it I expreffed furprize at this being allowed; but they faid they were permitted to fpend 2 *d.* in the fhilling of what they earned, as they pleafe; and they laid it all out in tea and fugar to drink with their bread and butter dinners.

Indulgence renders it neceffary to let them do as they pleafe with it, but it would be better expended in fomething elfe

Whatever they eat is perfectly good of the kind, the beft wheat, none but good *Warwickfhire* cheefe; the beft beef; and every article the fame no neighbouring poor live near fo well in their own cottages; and not one little farmer in ten. They are cloathed in a warm comfortable manner, and are in general pretty well fatisfied with their fituation; but the confinement difgufts them; they are not allowed conftant liberty without the yards (which indeed would be impoffible) and this they diflike.—A furgeon attends twice a week regularly; and oftener if neceffary.

The grand points in the eftablifhment are, the poor being better taken care of

N 3 than

than in the old parochial method; and at
the fame time a faving of 100 *l.* a year
made. Thefe two points are thofe principally to be attended to, in any difcuffion of
the merit of thefe eftablifhments; becaufe
it is impoffible they fhould unite without
exceedingly beneficial confequences flow-
ing from them. That the poor of all forts
are taken the utmoft care of, is a fact
indifputable, clear to the eyes of every
ftranger, as well as thoroughly known to
every perfon in this neighbourhood.

There remains a debt of 3600 *l.* which
will all be paid off fooner than may at firft
be imagined. If they paid off 100 *l.* a year
while they had the intereft of 4800 *l.* to
difcharge; now they have only the intereft
of 3600 *l.* to pay, they confequently liqui-
date 148 *l.* a year, which in the next ten
years will reduce the debt to 2120 *l.* The
ten years following, they will in the fame
proportion difcharge 208 *l.* a year, which
will clear the remaining debt in eleven
years. So that the fum total will be paid
off in 33 years from building the houfe.

Then (and not till then) they lower rates.

The

The total income is 1725*l.* a year, which enabled them, after maintaining their poor, to pay 192 *l.* a year in interest, and 100*l.* in discharge of debt, in all 292*l.* a year. They receive from the parishes in rates 1475 *l.* a year; consequently they can then immediately sink this sum 292*l.* which reduces it to 1183*l.*——which reduction amounts to *a fifth.*—And this seems the ultimate degree of benefit, in respect of lowering rates; and a matter of importance it is, when we consider that it is gained by the same measure, which adds so much to the advantage of the poor.

But there are four or five other houses of Industry in this county, and one in *Norfolk;* some of which I find have made vastly greater savings, even to the discharging more than half their debt in 10 or 12 years; such houses will in the end, and speedily too, sink the rates much more considerably.

Bosmere and *Claydon* hundreds have one of only 5 years standing. They borrowed 10,000*l.*; the rates amount to 2526*l.* annually, and the earnings 400*l* a year. Total income 2926 *l.* In these five years

they

they have paid off 1400 *l.* which has reduced the debt to - - £.8600
In 5 years more they will
  pay off the fame, £ 1400
Alfo the deduction of intereft, 280
                    —— 1680

The debt will therefore in 10 years,
  from the firft eftablifhment, be
  reduced to - - - 6920
In 5 years more the fame
  payment will be made, 1400
Alfo deduction from intereft, 620
                    —— 2020

The debt in 15 years, from firft
  eftablifhment, will be reduced to, 4900
In 5 years more, - 1400
Deduction from intereft, 1020
                    —— 2420

In 20 years, reduced to - - 2480
In 5 years more - 1400
Alfo the deduction of intereft, 1500
                    —— 2900

  In 25 years the whole debt paid. And
as they paid at firft 400 *l.* a year in intereft,
and 280 *l.* in difcharge of debt, together
    5   680 *l.*

680*l.* a year; the proportion of that fum to 2926 *l.* is the proportion in which the rates will be lowered. It is near a fourth.

It may be afked, how can thefe eftablifh-ments be fo beneficial to the poor, while they leffen the expences fo much? I re-ply; In two ways. Firft, in going cheaper to work with every thing than parifh officers can, who have not the fame advan-tages. Weekly allowances in the parifh, muft be given in proportion to the abilities of the poor to gain what they want. Diet of all forts, firing, cloaths, &c. are all procured by them at the deareft rate. If they buy cheefe, it is by the pound; candles, fingle; foap half a pound; and as they have them from the moft paltry of all fhops, they confequently pay extrava-gant rates for the worft commodities. This runs through their whole expenditure—— they muft neceffarily be paid by the parifh, fufficiently to enable them to fupport all thefe difadvantages.

This is very different at the Hundred Houfe; advertifements are regularly in-ferted in the *Ipfwich* journal when any commodity is wanted, that the truftees will

meet

meet at such a day to receive proposals, and view samples of such and such commodities. Every thing is bought in the great, and paid for at once——no private family lives so cheap. In the article of firing, what a vast difference between buying by the faggot, for various miserable fires, and a union of them into ship loads of coals? House-rent in the parishes was also a heavy article; but in what proportion to the rent of the Hundred House, cannot be ascertained.

The difference in the expence of surgery and medicine must be immense.

The second means of saving is this. The Hundred House pays no weekly allowances in the parishes; whoever wants assistance, must go to the house, unless they are really unable. This at once strikes off a very great expence; for in all parishes that have no workhouses, numbers of the poor thro' clamour, or the weakness of justices of the peace, obtain allowances that would not stir from their cottages for twice the sum: all such are cut off. Besides the numbers that betake themselves to a more industrious life, in order to keep at home in their

parishes,

parifhes, all having a much ftronger inclination for that than to go away.

These, I think, are two very powerful
reasons for the expence being lowered;
and in addition to them, the fuperior earnings ought certainly to be mentioned.——
But in refpect to the general good.——

It is evident that thefe houfes tend ftrongly
to reduce poor rates, and partly by creating
a new induftry. Are not thefe objects of
infinite importance! are they not the remedy of thofe evils, whofe enormity has
been the fubject of complaint for fo many
years throughout the kingdom? Is it not
therefore greatly incumbent on parliament,
to render univerfal, eftablifhments that have
been long experienced to work fuch good
effects? It is much to be wifhed that they
were made general.

I made the requifite enquiries into the
objections againft them; and I found but
few of any confequence.

Firft, The farmers complain that where
poor rates are lowered by them, the land-
lords take advantage of it, and raife their
rents in proportion.——

I reply.——So much the better; who of

4   common

Common fenfe ever fuppofed it a contrivance to put money in the pockets of farmers? If rates are lowered, it ought to be the gentleman's advantage; for his eftate always lets in exact proportion to the height of rates; and if he can let land that is worth 20 s. an acre for only 16 s. on account of heavy rates, furely he ought to have the benefit of raifing, when he has fo long laboured under the evil of finking?

But the farmers are piqued in many hundreds, and will never agree to the meafure.

Secondly, It depopulates a hundred; for the poor not liking the houfe, the fervants let themfelves in other hundreds.

This objection exifts merely while the eftablifhment is local; make it univerfal, and it ceafes at once.—The reality of the matter was, however, exprefsly contradicted to me, by perfons on whom I can well depend. They affured me, that they felt no fuch evil.

Thirdly, The acts of parliament which eftablifh the Houfes, being extremely various, and yet *public* acts, they may be

very

very troublefome to lawyers in any future pleadings on them.

One act *might* comprehend the whole kingdom. There is no *neceffity* for every hundred to have a diftinct act. But fuppofe the cafe; let thefe gentlemen take fo much the greater pains.——Thofe who are fo ready with abridgements in 500 folio's; may juft as well turn over 5000.

Fourthly, Gentlemen will not attend the truft—it then becomes a jobb in the hands of farmers and tradefmen.

This objection holds equally againft all public works executed by commiffioners; fuch as turnpikes, drainages, navigations, harbours, &c. &c.—It is too difficult a thing to *force* people to do their duty; and yet we find the works performed. Many are careful enough to attend; fome won't, and then evils may arife which force them to it but in fome way or other the bufi-nefs is done, without any flagrant or ftriking impofitions. Thus it would be with Houfes of Induftry. Some have been erected thefe dozen years, and yet I could not find that any mifchiefs had arifen from a want of attendance.——making fuch a

progrefs

progrefs in paying off the debt, does not carry that appearance.

Upon the whole, the objections that have been made to thefe eftablifhments are by no means folid: but fuppofing they were; are we to enjoy none of the benefits of improvement, becaufe objections are ftarted? What good is gained without its attendant evil? Make a navigation, you wafte land to convert it into water; and you cut through people's properties. Make a turnpike—you tax the whole country. If you will execute no improvement but what may be performed without the leaft objection—you for ever tye your hands from doing good. Compare the advantages with the inconveniences:—View the fcale —and then determine. It fhould be the bufinefs of cavillers alone to ftart objections, that will not, united, overturn the benefit propofed: For a nation to conduct itfelf by fuch ideas, is to revolve into the barbarifm of the darkeft ages.

The hufbandry of the neighbourhood of *Ipfwich* is in general very good. About *Bramford*, farms rife from 50 *l.* to 250 *l.* a year;

year; the average from 80 *l.* to 120 *l.* The foil in fome places is all ftrong clay; in others good loams: much gravelly loam, equally good for both turnips and wheat; lets from 10 *s.* to 15 *s.* an acre; average 12 *s.* 6 *d.* The rent from hence to *Hadleigh*, about 13 *s.* The courfe of crops,

1. Turnips   4. Wheat
2. Barley   5. Peafe or beans.
3. Clover one year

And,

1. Turnips   4. Wheat
2. Barley   5. Oats.
3. Clover

This addition of oats is bad.

Upon the clay foils it is,

1. Fallow   4 Wheat
2. Barley   5 Beans
3. Clover   6 Barley.

Admirable! No courfe can exceed this.

They plough but once for wheat, fow 2 bufhels, and get 26 bufhels on an average. For barley they ftir three or four times; fow 3 bufhels *per* acre, and get 4 quarters on an average. They plough but once for oats; fow 4 bufhels, and reckon the mean product at 4 $\frac{1}{2}$ quarters. They fometimes

fow

fow colefeed for feed, and never fail of getting fine wheat after it.

They give from 4 to 6 earths for turnips; always hoe them twice; feed them on the land with fheep or fattening oxen. They mow fome of their clover for hay; and fome they feed the firft growth, and mow the fecond for feed, they never fail of great crops of wheat after mown clover—but they dung the ftubble.

In refpect to manuring, they are excellent farmers · they form compofts with all their farm-yard dung, mixing it well with what they call chalk, but which I found on trial to be excellent marle. They put about a third part of chalk. Some farmers have limed their land, and with good fuccefs. All chop their ftubbles, and ftack their hay at home. All the way from *Ipfwich* o *Shotley*, and fo to *Maningtree*, through the hundred of *Sampford*, they are admirable hufbandmen, and have excellent land to work on: they ufe great quantities of fea ouze, and find it of great ufe; particularly in forming compofts with their farm-yard dung, which, when well mixed together, they fpread on their light lands.

They

They form thefe heaps from the fea, and their yards in fpring, and mix them well together through the fummer for fpreading on the clover lays for wheat.

All wheat throughout th's country that is weedy, is as regularly hand-hoed as their turnips; the price 6 s. an acre. They alfo hand-hoe all their beans twice; and never fail of fowing wheat after them.

About *Wolton* and *Felixton* the foil is remarkable rich. Their common courfe is,

1. Beans   2. Wheat.
and fo on for ever.

Nathaniel Acton, Efq; of *Bramford*, to whom I am obliged for the preceding particulars, has tried various experiments, that cannot fail of being particularly ufeful. Among other crops he has cultivated carrots with fuccefs.

Experiment, No. 1.

In 1768, two acres of good light turnip loam were trench ploughed, and carrot feed harrowed in in *March* without manuring. The plants arofe very regularly, and were hand-hoed three times, at the expence of thirty fhillings an acre; and taken up at once as foon as the tops withered. They were laid up for winter ufe, and applied chiefly to the feeding horfes, who all did excellently well on them. Mr. *Acton* found that fuch parts of the heap, as were not packed clofe together after being well dried, were apt to rot; but all that were dry and clofe laid, kept perfectly found.

Experiment, No. 2.

In 1769, an acre of the fame foil received the fame culture; thrice hand-hoed, at the above expence; and being carefully dried before they were laid up, and packed clofe together, none were rotten. Taking up 1 *l.* an acre. Given to horfes inftead of oats; and they never did better.

Experiment, No. 3.

This year, 1770, he has one acre; a very fine regular crop, cultivated in the preceding manner, and will turn out as good.

Refpecting the produce, Mr. *Acton* has found but little variation—he has had them accurately meafured—and finds that the quantity is 6 bufhels *per* rod, or 960 bufhels *per* acre: thefe at 8 *d.* a bufhel, the *Bram-ford*

ford price, come to 32 *l*. But I beg leave once more to obferve, that I have found carrots to be worth 1 *s* a bufhel in feeding cattle, at which price thefe crops have been worth 48 *l*. an acre.—But whether the value is 24, 32, or 48 *l*. is not of much confequence; for take the loweft price, and you will find no crop that *Britifh* fields produce equally profitable.

Experiment, No. 4.

April 3d, 1770, fome cabbage feed was fown on a bed of rich ground; both the great *Scotch* fort, and Mr. *Reynold*'s turnip-rooted cabbage. *June* 23d, they were tranfplanted into the field; the foil a rich black loam; the firft fort 3 feet by 2, the latter 2 feet by 18 inches. I viewed both crops with great pleafure; they were uncommonly fine · the *Scotch* plants 3 feet over, and *Reynolds* 2 feet; both of a deep green and remarkably luxuriant I think the turnip cabbage bids fair for being the largeft crop I have yet feen of them. Mr. *Acton* gives both forts fair play, for he keeps them as clean as a garden.

Experiment, No. 5.

The *Egyptian* turnip has been tried by this gentleman in some small experiments to see if it would do for the spring food of cattle—the root proves of a trifling size, but the leaves remain in full luxuriance through the sharpest winter; no frosts affect them; and it sprouts fresh very early in the spring.

Experiment, No. 6.

In planting, Mr. *Acton* has tried the *Turin* poplar, and finds that it shoots 10 feet in a year, and perfectly straight. He has also measured the shoots of the *Norfolk* willow, 12 feet long. Larches thrive greatly here; they are worth 1 s. 6 d. each in 9 years; which is an astonishing profit, and beats the finest husbandry.

Experiment, No. 7.

This gentleman has in the present year a remarkable instance of the quick vegetation of lucerne, even the first year of sowing. In 1769, two acres of a fine light rich loam were cropped with turnips; the land was ploughed quite fine after feeding

them

them off, and in the fpring drilled with lucerne; the feed failing, it was ploughed up, and again drilled in *July*, and in a month was 12 inches high; it has been hand-hoed thrice I found it as clean as a garden. The rows are equally diftant; 22 inches afunder, very ftraight, regular, and not ftraggling; which circumftances I mention, as it was drilled by hand in the furrow after the plough. It promifes to be an excellent crop,

Experiment, No. 8.

In Mr, *Acton*'s grafs land, one of the moft troublefome weeds he has met with, is the common nettle, and fo difficult to extirpate, that it has foiled him in many attempts. He tried an experiment in one fpot on grubbing them; the place was grubbed clean with a pick-ax, the roots taken out, and the furface levelled—the nettles came again in as full luxuriance as ever. 'He then tried mowing them as faft as they grew high enough for the fcythe; and this method by perpetual bleeding fucceeded; it is the only one on which he can depend. It is always of importance to

O 3

know

know those methods, which have proved most successful in the destruction of every weed; in this respect, matters seemingly of no consequence, are oftentimes passed over by inattentive persons, until they find themselves in a situation that shews the impropriety of slighting such information. Mowing less than three times a year will not destroy them.

Experiment, No. 9.

In 1769, nine acres were cropped with turnips and fed on the land. In 1770, it was sown with barley and grasses for a meadow; the seeds 12 *lb.* an acre of white *Dutch* clover, and 3 sacks of fine dressed hay-seeds I viewed the field, and found the ground covered with a luxuriant growth.

Experiment, No. 10

Another field was cropped with turnips in 1768, fed off for barley in 1769, and seeds sown with it, 4 sacks *per* acre of fine hay-seeds, 4 *lb.* of trefoile, 4 *lb.* of white clover, and 4 *lb* of red clover. After the barley was carried off, it was well manured from the compost dunghill. And this

year,

year, 50 *C. wt.* of hay *per* acre was mown; and the after-grafs coming on with great luxuriance.

Mr. *Acton*'s common hufbandry is excellent, and his crops good. His courfe of crops is,

1. Turnips, well hoed twice, and worth 35 *s.* an acre.

2. Barley, 5 quarters *per* acre.

3. Clover, which yields 4 ¼ tons of hay at 2 mowings.

4. Wheat, on one ploughing, always hand-hoed at the expence of 6 *s.* an acre; the produce 4 quarters *per* acre.

He manures his fields richly; ufes a clayey marle, very rich, if we may judge from the ftrong effervefcence with acids; he lays from 50 to 90 loads an acre; the ftrongeft effect of it is cleaning the land from all weeds, which it does in an uncommon manner; nothing deftroys poppies more. He makes compofts of pot-afh, cow-dung, horfe-dung, and turf, which he mixes well together, and finds it a great improvement. The pot-afh, 12 *s.* for 70 bufhels. He lays 15 loads an acre of this compoft.

In

In the management of his farm-yard he is alfo very attentive to the raifing dung; he confines all his cattle the winter through, and conducts all the urine that runs off, into a pit, where he abforbs it all in ftraw. This is a very good method. It is an un-accountable circumftance that nine tenths of farmers, gentlemen as well as others, give fo little attention to this very important part of their bufinefs.

Mr. *Acton* has contrived his cow-fhed extremely well; it has a hay-ftack yard behind it, and the racks are open to it, fo that the hay, without any trouble, is thrown directly from the ftack into it. His cart horfes are never confined to the ftable, but have a yard to run about at pleafure with an open fhed, under which they run, with a rack and manger for their oats and hay.

- Covered drains this gentleman has made in his wet fields with very great fuccefs; he has found the value of the land doubled by their means : before they were made, it was in vain to fpread any manure, the effect was fo trifling; but fince the drainage every fpoonful takes effect.

From

From *Bramford* to *Hadleigh*, the foil is heavier than around *Ipfwich*; they have not the fame command of turnips About *Hadleigh* is much fandy loam called woodcock land, lets on a medium at 15 s. an acre. Poor rates are 3 s in the pound more, and tythe 4 s an acre. The country from hence to *Lauenham* runs at 12 s. an acre; to *Stow-Market* 10 s. 6 d., and to *Colchefter* 14 s.

Farms here, rife from 40 l. to 300 l. a year.

Their courfe of crops is,

1. Turnips	3. Clover 1 or 2 years
2. Barley	4. Wheat,

The products;

Of Wheat, 4 quarters *per* acre.

Of Barley and oats, 4 quarters 2 bufhels.

Of Peafe 2 ½ quarters.

Of Beans the fame.

Clover they mow once for hay, and get 2 ton an acre. Their turnips are worth from one guinea to three——average 1 l. 11 s. 6 d.

They feed much clover with hogs, which they find a very profitable application of it. Turn them in in *May* of all fizes, and

keep

keep them in it without their coming home, till the stubbles are ready for them. The dairy wash is all kept for young pigs. This management is common here.

Many of their turnips they apply to fattening beasts; *Scotch* cattle, and also the *Yorkshire* long and short horned They give from 7*l*. to 9*l*. in *August*; turn them into stubbles, and then to turnips in the field. Some they buy at 3*l*. to 4*l*. 10*s*. and sell at 40*s*. advantage. Others buy larger cattle to eat off the after-grass, and then they are put to turnips; and from turnips in the spring to the summer's grass; and sell fat in *July*. But many go off fat from the turnips. This system of giving them first the after-grass, and selling fat from turnips, they justly reckon a very profitable one.

There are large tracts of rich meadow here, that let to 35*s*. an acre. They apply it to grazing and mowing; 2 acres will carry 3 cows through the summer: the crops of hay 2 tons an acre. A good cow will give 8 or 9*lb*. of butter a week.

Their principal sheep husbandry is to buy wether lambs in *August*, which they

turn

turn into their ftubbles; then they put them to turnips, making them follow the fatting beafts In the fpring they turn them into the clovers, and keep them there till fat, which will be in *July* or *Auguft*: they always double their money, and fometimes do more.

In tillage they reckon 7 horfes neceffary for 100 acres of arable land; they ufe 3 in a plough, in light work but 2, and do an acre a day; the depth 5 to 7 inches and generally plough up their ftubbles before *Chriftmas.*—Wheel ploughs only ufed.

They reckon 500*l.* neceffary for ftocking a farm of 100*l* a year.

The employment of the poor here, is the woollen manufacture. Many fpinners and combers; the latter earn 8*s.* or 9*s.* a week; the fpinners 4*d.* a day. All drink tea; many of them thrice a day.

LABOUR.

In harveft, 2 *s.* a day and beer.

In hay-time, 1 *s.* 6 *d.* and ditto.

In winter, 1 *s.* 2 *d.*

Reaping 4*s.* an acre

Mowing, making, and cocking grafs for hay, 4*s.* an acre.

Hoeing

Hoeing turnips, 4 *s*. and 2 *s*.

Thrashing wheat, 2 *s*. 4 *d*. a quarter

——————— barley and oats, 1 *s*. a quarter,

Head-man's wages, 10 *l*. to 10 *l*. 10 *s*.

Next ditto, 7 *l*.

Lad's, 3 *l*.

A dairy-maid, 3 *l*.

Other maids, 2 *l*. 10 *s*.

Women will not work in harvest, only glean.

PROVISIONS.

Bread,   - -   1 ¼ *d. per lb*.

Cheese, - -   4

Butter, - -   9   *per* 20 ounces,

Beef,   - -   3 ½

Mutton, - -   4

Veal,   - -   3 ½

Pork,   - -   4

Milk,   - - · ½ *d. per* pint.

Potatoes, - -   4 *per* peck.

Labourer's House-rent, 40 *s*,

——————— firing, 30 *s*.

The particulars of a farm as follows.

300 Acres in all	16 Horses
250 Arable	6 Cows
50 Meadow	18 Young cattle
£.200 Rent	40 Swine

62 Acres Turnips	4 Men
62 Barley	1 Boy
62 Clover	2 Maids
62 Wheat	4 Labourers

All this country has been chalked; the quantity generally 10 waggon loads an acre. But now they mix it with farm-yard dung, and reckon this management of it the beſt huſbandry.

Many of them chop their ſtubbles; and all ſtack their hay at home.

Some of my readers may perhaps remember a paſſage in my *Six Weeks Tour*, wherein I gave an account of a field of lucerne of doctor *Tanner's*. On coming again to *Hadleigh* I was very deſirous of ſeeing it, and having further information concerning it, as it is now ſeven years old. The Doctor was ſo obliging as to ſhew it me · I found the field very regularly planted; the bare ſpots quite inconſiderable; the verdure fine, and very few weeds in it. The Doctor expects it to laſt 10 years longer. Reſpecting the produce, it is as great as ever: He has a very clear way of deciding the value of it, from the particular circumſtance of always feeding three

ſmall

fmall meadows before he had the lucerne, and always mowing them fince: they yield juft 14 loads of hay weighed dry in the winter; and the average price is 40 s. a load: the four acres of lucerne, therefore, fave him 28 l. in hay, befides maintaining 80 fheep a month every autumn, which at 3 d. a week, comes to 4 l.; the whole produce is therefore 32 l. the four acres, or 8 l. per acre. This is greatly to the honour of broad-caft lucerne, and proves very clearly its immenfe importance.

If the firft crop was mown for hay, the produce would be 30 C. wt. an acre; and the Doctor finds a load of it to be as good as a load and half of any other hay. I examined a parcel of the hay, and never faw any that equalled it either in fcent or colour, and the leaves were all on.

It is the only food of his cows; and none give better milk, cream or butter; the butter is uncommonly excellent. Some of his horfes are fed totally on it, without either oats or hay; I faw them, and they are quite fat, with marbled coats, though conftantly worked.

It

It is manured once in four years, with about 12 loads an acre.

Upon the whole, Doctor *Tanner* is clear in the uncommon advantages of sowing lucerne broad-caft. The only culture it requires, is a thorough harrowing in *February* or *March*, and fcattering a little feed in the patches where it fails : and the convenience of fo fmall a portion of land maintaining fuch a great ftock of cattle, is unequalled in any other crop.

The country is pretty rich, and well cultivated to *Lavenham*, and fo on to *Haftead*; about which place the foil is chiefly clay, or clayey loam of a loofe nature, hollow and damp : lets from 9*s.* to 20*s.* an acre; average about 14*s.* 6*d.* Farms rife from 20*l.* to 130*l.* a year   The courfe of crops on their ftiff land, is

  1. Fallow   3. Barley

  2. Wheat;

and a vile one it is.   On the lighter land;

  1. Turnips   3. Clover

  2. Barley   4. Wheat;

which is far different.   They plough five or fix times for wheat, fow 2 bufhels, and reap on a medium 2 $\frac{1}{4}$ quarters.   For bar-

            ley

ley they ftir 2 or 3 times; fow 4 bufhels, and 3 quarters the average crop. For oats they plough but once, fow 4 bufhels, and reckon the mean produce 3 ½ quarters. *Edward Manning* of this place has had 40 quarters from 4 acres; and *Michael Mortlock* 15 quarters an acre, which is the greateft crop I ever heard of. They plough but once for peafe; fow 2 bufhels an acre; very feldom hoe them; the crop 2 ½ quarters.

For turnips they plough five or fix times; hand-hoe twice; and reckon the mean value 40*s.* an acre; ufe them for fheep, and fome few for fattening beafts.

Clover they both feed and mow for hay; get from 20 to 30 *C. wt.* an acre at one cutting. Some they feed; get 4 bufhels an acre on an average, fometimes 8. They reckon the wheat as good after feed as hay, but rather better after feeding than either, but never fo clean.

Folding fheep is never practifed. But all the farmers chop their ftubbles, and ftack their hay at home; and fome bring dung from *Bury*.

Many of them are very good farmers in

5   the

the article of draining: They make all covered drains; 32 inches deep, 2 ½ inches wide at bottom, and a ſpit at top; the price of digging and filling from 3 *d* to 4*d*. a rod· but of late years they have got into the way of ploughing the firſt ſpit, by going a bout or two with the common plough, and then digging one or two ſpits, in which manner they pay only 2 *d* a rod. They fill firſt with buſhes, and then with wheat ſtubble.

The beſt graſs-land lets at 20 *s*. an acre; they apply it all to the dairy; and reckon that an acre will carry a cow through the ſummer. The breed, a little mongrel ſort; they give on an average 4 gallons of milk a day; but good ones 8 gallons; the annual product 5*l*. They underſtand very well the management of hogs depending on cows; for they keep at the rate of 2 ſows, and all the pigs bred by them, to every 10 cows. The winter food of their cows is ſtraw, with ſome hay and turnips at calving.

Their flocks riſe from 20 to 80; the moſt common ſheep huſbandry is to buy old crones as they call them, that is, old ewes, in *September*, at from 5*l*. to 8*l*. a

VOL. II. P ſcore.

fcore. Thefe they keep a year, and fell the couples fat from 16*l.* to 19*l.* a fcore.

In their tillage, they reckon 6 horfes neceffary to 100 acres of ploughed ground, ufe 2 in a plough, and do an acre a day. The annual expence of a horfe they reckon at 7*l.* They do not break up their ftubbles till after barley fowing The price of ploughing 4*s* an acre; the depth 4 or 5 inches. They all cut ftraw into chaff.

They calculate 400*l.* to be requifite for ftocking a farm of 100*l.* a year.

Land fells at 30 years purchafe.

Poor rates 3*s.* in the pound: the employment fpinning wool, at which a woman earns 4*d.* a day. They all drink tea.

The farmers carry their corn 25 miles.

The particulars of farms.

160 Acres in all	1 Maid
120 Arable	3 Labourers
40 Grafs	24 Acres Wheat
£. 108 Rent	24 Barley
8 Horfes	24 Fallow
10 Cows	24 Clover
6 Young cattle	10 Turnips
60 Sheep	14 Peafe and
1 Man	beans.
1 Boy	

Another :

150 Acres in all	1 Boy
75 Arable	3 Labourers
75 Grafs	2 Men
£. 120 Rent	20 Acres Wheat
6 Horfes	20 Fallow
20 Cows	10 Barley
5 Young cattle	10 Clover
50 Sheep	5 Turnips
2 Maids	10 Oats.

From *Hadleigh*, another way, I took the road to *Maningtree*, through a country rich and very well cultivated. In that part towards *Hadleigh*, the hufbandry is pretty much the fame as in the account I gave above. About *Maningtree* it refembles the methods around *Ipfwich*. They ufe much rich marle from *Kent*, which is brought by fhipping; they call it chalk.

At the village of *Lawford*, very near to *Maningtree*, lives a moft ingenious fmith, Mr. *John Brand*; whofe mechanical abilities would do honour to a fuperior ftation. He has invented various implements of hufbandry, of which I have myfelf had near feven years experience, and will venture to affert that he has failed in no-

thing.

thing. Among other things, he makes an
iron fwing plough, to be drawn by a
pair of horfes, which much exceeds any
plough I have yet feen, in cutting a true,
regular furrow, well cleared of the loofe
moulds; or in turning over grafs land; at
the fame time, that in ftrength and duration
it is far preferable to all. The eafe and
fimplicity of the variations are excellent.
He has alfo invented other iron ploughs for
4 and 6 horfes, for ploughing from 1 to 2
feet deep.

Another machine of very great utility, is
an horfe-rake on wheels, for raking fpring
corn ftubbles, which performs in a very
complete manner, and will in level fields
rake hay.

Likewife a hand-mill for grinding wheat,
which anfwers (as I have been informed by
feveral perfons) exceedingly well.

He has made feveral other tools, that
have been tried and approved by many
farmers. He has fo quick a comprehenfion
in thefe matters, that I have but little doubt
but he would execute any new idea ftarted
to him with uncommon fuccefs. Defcribe
the powers required, and the force you
will

will allow, and I believe no man in *Britain* will fooner perform it

I cannot but recommend this very ingenious mechanic to the attention of the public,—he has abilities far fuperior to the obfcurity in which he lives.

From *Maningtree* to *Colchefter*, the country is all rich and excellently cultivated. I made enquiries into it, and found their methods quite fimilar from thence beyond *Colchefter*. About that town, and moft of the way to *Witham*, they excell greatly.

About *Lexden* and *Stanway*, farms rife from 20*l.* to 1000*l.* The foil is a fancy gravel, with fome brick earth; lets from 12*s.* to 20*s.* an acre. From *Colchefter* to *Witham* about 13*s.*

The courfe of crops,

1. Turnips   3. Clover 1 year
2. Barley   4. Wheat:

and fometimes the following crops added to thefe;

5. Beans or peafe   6. Wheat.

After beans, they plough twice or thrice for wheat; fow 2 $\frac{1}{2}$ bufhels an acre, and reap 3 $\frac{1}{2}$ quarters on an average; they have fometimes to 5 $\frac{1}{2}$ quarters, but it is all

hand-

hand-hoed. They ſtir their turnip land four times for barley; ſow 4 buſhels, the end of *March*, and through *April*; the mean produce 6 quarters. For oats they plough from once to 3 times; ſow 5 buſhels, and gain from 6 to 10 quarters; 8 the average.

Their turnips they always hand-hoe twice; the crops are generally worth 3*l.* an acre. One acre will fatten a beaſt of 40 or 50 ſcore in the field, to eat the turnips on the land.

For peaſe they give but one earth; ſow 2 buſhels an acre, hoeing them into drills at 3*s.* or 3*s.* 6*d.* an acre expence. They hand-hoe them thrice, ſo as to keep them as clean as a garden; the expence is 3*s.* the firſt hoeing; 2*s.* 6*d.* the ſecond, and 2*s*, the third. The average produce 4 quarters; ſometimes they get 5 or 6. They likewiſe plough but once for beans; dibble them in, in rows 9 inches aſunder; 2 buſhels of ſeed *per* acre; and always give the ſame hoeing as to peaſe, and at the ſame expence. The crops are never ſmall, generally from 5 to 10 quarters an acre; ave

rage

rage 6 or 7. Ufe both the horfe and tick bean.

Colefeed they fow both for food and the feed; they feed it in *April* with fheep and fwine, after the turnips are gone, and then plough it up for a crop of turnips

Much of their clover is fed by fheep, hogs, and horfes; when they mow for hay, they get great crops; 2 loads an acre at a cutting, and fometimes 3; and reckon that an acre in food and hay, pays 4*l*. 4*s*. on an average. A good deal of chalk is ufed about *Colchefter*, and all the way to *Maningtree*; and likewife yet more towards and about *Maldon*. It comes all from *Kent*. The farmers give 7 to 8, and 9*s*. a waggon load for it; and many of them fetch it feveral miles; even from 6 to 10. They lay 7 loads an acre, and all agree that it lafts longeft, and at the fame time does beft on ftiff lands. the fandy and gravelly loams are not fo profitable to chalk as the clayey ones, and ftiff clays. on the latter it lafts from 30 to 40 years; but on the former it holds good for 15 years. I have, with them, called it chalk; but I found from trial that it is a very rich marle.

P 4   Great

Great quantities of dungs of all forts are brought from *Colchefter*; the price 5*s.* or 6*s.* a waggon load, and they lay 7 or 8 on an acre.

All chop their ftubbles; and ftack their hay at home. But no folding fheep is practifed.

Much foot is bought at 6*d.* a bufhel, they fow it on their paftures.

Malt duft they fow on the barley tilth.

In their tillage they reckon 4 horfes neceffary for 100 acres of ploughed ground; ufe 2 in a wheel plough, and do from 1 to 2 acres a day. They ftir 5 or 6 inches deep; the price 4*s.* an acre · the ftubbles are all broken up before *Chriftmas.*

In the hiring a farm of 300*l.* a year, they reckon 2000*l.* neceffary to ftock it, if the land is at all out of condition.

Land fells at 30 years purchafe   Tythes are 3*s.* 6*d.* in the pound. Poor rates 3*s.*; in *Colchefter* 6*s.* or 7*s.* In fome parifhes in that town they rife to 16*s.* or 17*s.*

Agriculture is here carried on in general with very great fpirit; for the farms are chiefly large, and the farmers rich. fome of them are worth from 30,000*l.* to 40,000*l.*; many above 20,000*l.*

The

The following are the particulars of a farm.

400 Acres in all	8 Cows
360 Arable	90 Acres Wheat
40 Grafs	90 Barley
£.330 Rent	90 Clover
12 Horfes	90 Turnips.

From *Witham* towards *Chelmsford*, about *Boreham*, &c. the foil is heavier than at *Colchefter*; being a mixed clayey loam; lets from 10 *s*. to 12 *s*. Farms are from 100 *l*. to 150 *l*. a year.

The courfe,

1. Turnips	3. Clover
2 Barley	4 Wheat.

Here the good farmers ftop; but bad ones add,

5. Oats.

The products :

Wheat, 3 quarters.
Barley, 5 ditto.
Oats, 6 ditto.
Peafe, 3 ditto.
Beans, 5 ditto.

Both peafe and beans are all hand-hoed. Many turnips cultivated on clayey foils too

heavy

heavy to feed off, but they draw them for sheep, cows, and beasts.

A great spirit of manuring is found throughout all this country. They bring some chalk from *Maldon*; give 8 *s*. to 10 *s*. a waggon load for it, and lay from 6 to 8 loads an acre. 6 or 7 miles carriage makes this so great an expence, that they have of late years tried to substitute their own clay for it · they lay 60 loads an acre; and from the observation they have made, think it will last a lease of 21 years.

Lime they also use; lay a bushel to a square perch; it lasts 7 years; but more, if mixed with dung and earth.

LETTER XVI.

BEFORE I proceed in my journey, I
shall here make a pause, to observe
in general, that part of the country through
which I have lately passed, is as remarkable
for excellent husbandry, I apprehend, as
any in the kingdom. The uncommon exertions of spirited culture on the sands near
Woodbridge, I have already remarked. The
great fertility of the soil, and the incomparable use they make of it, I have observed
above; particularly their course of crops
being so well adapted to keeping the land
free from weeds: the culture of carrots;
the drill and hoeing management of pease
and beans; the singular use of crag as a
manure; their noble breed of horses, with
several other particulars, that stamp an ex-
cellence seldom found among common farmers.

After this country, comes the tract of
land in the neighbourhood of *Ipswich*,
which is cultivated in a very complete

manner,

manner, and a fpirited ufe made of various manures. Moft of *Sandford* hundred boafts a hufbandry of a fuperior kind;
marle is much ufed; great things are done
with the affiftance of fea ouze; at the fame
time that all other manures are perfectly
well underftood. From *Maningtree* to *Colchefter*, and thence to *Witham*, the farmers
are perfectly enlightened; throughout this
tract as well as the laft, all the peafe and
beans are kept as clean by hand-hoeing,
as turnips in other places, but at a much
greater expence; wheat alfo receives the
fame operation, which I think is a certain
mark of the farmers having extreme juft
ideas of hufbandry; for without fuch, they
would never arrive at fo unufual a practice.
Marle, called chalk here, they ufe, I believe, at a much greater expence than any
people in the kingdom; for many of them
go from 6 to 10 miles, and give from 8*s*.
to 10*s*. a waggon load for it: this is acting
with a fpirit that cannot be exceeded.
Town manures at *Colchefter* fell at 5*s*. a
load: foot, &c. &c. are ufed in large
quantities; and thefe noble exertions are

I   not

not the effect of low rents, as some fondly imagine they must every where be; on the contrary, this whole country is let at good rents; that is, from 12s. to 25s. an acre. and various places, in which all these circumstances unite, pay 16s. or 18s an acre round; and some 20s. Such a rent by no means frightens these sensible men, they expend great sums of money in the purchase of manures, and spare no expence in hoeing, notwithstanding that of rent.——— What is the consequence of this? Their rich soils so thoroughly manured, produce vast crops without damage from weeds, for their perpetual hoeing totally destroys them. The effect is answerable—from 4 to 5 quarters an acre of wheat; from 5 to 10 of barley; from 6 to 10 of oats; 5 or 6 of beans; and all other crops proportioned— with farmers worth from ten to forty thousand pounds These shew sufficiently that the above spirited practices form what might emphatically be called TRUE HUSBANDRY. Those who exalt the agriculture of *Flanders* so high on comparison with that of *Britain*, have not, I imagine, viewed with attention the country in question. It is difficult to imagine common crops cultivated in greater perfection.

LETTER

LETTER XVII.

FROM *Chelmsford* to *Dunmow* the soil is various, but chiefly heavy; near the former place it is all turnip land, but afterwards clay, at 12 s. an acre.

From *Dunmow* to *Hockerill* it is all clay, at 15 s an acre: the whole country quite flat, and all hollow drained. I observed a large portion of the land was summer fallow, and ridged up in 3 feet lands ready for wheat, lying in a most neat and clean manner; but no turnips in the country. The borders of the arable fields are all dug away, from a foot to 18 inches deep, and carried on to the land, which drains the fields at the same time that much manure is raised.

The crops here amount nearly to the following products, Wheat, 3 ½ quarters *per* acre; Barley, on summer fallow, 5 quarters; Oats, 6 quarters, Pease, 3 quarters; Beans, 4.

From *Dunmow* to *Braintree* the soil is chiefly clay; and lets at 15 s.

From

From *Dunmow* to *Thaxtead*, and from thence to *Clare*, the fame; with fome fpots of turnip land.

From *Hockerill* to *Ware*, near the former place, the farmers are very neat; but they have fome practices by no means defenfible, though followed from an idea of good hufbandry. They often fow barley after turnips, and then fummer fallow for wheat; which is as extraordinary a courfe as ever I met with. I enquired particularly into the reafon of ever omitting clover in fuch a cafe, and was anfwered, that clover fouls and fpoils the land. however feveral of them have better ideas, and practife the excellent hufbandry of, 1. Turnips. 2. Barley: 3. Clover: 4. Wheat; and they find it to anfwer extremely well. Land here lets at 15*s.* an acre · their crops are, Wheat, 3 ½ to 5 quarters; Barley, 5 to 7; Beans, 3 or 4.

About *Youngsberry*, the feat of *David Barclay*, within 3 miles of *Ware*, the hufbandry is various. Farms rife from 30*l.* to 300*l.* a year, but on an average are 100*l.* to 150*l.* The foil may be diftinguifhed moft properly into heavy and light; that

is,

is, turnip land, and such as will not bear that root. The rent at an average 12 s. an acre.

Their courses,

1 Fallow	3 Pease.
2 Wheat	

1. Fallow	3. Beans and oats
2. Wheat	mixed.

Also,

1. Fallow	3. Pease.
2. Barley	

Likewise,

1. Turnips	3 Pease.
2. Barley	

They plough three times for wheat; sow 2 bushels and a peck, and gain 20 in return. They plough, in summer fallowing, thrice for barley; turnip land but once; sow 4 bushels an acre in *March*, and gain 30 bushels on an average For oats they give but one earth; sow 4 bushels, and reckon the mean crop at 4 quarters.

For pease they stir only once; sow 4 bushels, never hoe them; the produce at a medium 16 bushels; 60 bushels were once produced by an acre, after turnip land barley

VOL. II   Q   Their

Their culture of beans is, I think, as bad as in any part of *England*; they always mix them with oats. First, they sow 2 bushels an acre of beans, and some time afterwards they harrow in 1 ½ of black oats; the crop of both, about 20 bushels

The oats constantly shell, and are half loft before the beans are ready to cut; and to remedy this in part, they are induced to cut the beans too soon, and then as surely find them a thin and hollow sample. they own these disadvantages, and yet persist in such a slovenly method. I should also add, that this custom quite excludes the moft profitable one of hand-hoeing. It much behoves the good husbandmen of this country to discountenance so execrable a practice.

They plough thrice for turnips; hand-hoe them once, and eat the crops off with sheep: the average price, 35 *s*. an acre.

They generally mow one growth of their clover crops, and feed one, the produce of the firft 1 ¼ load of hay an acre. many keep it 2 years on the ground, but it is reckoned beft to have it only one. Some mow twice for hay; get 1 load at the

second

I

fecond cutting; and others leave it for feed: Wheat they reckon beft after feeding.

In their manuring, they depend pretty much on folding fheep, but do not practife it in winter, except on very dry land. They fold once in a place: 230 fheep will do an acre in a week. They fold all forts, but reckon a wether fold much the beft.— They chop their ftubbles for littering the farm-yards; and ftack all their hay at home, not much for fale. Chalk they fpread on their lands, about 20 loads an acre; it does beft on heavy foils; lafts 6 or 7 years.

Afhes they fow on light land, chiefly on clover, 20 bufhels an acre, and find the improvement great.

Malt-duft they ufe at the price of 7s or 8s. a quarter; ufe from 3 to 4 per acre. Pidgeon's dung they fpread on barley land, 20 bufhels an acre; and find that it beats all other manures.

Under ground drains are common; they find the improvement remarkable. They plafh their hedges, but have fcarcely any ditches, even in the clay land.

Good meadow land lets at 30s. an acre;

Q 2   they

they mow it all, and get 1 ½ load of hay an acre; two acres will keep a cow through the fummer. A good cow will give 3 gallons of milk a day during half the feafon; and 5 *lb.* of butter a week · the total annual produce 5 *l.* They keep about 15 hogs to 10 cows. A dairy-maid will take care of 10. The winter food chiefly grafs, but hay at calving; they keep all in the yard except at calving. In fatting cattle, they buy in beafts in *Auguft,* that are forward in flefh; they put them to the eddifhes, and from thence to turnips, upon which they are kept four months; but they are drawn and thrown on grafs land, a beaft of 100 ftone (8 *lb.*) will be fattened by an acre and half.

Hogs fattened to 40 ftone; but 26 the average.

Flocks of fheep rife from 100 to 400. The profit they reckon at,

Lamb,	-	-	0	8	0
Wool,	-	-	0	3	0
			0	11	0

The management of fheep is various. They buy in wethers, 2 years old, in *October,* or *November,* at 14 *s.*; keep them one year; firft they are put to ftubbles

3 and

and then to fome turnips; after that they have fome clover, from which they are fold fat: they are folded all fummer through.

The average fleece 6 *lb*.

In refpect to the rot, they hold that the diftemper is by no means owing to a quick luxuriance of growth, diftinctly taken, but to overflowings of grafs land; no rot known but from the latter caufe.

In their tillage, they reckon 4 horfes neceffary to 100 acres of arable land: they ufe 4 in a plough, with a driver; do an acre a day, from 4 to 5 inches deep; the price 6 *s*. or 7 *s*. an acre. The annual ex-pence of a horfe they reckon at 10 *l*. 10 *s*. The weekly allowance of oats, is 10 bufhels to 4 horfes. They do not break their ftub-ble till after *Chriftmas*. Both wheel and fwing ploughs ufed. The hire of a cart, 4 horfes, and a driver, 10 *s* a day.

In the hiring and ftocking farms, they reckon 1200 *l*. neceffary for 200 *l*. a year.

Land fells at 30 years purchafe.

Poor rates 3 *s*. in the pound; 20 years ago were not 1 *s*. 6 *d*.; only 1 *s*. in *Ware*, becaufe they have a poor workhoufe, wherein hemp is fpun for ropes, and

thread for netting and facking. Tythes
are chiefly compounded; Wheat 4s. or 5s.
an acre; Barley the fame; Oats 2s. to 2s.
6d; Turnips 1s. to 2s.; Clover 1s.

The employment of the poor women,
&c. fpinning, at which they earn 4d. a
day. All drink tea twice a day.

Moft of the farmers have leafes.

LABOUR.

In harveft, 36s. to 40s. and board.
In hay-time, 1s. 6d. a day.
In winter, 1s. 2d.
Reaping, 4s. to 5s.
Mowing barley and oats, 1s. to 1s. 6d.
——— grafs, 2s.
Hoeing turnips, 4s. to 5s.
Plafhing a hedge, 4d. a rod.
Thrafhing wheat, 3d. a bufhel.
——— barley, 2d.
——— Oats $1\frac{1}{2}$d.
——— peafe and beans, 1s. for 5 bufhels.
Head-man's wages, 8l.
Next ditto, 7l.
Lad's, 3l.
Dairy-maid, 5l.
Other ditto, 4l.

Women

Women *per* day, in harvest, 1 *s.* and board.

——— ——— in hay time, 8 *d*

——— ——— winter, 6 *d*

Value of a man's board, washing and lodging, 5 *s.* a week.

There is no rise of labour by the day; but the good labourers will only work by the piece, which was not the case formerly.

PROVISIONS.

Bread,	-	-	1 ½ *d. per lb.*
Cheese,	-	-	4
Butter,	-	-	8 ½
Beef,	-	-	3 ¾
Mutton,	-	-	4
Veal,	-	-	5
Pork,	-	-	3 ¾
Bacon,	-	-	6
Milk,	-	-	½ *d. per* pint.
Potatoes,	-	-	3 *per* peck.
Candles,	-	-	7 ½ *per lb.*
Soap,	-	-	6 ditto.

Labourer's house-rent, 40 *s.*

——— firing, breaking hedges and cutting trees

The following are the particulars of a farm here.

300 Acres in all	20 Oats
30 Grafs	20 Peafe
270 Arable	10 Clover
£. 180 Rent	20 Turnips
8 Horfes	100 Fallow
8 Cows	3 Men
200 Sheep	2 Boys
20 Young cattle	2 Maids
40 Acres Wheat	4 Labourers.
40 Barley	

David Barclay of *Youngsberry* has executed fome experiments in agriculture that
are of confequence. I am much indebted
to him for the following particulars, as well
as the preceding account of the common
hufbandry around him.

WINTER TARES.

Experiment, No. 1.

Upon a ftrong mixed foil, not fo heavy
that it would not do for turnips, ten acres
were fown with winter tares, after barley,
on one ploughing, 2 ½ bufhels *per* acre.
The fecond week in *May* they were begun
for foiling horfes: they lafted 25 horfes 9
weeks, which, at 2 s. 6 d. a horfe *per* week,
come to 2 l. 16 s. an acre. No manure

was

was ufed, and the tares were off time enough for turnips.

MANURES.

Experiment, No. 2.

A field of turnip land gravel was manured for wheat, with trotters from *London*, rabbits dung, and the fheep fold. Six quarters an acre of the trotters coft,

		£.	s.	d.
at 7 s. a quarter,		2	2	0
Carriage, 1 s. 6 d. - -		0	9	0
Per acre, - -		2	11	0
Rabbit dung 10 quarters, at 2 s.		1	0	0
Carriage, 1 s. - -		0	10	0
Per acre, - -		1	10	0

The other folded; 40 herdles, 10 of each fide, 8 feet each, for 230 fheep.

The effect was; the trotters produced 25 bufhels *per* acre; the fold, 20 bufhels; and the rabbit dung 15 bufhels.

	Bufhels.
Trotters, - -	25
Fold, - -	20
Superiority, - -	5

Which at 5 s. is 1 l. 5 s.

Trotters,	-	-	25
Rabbits dung,	-	-	15
			—
Superiority,	-	-	10
			—

At 5 s. is 2 l. 10 s.

It appears clearly from hence, that the trotters are vaftly fuperior to the rabbit dung, and fomething better than the fold: indeed the rabbit dung is fo fmall a produce, that one can hardly fuppofe it did any benefit at all.

Experiment, No. 3.

Coal afhes fifted fine, were compared with dung as manure for grafs-land. 160 bufhels *per* acre were fpread, at 3 ½ d. a bufhel, all expences included. On the other part, 16 loads an acre of dung, quite black and rotten, that had been turned over and well mixed together. The refult was, that the afh'd part produced a load and three quarters of hay *per* acre; the dunged ¼ of a load: much white clover with the former, but none among the latter. Before the manuring, the products were not more than ½ a load an acre. I viewed the after-grafs of the trial, and could

could trace exactly, by the thickness of the grafs and the verdure, where the afhes were laid

Experiment, No. 4.

Rape oil cake duft was tried on barley, fowed with the feed and harrowed in; 2 quarters *per* acre, at 15*s.* a quarter. The effect remarkably great; the crop 5 quarters *per* acre, which is much more confiderable than ever feen on the land

Experiment, No. 5.

Malt-duft Mr *Barclay* has tried for barley; 4 quarters *per* acre, at 7*s.*; and from the appearance of the crop, has great reafon to think that it anfwered well.

DRAINING.

Experiment, No. 6.

Above fifty acres of wet, heavy, loamy clay, and clayey foil, were drained in one winter by covered drains. The leading drains were cut 28 inches deep; and the branches 22 inches; 3 or 4 inches wide at bottom, and 9 at top. The digging and filling the 28 inch ones, 3*d.* a rod; and the

the 22 inch, 2 *d*. They were filled with black-thorn bushes at 9 *s*. a load, of 80 large faggots—3 loads did the drains of an acre of land, cut within a rod of each other. The improvement of these drains is strongly visible, though done only last winter.

CABBAGES.

Experiment, No. 7.

Three acres of strong clay land were summer fallowed last year, and the beginning of this. The feed of the great *Scotch* cabbage, &c. was sown in *April*, and the plants set on 3 feet ridges, 2 feet from each other, the 24th of *June*. They were horse-hoed twice with a shim, which cuts the land without turning a ridge . the rows hand-hoed twice; and after that the furrows struck with a common plough, earthing up the plants.

The shim with one horse did 3 acres a day. Befides the great *Scotch*, fome brown cole, and turnip cabbages were planted, all of which are in a very thriving condition, and to the honour of the cultivator, as clean as a garden.

DITCHING.

Experiment, No. 8.

By a comparifon between the cutting a ditch with fpades in the common manner, and ploughing it, it appeared that a ditch 30 rod long, cut by the fpade,

coft	-	-	-	£ 3	0	0

By ploughing, 6 horfes and 20 men did 30 rods in one day.

20 Men,	-	-	-	1	3	4
6 Horfes,	-	-	-	0	12	0
				1	15	4

The fpade,	-	-	£ 3	0	0
The plough,	-	-	1	15	4
Superiority of the latter,		1	4	8

In the labour of the 20 men, is included their paring down and finifhing the fides of the ditch, and the bank. This is certainly a very confiderable improvement, and deferves the attention of all who cut new ditches.

FATTING BEASTS WITH OIL-CAKE.

Experiment, No. 9.

In 1769, ten oxen were bought and put to lint-feed cake.

They cost,	-	-	£ 60	0	0
Commiffion,	-	-	0	15	0
Driving, &c.	-	-	0	8	0
December 30.—6250 cakes,	-	33	0	0
Carriage of 4 waggon loads, at 21 *s*.	-	-	-	4	4	0
November 6. to *April* 10. Four months hay, 6 *lb*. each *per* diem, at 40 *s*. a load,	-	10	14	0
Labour,	-	-	-	7	0	0
Two of them 3 weeks at grafs, at 6 *s*.	-	-	0	18	0
Four had an acre of turnips,	-	2	0	0
			118	19	0

Produce.

By 10 oxen received,	-	120	0	0
Expences,	-	-	-	118	19	0
Profit,	-	-	-	1	1	0

The

The beafts were well littered with ftraw, and raifed a vaft quantity of dung; they were ftalled, and never let out; water was given in pails thrice a day. A thoufand cakes, which come to 5 *l.* 5 *s.*, weigh 1 ton 7 *C. wt.* 3 quarters.

I muft obferve on this account, that the clear profit in money is by no means the objeꝗt;—the dung is the great advantage. Thofe who can command ftraw, ftubble, fern, or other litter, and can convert it into the richeft dung without lofs on the ox account, will make a very great profit in the high improvement of their land. No manure exceeds the dung of oil-cake fed beafts; it is the moft fertile of all. Had Mr. *Barclay* bought the ftraw, and meafured the dung, the truth of this obfervation would be fufficiently clear But I muft further remark, that the charge of 7 *l.* for attendance feems very high. In a convenient ox-houfe that expence might be much reduced; witnefs the practice of Mr. *Moody* of *Retford*

HEDGES.

Experiment, No. 10.

In fencing, Mr. *Barclay* has made a trial of tranfplanting old quick ftubbs to form a new hedge. He was very doubtful of their fuccefs, but none could thrive better this reminds me of the fame practifed to a large extent by the Rev. Mr. *Hall* in *Yorkfhire.*

SPIKY ROLLER.

This implement (procured of *John Arbuthnot* Efq; of *Mitcham)* has been ufed on fome very ftrong cloddy land in fummer fallowing with very great fuccefs; it reduced fome very rough land, at twice going over, to a fine tilth, at a feafon when a plough could not have been of the leaft fervice. The expence of the operation as follows :

	£.		
5 Horfes, -	0	10	0
1 Man, - -	0	1	6
	0	11	6

It rolls 1 ½ acre, twice in a place, *per* day;

the

the expence confequently is 7*s*. 8*d*. an acre *.

From the activity and judgment with which *David Barclay* begins his hufbandry, the public has no flight reafon to expect that it will be of general utility: his readinefs in trying, and his accuracy in relating, will render his experiments very valuable.

At *Efenden*, in the way from *Ware* to *Hatfield*, Sir *William Baker* has built a barn, which is the moft coftly one I have feen. It is 84 yards long, 15 broad; the whole raifed on capt ftones, fo that a moufe cannot get into it: The whole floor is equally for thrafhing. The fides, &c. are boarded and painted blue, and the roof is flated.

I croffed

---

* YOUNGSBERRY is a plain neat edifice, built by Mr. *Paine*, the fituation very beautiful, on the brow of a waving hill, fcattered with trees. It commands a fine view of rich inclofures, various from the inequalities of the country.

In the vale, which winds at the bottom of the hill, Mr *Barclay* has cut a large river, that enriches his profpect greatly, and gives the whole fcene a livelinefs which (however pleafing) it could not otherwife poffefs.

I croffed from *Hertfordſhire* into *Surry*, paſſing through *Clapham* † in the way to *Peterſham*, where I had the pleaſure of viewing the farm of Mr. *Ducket*, whoſe mechanical abilities are ſo well known by the invention of two moſt excellent ploughs.

All his fields are ſand, of two ſorts; one very light and rather poor; the other is moiſt, black, and good. Moſt of his ara-

ble

---

† At this place Mr. *Thornton* has an orna-mented paddock, laid out in an agreeable man-ner; in ſome particulars, different from the common method of ſketching them. It conſiſts of a varied lawn well ſcattered with ſingle trees and ſome clumps, and ſo incloſed with wood as to be perfectly rural, though ſo near *London* A gravel walk runs around the whole, and encom-paſſes ſeveral meadows, to the extent of more than two miles. It is in moſt places ſhaded thickly with wood; and on one ſide very well broken with ſome old oaks, &c. that grow out of it. Almoſt in front of the houſe it leads to a *Gothic* bench, that is light and pleaſing. At each end it concludes in a ſhrubbery, which joins the houſe, and is in ſeveral inſtances very beauti-ful. a ſmall river winds through it, gently bounded by riſing hillocks, and ſmooth green ſlopes, very well varied, and ſpotted with ſhrubs and trees in a judicious manner. The bends of the water are natural, and the union with the

lawn

ble crops are cultivated in the drill method:
His turnips, barley, oats, and wheat, are
chiefly in rows. the turnips 12 inches to
2 feet afunder; the wheat and oats from 9
to 12 inches, equally diftant. He hand-
hoes all thefe crops fufficiently to keep them
clean; and finds, from repeated experience,
that the crops are better than in the broad-
caft mode, at the fame time that the land is

R 2 kept

lawn and wood well imagined. To the right it
feems loft in the retiring grove These circumftances are all executed with real tafte, and if a
few others were a little altered, the whole place
would (in its ftile) be complete Among others,
the looking from the lawn on to a bridge, which
on croffing, you find, has no connection with
the water, the end of the river appearing full
in view,—this is not quite the thing —The
chevaux de frize pales, with part of the lawn
from the paddock, are too near the water, they
juft cut a flip of mown grafs along the banks,
which is a mere edging, befides the pales themfelves are feen, and that clofe appearance of *art*,
and *boundary*, hurts the effect of the river ——
Perhaps alfo, the benches in the walk are too
frequent As to the rock work grotto, it is
(the lanthorn excepted) extremely well executed;
but in too wild a ftile for a gentle ftream, and a
fmooth fhaven lawn fpotted with fhrubs,—it
requires a romantic fituation on the banks of a
rapid ftream tumbling over broken fragments

kept much cleaner.—And one application of this mode is particularly useful.—he sows clover seed over his wheat or spring corn, just before the last hand-hoeing, which operation covers the seed in the compleatest manner. I viewed the crops, and found the clover as regular as possible.

Mr. *Ducket*'s hedges are remarkably neat—they are of white-thorn only, very well plashed to secure them at bottom, and afterwards kept regularly clipped. The management of his borders, also, do him credit; he found them wide and quite over-run with bushes and rubbish; all this he has grubbed up, so that the plough goes quite to the hedge—the fields are the neater, at the same time that much land is gained.

All the tillage of his land is performed with ploughs of his own invention. first, with a trenching one with two shares, &c. that work one below another, paring off the turf or surface of the land, and turning it over; the lower one follows in the same furrow, and raising fresh earth buries the first. In this manner it cuts 12 inches deep with 4 horses, and does an acre a day. One

very

very important ufe of this plough, is the burying twitch in fand land. Mr. *Ducket*'s method, when his land is run much to twitch, is to bury it fo deep as to admit the fucceeding tillage *above* it; a large quantity of twitch buried, turns to excellent manure; but if not fown with hoeing crops, it will not be deftroyed; hand-hoeing with this management will totally deftroy its growth; but while it is rotting, it holds the land together and is of great fervice. This method Mr. *Ducket* finds to be far preferable to ploughing fhallow, and trufting to the harrows for tearing out the twitch The other is a trebble plough on one bent beam. It turns three furrows at once; works with 4 horfes, and does from 3 to 4 acres a day.

I fhould give drawings of thefe moft excellent implements, but the Regifter of the Society at *London*, is about to publifh a work which will include them

They anfwer the purpofe extremely well; and not only on fand, but alfo on ftiff foils, as I have been for fome time a witnefs, in the fields of a gentleman whofe hufbandry I fhall prefently come to.—The trench

R 3   plough

plough cofts 8 *l.* 8 *s.* ; and the trebble one 9 *l.* 9 *s.*

The method in which he drills his crops, of whatever fort, is the following. The land, when ready for the feed, is harrowed flat; then the drills are ftruck with a plough made on purpofe

See Plate VIII. Fig. 1.

From a to b. ——— 4 feet.

     d — e. ——— 5 ———

     a — c. ——— 0   8 inches.

     f — h. ——— 4   0

     f — g ——— 2   4

     e — o. ——— 2   6

     n. ——— fcrew holes to vary the diftances of the fhares. The bottoms of the fhares in the fhape of a boat, and fhod with a narrow ftrip of iron; they are 4 inches thick, and 12 high from the ground.

For the furrows to be ftraight, the outward fhare goes in the laft furrow of the preceding fet. When they are made, the corn, &c. are fown broad-caft, and the land harrowed; nine tenths of it rife in the rows, and very regularly.—The price of it 3 *l.*

Mr,

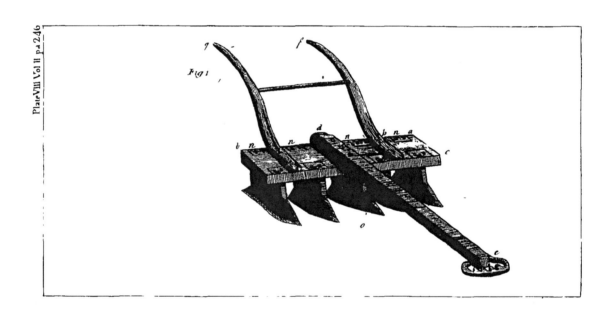

Plate VIII Vol II p.a 246

Fig 1

Mr. *Ducket*'s beft meadow on the banks of the *Thames* (an excellent one for cows) confifts at leaft half the herbage of burnet : the reft vernal, white clover—cow grafs— wild trefoile—and narrow leaved plantane.*

As to the common hufbandry about *Richmond* and *Peterfham*, it is difficult to give

---

* RICHMOND Gardens have been lately altered : the terrafs and the grounds about it, are now converted into a waving lawn that hangs to the river in a moft beautiful manner the old avenue is broken, and the whole clumped in fome places with gioves ; in others with knots of trees, and a very judicious ufe made of fingle ones no traces of the avenue are to be feen, though many of the trees remain. The lawn waves in a very agreeable manner, and the wood is fo well ma- naged, that the views of the river vary every moment. A gravel walk winds through it, which commands the moft pleafing fcenes The river, noble as it is, is not the only object that feafts the eye, on the other fide of the walk the grounds are thrown into fuch various forms, that they no where fatigue the eye, in one place the lawn fpreads over a moft beautiful vale, and breaks among the woods, in a ftile that muft command attention, in fome fpots retiring into the groves, and contrafting its lively green with the darker fhades of wood ;—in others it fwells into gentle hillocks fcattered with fingle trees, and rifes into a hill that compleats the inequality

R 4   of

give an account of it; the greateſt part of the country is occupied by the ſeats, gardens, and lawns of the nobility and gentry. the few farms here, riſe from 40 *l.* to 200 *l.* a year; in general about 60 *l.* 80 *l.* or 100 *l.* a year. The ſoil of two ſorts, either ſtiff loams,

of the ſpot a flock of ſheep ſcattered about the ſlopes, add uncommonly to the beauty of the ſcene It is, on the whole, a mild agreeable landſcape, which ſeems created by the hand of unpreſuming Taſte.

After this, the walk retires into thicker plantations, and winds through them with as much variety as the ground affords, the wild ſhrubby land is well managed, and contraſts the more dreſſed parts of the garden.

At *Kew* are many very fine exotic plants, with a great variety of trees not common

The view from *Richmond* hill would figure in the fineſt parts of the north of *England*, where a bolder inequality of country preſents ſuch amazing ſcenes. The noble bend of the river at the foot of the hill, which preſents ſo fine a ſheet of water, is well contraſted by thick woods, and the iſlands give a ſtriking variety to the ſcene. The ſurrounding country is rich, and cut into innumerable incloſures, nor are there more houſes than ſufficient to throw a chearfulneſs over the whole, a fortunate circumſtance ſo near *London* But the point of view being quite a town is very unhappy.

loams, tending pretty much to clay, or
mere fands ; fome of the latter do not let
at more than 10 *s.* or 12 *s* an acre ; the
meadows let at 40*s* —the average of the
neighbourhood, from 20*s.* to 25*s.*—As to
the courfes of crops, they are as various
as the private opinion of every farmer ; but
in general, they croud in crop upon crop
as faft as poffible. Wheat and rye produce
3 quarters, Barley 4 ; Oats from 2 ½ to 10 ;
the average 5 ; Tick beans, on their ftrong
land, 4 quarters. They hoe their turnips
but once ; and reckon the value 40*s* to 3*l.*
They mow much of their clover for foiling ;
it yields in hay, at two cuttings, 3 ½ loads.

LABOUR.

In harveft, 2*s.* 6*d.* a day and board.
In hay-time, 2 *s.* and beer
In winter, 1 *s.* 6*d.* to 1 *s* 8*d.*
Reaping, 7*s.* to 16*s.*
Mowing barley, 1 *s.* 6*d.* to 4*s.*
Mowing, making, carrying, and ftacking
    hay, 10*s.* 6*d* ; but the farmer finds a
    loader.
Hoeing turnips, 6*s.*

Men's

Men's wages, 8 *l.* 8 *s.*
Lad's, 2 *l.* 10 *s.* to 4 *l.*

PROVISIONS.

Bread,   -   -   1 $\frac{1}{4}$ *d per* pound.

Cheefe,   4 $\frac{1}{2}$

Butter,   -   -   9

Beef,   -   ' -   2 $\frac{1}{2}$ *d.* coarfe joints

Mutton,   4 $\frac{1}{2}$

Veal,   -   -   5

Pork,   -   -   4 $\frac{3}{4}$

Bacon,   -   -   8

Milk,   -   -   1 *d. per* pint.

Houfe-rent, 5 *l.*

LETTER XVIII.

I Proceed to the register of the experiments of *John Arbuthnot*, Efq, of *Ravenfbury*, with the fatisfaction of knowing that I fhall lay before the public, as ufeful knowledge as was ever yet received in the walk of hufbandry. Their genuine merit renders any further introduction unneceffary.

The moft familiar method of arranging them will be under the following heads.

I. LAYING LAND TO GRASS.

II. THE CULTURE OF LUCERNE.

III. THE CULTURE OF MADDER.

IV. EXPERIMENTS ON THE DRILL CULTURE OF SEVERAL CROPS.

V. EXPERIMENTS TO ASCERTAIN THE BEST COURSE OF CROPS.

VI. MISCELLANEOUS EXPERI-
MENTS.

VII. IMPLEMENTS.

I. LAYING LAND TO GRASS.

Experiment, No. 1.

In 1756, feventeen acres were laid down
with oats, fucceeding a fummer fallow;
the feeds ufed were,

2 Sacks *London* hay feeds;

20 *lb.* of white clover.

The two firft years the product was very
good, amounting to 2 loads an acre of hay;
but it declined much afterwards. The
graffes that appeared, confifted chiefly of
meadow poa—red robbin—fome *dactilus*,
or orchard grafs—and a fmall proportion of
ray-grafs. The white clover difappeared
quite, owing to the wetnefs of the land
preventing its trailing branches ftriking
root. Four of thefe acres were hollow
drained in 1766, which has gradually improved the herbage, infomuch that thofe
parts in which the white clover died away,
are now thickly covered with it.

Experiment, No. 2.

Mr. *Arbuthnot* has laid, at different times, 70 acres, in various methods ·——— firſt, 31 acres, with oats, on a ſummer fallow; the ſeeds,

20 *lb.* of white clover;

10 *lb.* of lucerne;

And 1 buſhel of ray-graſs.

This field, for two years after the firſt laying, produced 2 loads of hay *per* acre; but ſince that time (ten years ago) it has gradually diminiſhed. The white clover has diſappeared, except in dry patches, which has been owing to the wetneſs of the ſoil. After the firſt year, the lucerne has never made any appearance; but the ray-graſs has kept its ground.

The goodneſs of the crops the two firſt years, Mr. *Arbuthnot* attributes to the ſtaple of the ground being then pervious to the rain, and conſequently draining itſelf; but when the land ſubſided, the water was retained on the ſurface, to the deſtruction of the tender graſſes. The white clover is a plant that trails on the ground, but does not ſtrike root except in ſpots dry enough to admit it; which was

I   the

the occasion of the above-mentioned partial failure. These 31 acres have since been drained by under-ground cuts, which has brought the white clover in much greater abundance.

In 1766, it was manured at the rate of 30 loads an acre with river mud, in which were many small shells. No benefit was seen the first year; which he attributes to the servant having injudiciously rolled it with an heavy roller in the spring when too wet: this manuring was before the draining; the mud took no effect till after that operation.

In the wettest parts of the field there appeared a very pernicious grass called red robbin; in arable land, the *Surry* farmers call it water-grass. it is there very difficult to extirpate; for though only fibrous rooted, yet burying will not destroy it; it must be extracted like couch: in grass land it comes very late, and yields nothing.

Experiment, No. 3.

Ten other acres were likewise sown with oats on a fallow; the seeds,

2 Sacks

2 Sacks of hay feeds from the Horfe Guards, chiefly confifting of crefted dog's tail—narrow leaved plantane— barley grafs—and innumerable daifies. 20 *lb*. White clover.

This field has continued a good pafture, without declining like the preceding ones; but it has not produced a good burthen of hay. The reafon of its not falling off after the fecond year like the reft, is the foil being a black loam, which does not fubfide into fo retentive a mafs as the other wetter an ds. The product of the hay being but fmall, arofe from moft of the above mentioned grafses running chiefly to bents, inftead of thickening on the ground like many other forts

Experiment, No 4.

Seven acres more were fown with tares; the ftubble ploughed up and hollow drained; oats thrown in at fpring, and with them 2 facks an acre of *Suffolk* hay feeds, and 20 *lb*. white clover. The whole was manured after the oats were off. This has proved a good pafture ever fince, and has yielded large crops of hay, but the grafs has confifted chiefly

chiefly of the *holchus*, believed to be a very bad fort—some *dactilus*—a fmall quantity of meadow fefcue—and a little meadow fox tail, and great poa;—and it is remarkable that no vernal has appeared.— This field has remained quite dry ever fince, even in the depth of winter—though the fame foil undrained has been too wet for cattle to ftir on.

Obfervation.

Mr. *Arbuthnot* remarking that ray-grafs generally run to feed before the white clover made any bottom in the fpring, and efpe-cially on land undrained; he has ufually fed the pafture until the end of *May*, and then laid it by for hay. This conduct has given the white clover time to bottom, fo that he has often mown a load of hay an acre on land, which, in other management, would not near equal the produce. A hint that may prove very ufeful to many culti-vators;—for feeding ray-grafs late in the fpring without damaging the crop of hay, is a very great acquifition in fheep feed.

II. LUCERNE.

Experiment, No 5.

In the year 1759, twelve acres of a black, deep, fandy loam were fown with barley, after turnips, and with it 10 *lb. per* acre of lucerne broad-caft. The corn was mown and carried, but nothing done to the lucerne.

1760.

This year it was mown for foiling horfes, &c. but the produce weak; not confider-able enough for a particular valuation.

1761.

This year the crop came to perfection. Early in the fpring it was crofs ploughed with a round fhare, and harrowed. Mowed it thrice, each time for hay; the product of the three, four tons *per* acre of the beft hay ever ufed. The team men would not at firft ufe it; but they were at laft fo pre-judiced in its favour, that when done, they lamented the lofs. After the mowings, there was an aftermath, which yielded fome food for cows and fheep. Between each cutting it was harrowed; and likewife

in

in autumn. The average price of common hay is 45 s. a load, but Mr. *Arbuthnot* valued this of lucerne at 55 s., in which valuation his men agreed.

1762.

This year the culture was the same as the preceding, and also the crop; it was again mown thrice.

1763

The same culture and product. a latter growth the end of *September* was cut off in one night by a flight frost· hardy as the plant in general is, yet the shoots are extremely tender, they will bear no frost The natural grafs made so formidable an appearance, that the autumnal harrowing was omitted, from an idea that it would be ineffectual.

1764.

In the spring of this year, one acre was ploughed up and planted with madder, the remaining eleven were mown twice, but had no harrowing; the product 44 tons of dry hay; but more than half was in the first crop, and much of it natural grafs.

1765

In this fpring, ploughed it up for madder; the lucerne declined, owing, as apprehended, to a want of more regular and fevere harrowing, as it has been found that the feveieft operation of that fort will not damage the plants. *Rocque*'s harrow was ufed.

In refpect to making it into hay; the luceine is fo ftalky that it does not fettle foon, it was therefore ftacked veiy green —the heat that refults from fap (not wet) is beneficial It was always cut as foon as there appeared a general fcattered bloom.

Expences and Produce.

1760		£		
Rent,	-	1	0	0
Tythe and town charges,		0	6	0
Three ploughings	-	0	13	6
Seed and fowing,	-	0	12	0
Three harrowings,	-	0	4	6
Mowing, &c.	-	0	5	0
		3	1	0
By green food,	-	1	0	0
Lofs,	- -	2	1	0

		£.		
1761.	Rent, &c. -	£.1	6	0
	Ploughing, - -	0	4	6
	Four harrowings, -	0	6	0
	Mowings; first, -	0	3	0
	second, -	0	1	6
	third, -	0	1	6
	Making, raking, carting, and stacking thrice,	1	0	0
		3	2	6
	By 4 loads of hay, at 55 s. - -	11	0	0
	After-grass, -	0	5	0
		11	5	0
	Expences, -	3	2	6
	Clear profit, -	8	2	6
1762.	The same as in 1761.			
	Product, - -	11	5	0
	Expences, -	3	2	6
	Profit, -	8	2	6
1763.	Rent, &c. - -	1	6	0
	Three harrowings, -	0	4	6
	Mowing, - -	0	6	0
	Making, &c. -	1	0	0
		2	16	6

By 4 loads of hay,		£.11	0	0
Expences,	-	2	16	6
Clear profit,	-	8	3	6
1764. Rent, &c.	- -	1	6	0
Mowing twice,	-	0	4	6
Making, &c.	-	0	15	0
		2	5	6
By 4 loads of hay,	-	11	0	0
Expences,	-	2	5	6
Clear profit,	-	8	14	6
1761. Profit,	- -	8	2	6
1762. Ditto,	- -	8	2	6
1763. Ditto,	- -	8	3	6
1764. Ditto,	- -	8	14	6
		33	3	0
1760. Lofs,	- -	2	1	0
Profit in 5 years,	-	31	2	0
Which is *per* acre *per ann.*		6	4	4
And on the 12 acres,		74	12	0

Wheat, to equal this profit, muft yield 5 quarters an acre, and that *every* year. If

S 3   this

this does not prove the vaft profit of lucerne; nothing can   Nor fhould we condemn for lafting no longer a grafs that will continue four years in fuch full perfection. In other methods of culture it has remained much longer—but that is not the leaft reafon for rejecting a fhorter duration. Such a culture may poffibly be found more beneficial than the more lafting, and at the fame time more expenfive modes;—for fuch a term of five years, in a courfe of feveral crops, will be found uncommonly profitable.

Mr. *Arbuthnot*, from the experience of this crop, as well as more general obfervation, recommends the broad-caft culture of lucerne intended for hay, becaufe it is neceffary that the ground fhould be quite covered with plants, to prevent the dirt or duft fticking to the hay   But if it is defigned for foiling, then he recommends drills equally diftant, 18 inches afunder. It is abfolutely neceffary to harrow it crofs and crofs in both fpring and autumn, it fhould be done till the land has the abfolute appearance of a fallow, and alfo be manured every autumn, before the harrowing, with fine rotten compoft. The fpring harrowing as early as the feafon will admit; if the young fhoots fpring before you can get on, do not therefore defift from harrowing; you had better deftroy them totally than omit that operation, which is effential to the goodnefs of the crop.

Experiment, No. 6.

In order to determine in what degree lucerne will bear very rough treatment, this gentleman wounded many plants in a fevere manner, quite to mangling them— others he cut off 3 inches below the ground; the refult was, that the latter plants were abfolutely killed, but the former not in the leaft hurt. the fact is, that the bulb may be wounded in any degree; if the leaft bit remains it fprouts prefently; but cut it quite off, and you deftroy the plant.

III. THE CULTURE OF MAD-DER, &c.

Mr. *Arbuthnot*, on his applying to huf-bandry, formed a general idea of the means of rendering it profitable. It appeared to him that common crops managed in a common manner, could not to a gentleman

S 4   yield

yield the fame advantage as to men who
attend to the loweft minutiæ of the bufinefs,
and live as much by frugality as agriculture. In fuch a ftile of hufbandry he
thought it not defirable to emulate them,
but rather to apply to the culture of fuch
rich vegetables, as would yield a profit
confiderable enough to pay for an accurate
expenfive culture, which would not only
be more beneficial, but at the fame time
require much lefs trouble and fatigue—and
not be liable to the numerous cafualties and
impofitions to which common crops are fo
univerfally open.

Among other plants, MADDER attracted
his attention, as an article of culture that
has as few objections to it as moft others—
it remains feveral years in the ground, confequently is lefs complex in its management
than fuch annual ones as hops—it is liable
to few accidents—and pays excellently for a
perfect culture: large quantities being conftantly imported from *Holland* to anfwer
our own demand, and the *Dutch* growing
moft of it themfelves, and having by mo-
nopoly raifed it to a moft extravagant price,
he determined with the fpirit which real

prudence

prudence dictates, to take a journey into
Flanders to examine the soil there preferred
for madder, and their management of the
crop. Afterwards, in a journey through
Holland, he also made enquiries into the
conduct of the crops, and the method of
manufacturing it; having obtained admission into their stoves, where he found a management more expensive, but no ways
preferable to what is practised by many in
England, this he did that he might enter upon
the culture himself, with that knowledge of
the business which was requisite for avoiding
great errors. Ill success in such pursuits, is
more often owing to hasty, premature
attempts, than to really natural obstructions
—It is oftener the moral, than the physical
capability that is wanting.

During his stay in *Holland*, he examined
their madder grounds with the minutest
attention; made every requisite enquiry for
gaining as complete a knowledge of the
culture as possible—and from thence was
convinced of the propriety of attempting it
at home. He took the opportunity of being in that country, to make himself further
acquainted with husbandry in general. He
travelled through all the provinces, and likewise

wife that region of good hufbandry, FLAN-
DERS, and being perfectly acquainted with
the *Dutch* and *French* languages, he was able
to gain whatever information he wanted;
accordingly he has introduced feveral
practices on his own farm, the hint of
which he caught in *Flanders*.

Experiment, No. 7.

He began his undertaking with trying
one acre in the year 1765. The foil a
deep black loam. It was dug 18 inches
deep in *March*, and planted with winter
plants—that is, with parts of the runners
and crown of the root on which the buds
are made for that year's growth. The rows
were equally diftant, 18-inches afunder,
and 6 inches from plant to plant As foon
as the fhoots were 10 inches high, the
plantation was hand-hoed; which operation was repeated twice more during the
fummer, fo as to keep the land quite free
from weeds.

1766.

In the fpring of this year, as foon as the
fhoots appeared, they were earthed up
with hand-hoes; and when 8 inches high,
they

they were moſt of them drawn for planting other land; after which the rows were earthed again. as ſoon as the freſh ſhoots were 8 inches high, they were drawn again —and after another earthing, the ſame for the third time. In autumn the beds were earthed again, and the haulm that remained, buried, by digging earth in the intervals and ſpreading it on the rows.

1767.

In this ſpring, plants were once drawn off and earthed as in laſt year; alſo hand-hoed twice   In autumn the crop was dug up with ſpades, and the madder clean picked. but the produce not exceeding 10 *l.* value; which was owing to the great damage the plants received from having ſetts ſo often drawn from them.

Expences.

		£.		
1765.	Firſt digging, -	£.8	o	o
	Planting, - -	I	I	o
	Plants, - -	15	o	o
	Hand-hoeing thrice, -	I	10	o
1766.	Hand-hoeing; thrice			
	earthing at the ſame			
	time; · - -	I	10	o
	Carry over -	27	I	o

Brought over, £.27	27	1	0
Digging the intervals,	1	0	0
1767. Hand-hoeing thrice,	1	10	0
Taking up, -	8	0	0
Three years rent, tythe			
and town charges, at			
1 *l.* 6 *s.* - -	3	18	0
Total expences,	41	9	0

Produce.

Value of the crop, -	10	0	0
Lofs, -	31	9	0

The balance is here called lofs; and im-
properly, becaufe this acre was but a nurfery for fucceeding crops; the value of the
plants drawn from it, amounted to 90 *l.*;
it fhould here, therefore, be efteemed the
mere price of the fets for the fucceeding
plantations.

From this experiment two very ufeful
facts are gained. firft, the expence of cultivation by digging, where no manure is
wanting, and the plants not purchafed,
amounts, on land of 20 *s.* to 26 *l.* 9 *s. per*
acre, including the expence of twice digging; but if the fame ground was again
planted, the total would of courfe be lefs.

I   Hence

Hence we find, that 6 *C. wt.* of madder, at 4*l.* a *C. wt.* will pay the expence of fuch cultivation.

Another circumftance of great confequence, is the damage the crop received by drawing plants from it—even to the total deftruction of the profit. This offers a leffon for the cultivators of madder, not to be free in taking plants from their crops. —If their plantations are annually increafing, all may poffibly be fpoiled by drawing: does it not therefore feem expedient to leave part * of the crop, enough as you judge for a fupply of plants till the fpring planting is over, and then take it up inftead of the autumn preceding.

Experiment, No 8

Seven acres of a fandy loam (a barley ftubble) was ploughed at *Michaelmas* with a ftrong wheel plough, 14 inches deep. Upon this ploughing it was manured with 10 loads (40 bufhels each) an acre of farm-
yard

---

* One acre of very good madder will yield plants enough for ten.

yard manure, which was turned in by landing up for the winter on to 3 feet ridges.

1766.

The beginning of *March* ploughed it again; reverfing the ridges thrown up the preceding autumn. The fame month they were planted with winter * plants, a fingle row on each ridge; the plants 18 inches afunder. The method ufed in planting was to draw furrows with hand-hoes, and then the fets were laid in them, and covered alfo by hoes. Moft part of the field mifcarried, owing to an unufual quantity of rain falling, and the fpring ploughing being given while the land was wet. The whole was therefore ploughed up, and in *May* it was again planted with fpring plants, bought at 8 *s. per* thoufand; the

---

* Winter Plants, are that part of the root on which the eyes are made, which are cut in lengths of 2 or 3 inches, in the fame manner as hop plants

Mr *Arbuthnot* does not approve their ufe, becaufe they remain fo long in the ground that they are fubject to rot, efpecially if it be moift and this he attributes to their wanting the fupport of fibres which they had when on the mother plant, and though from their great fucculency they will vegetate, yet they are very fubject to decay from moifture

the rows 2 feet by 18 inches, which is
15000 *per* acre; they were dibbled in.
During the fummer, the plants were kept
clean by three hand-hoeings; and in the
autumn the rows were covered by earth
dug in the intervals

1767.

This year the field was hand-hoed twice.

1768

And again the fame in 1768 In autumn
it was ploughed up with the great wheel
plough, to the depth of 18 inches, with
12 horfes. Men followed the plough with
pronged forks to throw the madder out of
the furrows, and women and children followed to pick it up. The produce 4 tons
4 *C wt.* on the 7 acres, at 4*l* 10*s. per C wt*

Expences per acre.

1765.	Firft ploughing, -	£.1	4	0
	Manuring, - -	3	10	0
	Landing up, -	0	7	6
1766.	Spring ploughing -	0	7	6
	Planting, - -	1	0	0
	Ploughing up, -	0	7	6
	Planting the fecond time,	1	10	0
	The plants, -	6	0	0
	Carry over, -	14	6	6

		£.	s.	d.
Brought over,		14	6	6
Three hand-hoeings,		1	10	0
Digging in autumn,		0	10	0
1767. Two hand-hoeings,	-	1	0	0
1768. Ditto, -	-	1	0	0
Taking up, all expences included,	-	7	0	0
Drying, at 3*s. per C. wt.*		1	16	0
Three years rent, tythe and town charges, at 22 *s.* -	-	3	6	0
Total, -	-	30	8	6

Produce.

		£.	s.	d.
12 *C. wt.* of madder, at 4*l.* 10*s.* -	-	54	0	0
Expences,	-	30	8	6
Clear profit,	-	23	11	6
Or *per annum,*		7	17	2
Product of the 7 acres,		378	0	0
Ditto expences,		212	19	6
Ditto profit,	-	165	0	6
Or *per annum,*		58	6	10

Obfervations.

Near 8 *l.* expence *per* acre was here in-
curred by accident; fo that the profit, with
better fortune, would have been above 30*l.*
an acre : and this fuppofition is not to be
flighted, as Mr. *Arbuthnot* candidly owns
it to have arifen from an error in ploughing when the land was too wet. However,
to take the fact as it really happened, the
profit is very confiderable . 7*l.* 17*s.* 2*d. per*
acre *per annum*, much exceeds what can be
gained from any common hufbandry : 5
quarters *per* acre of wheat gained every
year (which by the way is an impoffibility)
will not equal this amount ; at the fame time
that conftant crops of that grain, would be
without comparifon more hazardous and
troublefome : a ftrong proof of the juftnefs
of this gentleman's idea of the propriety
of adopting uncommon articles of culture.

Plants were drawn from this crop, but
not in abundance.

Experiment, No. 9.

Nine other acres of the fame foil were
ploughed 14 inches deep at *Michaelmas*

1765, and dunged with 10 loads an acre of yard dung, covered by landing up.

1766.

In the fpring it was planted with fpring plants, dibbled in rows 2 feet afunder, by 18 inches from plant to plant; and kept clean through the fummer by three hand-hoeings: and in autumn the furrows were dug, and the earth thrown over the plants.

1767.

This year it was kept clean by two hand-hoeings.

1768.

In *February*, a large compoft, confifting of farm-yard dung and fome afhes, laid on the headland and mixed well with a large quantity of virgin earth, was fpread on the land, and in the fummer it was hand-hoed twice. In autumn it was ploughed up, to the depth of 18 inches; and the crop when dry amounted to 12 *C. wt. per* acre, at 4*l.* 10*s.*—But three lands, of 3 rows each, were left for a further growth of three years longer, by way of experiment, to difcover the increafe of the root in ftanding three years extraordinary.

Expences.

			£	s	d
1765.	Ploughing,	-	1	4	0
	Manuring,	-	3	10	0
	Landing up,	-	0	7	6
1766.	Spring earth,	-	0	7	6
	Planting,	-	1	0	0
	Three hand-hoeings	-	1	10	0
	Autumnal digging,	-	0	10	0
1767.	Two hand-hoeings,	-	1	0	0
1768.	Manuring,	-	4	0	0
	Two hand-hoeings,		1	0	0
	Digging up,	-	7	0	0
	Drying, at 3*s*. a *C. wt.*		1	16	0
	Three years rent, &c.		3	6	0
			26	11	0

Produce.

	£	s	d
12 *C. wt.* of madder, at 4*l.* 10*s.* -	54	0	0
Expences, -	26	11	0
Clear profit, -	27	9	0
Or *per annum,*	9	3	0

T 2   Pro-

Product of the nine acres, - -	486	0	0
Ditto expences,	238	19	0
Ditto profit, -	245	1	0
Or *per annum*,	81	13	8

Observations.

It is to be remarked on this crop, that the produce does not exceed that of Experiment, No. 8, notwithſtanding the laſt year's manuring at the expence of 4*l.* an acre; it is true that the firſt planting of it ſucceeded, which might perhaps be a matter of conſequence in gaining time before the ſummer heats came on; not however to the amount of balancing a manuring of 4*l.*. it ſhould therefore ſeem that the manure ought to be ſpread on the land before planting, or at leaſt long before the laſt year of the crop, for then the plants have not time to avail themſelves fully of the advantage. The plants, Mr. *Arbuthnot* remarks, on this crop were too far aſunder, and the laſt dunging did not anſwer; as by earthing, it drew up ſhoots, that ſhewed the appearance of great increaſe, when the crop was taken up; but thoſe tops being more ſucculent than the other

part

part of the root, they withered in proportion to their fucculency.

The profit is very confiderable: 9*l.*
3*s. per* acre clear, is fuch a degree of
advantage as can never be expected in
any common hufbandry. make it as perfect as you pleafe, it will never arrive at
fuch a height.

Experiment, No 10.

In 1766, nine acres were fallowed, receiving in all fix earths the firft, 14 inches
deep, and landed up in autumn by the laft,
being at the fame time thrown on to 4 feet
ridges.

1767.

In the fpring it was manured at the rate
of 5 facks *per* acre of wood-afhes, and 5
quarters *per* acre of trotters; and the whole
covered by reverfing the ridges. It was
then planted with dibbles. 6 acres, one
row on a land; $2\frac{1}{2}$ acres, two rows on a
land; and $\frac{1}{2}$ an acre, one row on 2 feet
lands. Thefe variations were made by way
of trial, to difcover the moft profitable
method of planting. The fets in each,
one foot afunder.

This fummer the rows were hand-hoed
three times; and many hard clods being

tumbled

tumbled, by the firſt hoeing, into the furrows, they were cruſhed in pieces by a
ſmall ſpiky roller; an implement uſed by
Mr. *Arbuthnot*. The intervals were horſe-
hoed thrice with a ſhim, which cuts the
land and weeds, but does not bury them.
After each ſhimming, followed another implement; the double mould-board plough
with moveable earth-boards expanding
at pleaſure; this machine ſtrikes the looſe
earth from the furrows, which was raiſed
by the ſhim earthing up the beds. Theſe
operations were the ſame to all, except the
half acre planted on narrow lands, which
could only be hand-hoed. In autumn the
furrows were again ſtruck with the double
mould-board plough.

1768.

This year the beds were hand-hoed
thrice, and the furrows ſhimmed three
times; followed each time, as before, with
the double mould-board plough. On the
laſt hand-hoeing, two acres were ſown with
weld, as the madder plants ſtood thin on
theſe acres. The furrows in autumn ſtruck,

aſ

as before, with the double mould-board plough.

1769.

This year the rows were hand-hoed twice; and the furrows ploughed with the fhim and double mould-board plough thrice; but none of thefe operations to the two acres where the weld was fown. In *July* the weld was pulled; and in *October* the madder taken up with the great plough; laying two lands into one.

The products were as follow

No. I.   On the half acre, fingle rows on 2 feet lands, 6 *C. wt.*

No. 2.   On the fix acres, fingle rows on 4 feet lands, 8 *C wt. per* acre

No. 3.   On the 2 ½ acres, double rows on 4 feet, 10 *C wt. per* acre, and 72 *l*'s * worth of weld on the two acres—but the half acre, where no weld grew, was the beft part.

---

* *N B.* Weld was this year 12 *l* a load.

Account of No. 1.

Proportions *per* acre.

Expences.

1766.	Five ploughings, at 7 *s.* 6 *d* -	£.1	17	6
	One deep ditto, -	0	17	0
1767.	Five quarters of trotters,	3	0	0
	Five facks of wood afhes,	0	12	6
	Ploughing, - -	0	7	6
	Planting, - -	1	5	0
	Three hand-hoeings, -	1	10	0
	Striking furrows, -	0	1	2
1768.	Three hand-hoeings, -	1	10	0
	Striking furrows, -	0	1	2
1769	Two hand-hoeings, -	1	0	0
	Taking up the madder,	5	10	0
	Drying, at 3 *s.* -	1	16	0
	Rent, tythe, and town charges, four years,	4	8	0
		23	15	10

Produce.

12 *C. wt.*, at 4 *l.* 10 *s.*	54	0	0
Expences, -	23	15	10
Clear profit, -	30	4	2

Account of No. 2.

Expences.

		£	s	d
1766.	Five earths, at 7 *s*. 6 *d*.	1	17	6
	One deep ditto, -	0	17	0
1767.	Trotters and afhes, -	3	12	6
	Ploughing, - -	0	7	6
	Planting, - -	1	0	0
	Three hand-hoeings, -	1	10	0
	Rolling furrows with fpi-ky roller, -	0	0	8
	Horfe-hoeing with fhim thrice, at 8 *d*. -	0	2	0
	Ditto double mould-board plough, four times, at 1 *s* 2 *d*. -	0	4	8
1768.	Three hand-hoeings -	1	10	0
	Shimming thrice, -	0	2	0
	Double mould board plough, four times,	0	4	8
1769.	Two hand-hoeings, -	1	0	0
	Shim thrice, -	0	2	0
	Double mould-board plough, - -	0	4	8
	Taking up, -	5	10	0
	Drying, at 3 *s*. -	1	4	0
	Four years rent, &c.	4	8	0
		23	17	2

Produce.

		£		
8 C. wt. at 4l. 10s.	£	36	0	0
Expences, -		23	17	2
Clear profit,		12	2	10

Account of No. 3.

Expences.

1766.	Ploughing as before, -	2	14	6
1767.	Trotters and afhes, -	3	12	6
	Ploughing, - -	0	7	6
	Planting, - -	1	5	0
	Hand-hoeing, and horfe-			
	hoeing as in No. 2.	1	17	4
1768.	Ditto, - -	1	16	8
	Weld, feed and fowing,	0	1	6
1769.	Pulling, &c. the weld,	1	10	0
	Taking up the madder,	5	10	0
	Drying, at 3s. -	1	10	0
	Four years rent, &c.	4	8	0
		24	13	0

Produce.

10 C. wt. Madder, at 4l.			
10s. - -	45	0	0
Weld, - -	36	0	0
	81	0	0
Expences, -	24	13	0
Clear profit, -	56	7	0

5

Suppofing the weld not fown, the account would be,

		£		
Madder,	- -	£.45	0	0
Expences,	-	23	1	6
Clear profit,	-	21	18	6

Comparifon.

Single rows on 2 feet lands,	30	4	2
Double rows on 4 feet lands,	21	18	6
Superiority of the former,	8	5	8

Single rows on 2 feet lands,	30	4	2
Single rows on 4 feet lands,	12	2	10
Superiority of the former,	18	1	4

Double rows on 4 feet lands,	21	18	6
Single rows on ditto, -	12	2	10
Superiority, -	9	15	8

Profit *per* acre *per annum* on the fingle rows on 2 feet, -	7	11	$0\frac{1}{2}$
Ditto on the double rows at 4 feet, - - -	5	9	$7\frac{1}{2}$
Ditto on the fingle rows at 4 feet,	3	0	$8\frac{1}{2}$
Ditto on the madder and weld,	14	1	9

Total of the nine acres.

Expences.

Half an acre of No 1	-	11	17	11
Six acres of No 2.	-	143	3	0
Half an acre of No. 3 without				
weld, - - -	11	10	9
Two acres of ditto with weld,	49	6	0
	215	17	8

Produce.

No. 1. Half an acre,	-	27	0	0
No. 2. Six acres,	-	216	0	0
No. 3. Half an acre,	-	22	10	0
Ditto two acres,	- -	162	0	0
		427	10	0
Expences,	-	215	17	8
Clear profit,	-	211	12	4

Which is, on an average, *per*
  acre, - - -   23 10 3

And *per* acre *per ann.* -   5 17 6

Observations.

The great profit in this experiment is by
the fowing weld on the madder; but in
con-

confidering the culture of the latter plant, this circumftance fhould be thrown out of the account; the madder was however damaged by it, and the weld would have been as good a crop had no madder been on the ground, and probably a better. But a product by weld of 36*l.* an acre, for only 2 years, (fuppofing a fallow) and the culture not expenfive, appears to be an object of capital importance· Probably not many madder crops will pay better.

In the comparifon between the modes of culture, fomething fhould be allowed to No. 3. on account of the damage arifing from the weld.

It is extremely evident, that the nearer the rows, the greater the crop—at leaft to the proximity of 2 feet equally diftant Single rows at 4 feet, are not half fo advantageous, which is very remarkable. Two rows on 4 feet are almoft doubly more beneficial than the fingle ones, but though two rows on a 4 feet land amount in the whole to the fame as equally diftant at 2 feet, yet do they not near equal them in product; from which it fhould feem that the plants fhould be fpread pretty equally

over

over the land. If madder is obferved in
the taking up, it will be found that the
principal produce is the large roots which
fhoot immediately from the crown; take a
cubical foot of land furrounding one plant,
there will be much more crop in that fpace,
than in half as much again, or perhaps
double the fpace next adjoining; which
feems to account for rows equally diftant
2 feet, being better than 2 on 4 feet. How
much of the fuperiority is to be attributed
to the horfe-hoeing on both fides the rows,
cannot be decided from this trial.

The profit clear of 7*l* 11 *s*. 0*d*. ¼ *per* acre
per ann. on the beft crop, is extremely advantageous, and much exceeding the grofs *product* of the beft common hufbandry. The
fame obfervation is almoft as applicable to
the 5*l*. 9*s*. of the double rows. But the
3*l*. *per* acre on the fingle rows may be exceeded by common crops.

The profit of the weld and madder, 14*l*.
an acre, is great; and certainly demands
the attention of all who may have crops in
the fame fituation, more particularly as it
has been the general opinion that fuch land
was not proper for that vegetable.

Experiment, No. 11.

Four acres of an old lay were ploughed up at *Michaelmas* 1765, fourteen inches deep; the foil a deep fandy loam.

In 1766 it was fallowed; receiving four earths, the firft of which was alfo 14 inches deep. In autumn it was landed up

In fpring 1767, manured it with 3 quarters of trotters and 75 bufhels of lime *per* acre; which were turned in by ploughing down on to 4 feet lands. It was then planted with dibbles, 2 rows on each land, at one foot afunder. The whole was deftroyed by the fod or wyer worm; which mifcarriage was owing to its being an old lay.

Expences.

		£	s	d
1765.	Firft ploughing, -	0	17	0
1766.	Ditto. - -	0	17	0
	Three common earths,	1	2	6
	Landing up, -	0	7	6
1767.	Trotters, 3 quarters, -	1	13	0
	75 bufhels lime, at 9*d*.	2	16	3
	Ploughing down, -	0	7	6
	Planting, - -	1	5	0
	Two years rent, -	2	4	0
		11	9	9

The planting and the value of the fetts are the only charges here to be carried to the account of madder; the tillage and manuring being fo much value in the land for other crops. The field was ploughed up and fown with turnips.

This experiment fhould be a lafting warning againft ever planting madder on new land, for moft of it is full of this fod worm, and it is plain that one year will not deftroy them · Land fhould be thrown into one round of crops before the madder is planted; in that time the worm's food will be deftroyed, and no danger confequently remain.

Experiment, No. 12.

Four acres of the fame foil as No. 11. were followed through the year 1766, receiving 5 common ploughings, and one of 12 inches deep, and afterwards landed up in 4 feet ridges. In the fpring of 1767 it was manured with 3 quarters of trotters and 4 facks of wood-afhes *per* acre, and turned in by a common ploughing it was then planted with dibbles; one row on each land, the fets one foot afunder; and

that

that fummer hand-hoed thrice; fhimmed thrice; the furrows ftruck with double mould-board plough four times; and the clods broken by fpiky roller once.

In 1768 it was hand-hoed thrice again; alfo fhimmed thrice; and ftruck four times. In 1769 hand-hoed twice; and fhimmed and ftruck as often, ploughed up, the crop 12 *C. wt. per* acre, at 4*l.*

Expences.

		£		
1766.	Five ploughings, -	£ 1	17	6
	One ditto 12 inches deep,	0	17	0
	Landing up, -	0	7	6
1767.	Manuring with trotters,			
	3 quarters, -	1	16	0
	4 Sacks afhes, -	0	8	0
	Ploughing, - -	0	7	6
	Planting, - -	1	5	0
	Three hand-hoeings,	1	10	0
	Rolling, - -	0	0	8
	Shim thrice, -	0	2	0
	Double mould-board			
	plough four times,	0	4	8
1768.	Three hand-hoeings,	1	10	0
	Carry over, -	10	5	10

		£		
Brought over,		10	5	10
Shim thrice,	-	0	2	0
Double mould-board				
plough four times,		0	4	8
1769. Two hand-hoeings,	-	1	0	0
Shim twice,	-	0	1	4
Double mould-board				
plough ditto,	-	0	2	4
Taking up,	-	5	10	0
Drying,	- -	1	16	0
Four years rent, &c.		4	8	0
		23	10	2

Product.

12 C. wt. at 4 l.	-	48	0	0
Expences,	-	23	10	2
Clear profit,	-	24	9	10
Or *per* acre *per ann*		6	2	$5\frac{1}{2}$
Product of the 4 acres		192	0	0
Ditto expences,		94	0	8
Profit,	-	97	19	4

Observations.

If the remark made in Experiment, No.
11. be justly founded, this field was planted

in a difadvantageous manner, and yet we
find it produce a crop fufficient, at a low
price, to pay more than 6*l* an acre clear
profit, which I need not remark is more
than common hufbandry can yield It appears therefore very plainly from every
view we can take of madder, that it much
exceeds the farmer's culture

Experiment, No 13.

Six acres of deep black loam were trench
ploughed from luccrne in *March* 1767,
with *Ducket's* trenching plough, 14 inches
deep, and on that ploughing planted with
madder in equally diftant rows, 4 feet
afunder It was that fummer hand-hoed
thrice; the intervals ploughed with the fhim
and double mould-board plough thrice;
and in autumn the furrows were ftruck with
that implement, and the rows earthed with
hand-hoes

1768.

In this fpring plants were drawn from it
four times. It was in fummer hand-hoed
four times; horfe-hoed as before, thrice;
and the furrows ftruck in autumn

This ground was deftined for a nurfery,

being

being of loofe texture, admitting the plants
to be eafily drawn, which in ftronger land
is very troublefome and prejudicial to the
crop, as many break off fhort, and the
roots fubject to be much injured by the inftrument which muft neceffarily be ufed in
fuch land for taking up the plants.

1769.

Plants were again taken from it this
fpring as often as the laft. The horfe and
hand-hoeing the fame as before.

1770.

The crop came in courfe to be taken in
autumn 1769, but it had received fo much
damage by having plants drawn from it,
that Mr. *Arbuthnot* determined to let it
ftand for drawing more from it in the fpring
of 1770, rather than damage another crop
as well as this. It was therefore earthed
up twice in the fpring, and had plants
drawn from it as long as the planting feafon lafted. In *Auguft* taken up; crop
2 *C. wt. per* acre.

Expences.

		£		
1767.	Trench ploughing,	0	16	0
	Planting, - -	1	0	0
	Three hand-hoeings,	1	10	0
	Shim thrice, -	0	2	0
	Double mould-board			
	plough thrice, -	0	3	6
	Ditto ftriking furrows,	0	2	6
	Earthing up, -	0	5	0
1768.	Four hand-hoeings, -	2	0	0
	Shim thrice, -	0	2	0
	Double mould-board			
	plough thrice, -	0	3	6
	Ditto ftriking furrows,	0	2	6
1769.	The fame as 1768, -	2	8	0
1770.	Hand-hoeing twice,	1	0	0
	Twice earthing, -	0	10	0
	Taking up, -	4	0	0
	Four years rent, (at 1 *l.*)			
	tythe and town charges,	5	4	0
		19	9	0

Produce.

2 *C. wt.* at 4 *l.* -		8	0	0
Lofs, - -		11	9	0

U 3

Which is *per* acre *per ann.* £.2 17 3

Or the fix acres, - 68 14 0

Obfervations.

It has been already remarked, that drawing plants injures a crop fo greatly, that
whenever Mr. *Arbuthnot* often repeats the
drawing from the fame plantation, he gives
up the expectation of a crop, knowing
that it muft be thereby ruined. The lofs
upon this account therefore, is no objection
to the madder culture; it is the price at
which all the plants drawn from fix acres
are purchafed What principally demands
attention on this experiment, is the great
expence at which plants are procured when
they are drawn from a crop in the fpring.
Therefore, though it would not be proper
to leave the whole crop to be taken up in
the fpring for the fake of obtaining plants,
yet it is advifeable to leave fuch a proportion
of it as will fupply the required quantity
of plants; on an average one may reckon,
if the crop is good, that each ftool will produce in the different drawings from 30 to
40 plants, but it is not advifeable to truft to

too

too many drawings, as that may carry you too far in the spring, and endanger the new plantation from the drought

Experiment, No 14.

In 1767, fallowed 10 acres of a strong loamy soil, ploughed it 4 times, 13 inches deep In autumn manured seven acres of it with farm-yard dung, at the rate of 20 loads an acre, covered the dung by ridging the field into 3 ½ feet lands, manured the other three acres with trotters, 6 quarters *per* acre and left the whole well water-furrowed for winter

1768.

In *April*, planted one row on a land, by drawing a furrow with a *Suffolk* plough on the middle of the ridges, about 6 inches deep; spring plants were laid in the furrows by women and children, and earth drawn on them by men with broad hoes, and the furrows then struck with the double mould-board plough. The rows were hand-weeded twice; and the intervals thrice ploughed with shim and double mould-board plough, and in autumn the

U 4 furrows

furrows ftruck with the fame implement, The field was then water-furrowed.

1769.

This year the plantation was hand-hoed thrice, and the intervals ploughed four times with the fhim and double mould-board. In autumn the furrows ftruck deep.

1770.

Hand-hoed the beds twice; fhimmed the furrows twice, and each time followed it by the double mould-board plough.

Account of the feven acres.

Expences,

		£	s	d
1767.	Ploughing four times,	2	12	0
	Manuring, -	6	0	0
	Ridging up, -	0	7	6
	Water-furrowing, -	0	1	6
1768.	Planting, - -	0	18	0
	Hand-weeding twice,	0	12	0
	Shim thrice, -	0	2	0
	Double mould-board ditto,	0	3	6
	Striking furrows, -	0	2	6
	Water-furrowing, -	0	1	0
1769.	Three hand hoeings,	1	10	0
	Carry over, -	12	10	0

		£	s	d
Brought over,	£.	12	10	0
Shim four times,	-	0	2	8
Double mould-board ditto,		0	4	8
Striking furrows,	-	0	2	6
Water-furrowing,	-	0	1	0
1770. Two hand-hoeings,		1	0	0
Shim twice,	-	0	1	4
Double mould-board plough ditto,	-	0	2	4
Taking up,	-	4	0	0
Drying, at 3s.	-	2	5	0
Four years rent, (16s.) tythe, &c.	-	4	8	0
		24	17	6

Produce.

		£	s	d
15 C. *wt.* at 4*l.*	-	60	0	0
Expences,	-	24	17	6
Clear profit,	-	35	2	6
Which is *per* acre *per* annum,	- -	8	15	7
And on the 7 acres,		61	9	1

Account of the three acres

Expences.

	£	s	d
Every article the fame as the preceding, except manuring and drying, - -	5	12	6
6 Quarters an acre trotters,	3	12	0
Drying, at 3s. - -	1	16	0
	11	0	6

Produce.

	£	s	d
10 C. wt at 4l - -	40	0	0
Expences, - -	11	0	6
Clear profit, - -	28	19	6
Which is *per* acre *per ann*	7	4	11
And on the 3 acres, -	21	14	9
Profit by dunging, -	8	15	7
———— trotters, -	7	4	11
	1	10	8
Weight *per* acre from dung,	15	0	0
————————— from trotters,	10	0	0
	5	0	0

	£		
Product of the ten acres,	540	0	0
Expences ditto, -	206	14	0
Profit ditto, -	333	6	0
Which is *per* acre -	33	6	7
And *per* acre *per ann.*	8	6	7

Observations.

The great importance of applying the proper fort of dung is here apparent. Farm-yard compoft, it is plain, much exceeds trotters Top dreffings of all forts are too fmall in quantity, however rich, to laft with effect three years; they want, efpecially on ftiff land, the power of keeping it open, and aiding in pulverization. The profit of thefe crops are confiderable, and prove how important this culture certainly is.

Experiment, No. 15.

Three acres of the fame foil as No 14. were treated exactly in the fame manner as the feven acres of that trial. Crop the fame,

Expences.

Sundries as before,	-	£ 24	17	6

Produce.

15 C. *wt.* at 4*l.*	-	-	60	0	0
Expences,	-	-	24	17	6
Clear profit,	-		35	2	6
Or *per* acre *per ann.*	-		8	15	7
And on the three,	-	-	26	6	9

Experiment, No. 16.

Seven acres of land planted before with madder, and regiſtered in Experiment, No. 8. were again planted in 1769: It laid all winter in very high arched up ridges, after taking up the preceding crop. In *March* it was dunged with 25 great loads an acre of farm-yard dung, remarkably black, rich, and rotten. It was then ploughed into lands; ſome 3 feet wide, and ſome 4 feet; the latter were planted with two rows on each, 14 inches aſunder, and 10 inches from plant to plant: on the 3 feet lands, ſingle rows at 1 foot from ſet to ſet. The

method

method followed in planting, was drawing furrows with a little plough; laying in the plants by women and children, and covering them with hand-hoes. They were hand-hoed thrice during the fummer: horfe-hoed with the fhim four times, and with the double mould-board plough as often. As foon as the haulm fpread over the beds, the two rows were thrown into one by the double mould-board plough, the wings much extended, in the way that peafe are earthed; and on the narrow lands the earth thrown up to them by the fame plough. Thus the beds were left till autumn; when the furrows were ftruck deep with the double mould-board, and the earth drawn by hoes in upon the haulm.

1770.

In the winter great quantities of chick-weed appeared on the beds; owing, as believed, to the thickness of the dunging. This was all extracted by hand in the fpring. After which it was hand-hoed once more; fhimmed twice, and ploughed with double mould-board as often——in which manner it is left for autumn work.

It comes in courfe to be taken up in autumn

tumn 1771 It promifes to be far fuperior to any yet planted. Expences hitherto in-curred are;

		£	s	d
1769.	Manuring, -	.10	0	0
	Ploughing, with *Rother-*			
	ham ploughs, -	0	5	0
	Planting, - -	0	18	0
	Three hand-hoeings,	1	10	0
	Shim four times, -	0	2	8
	Double mould-board			
	plough ditto, -	0	4	8
	Ditto ftruck the furrows			
	twice, - -	0	5	0
	Earthing, - -	0	5	0
1770.	Firft weeding, -	1	10	0
	Second ditto, -	0	10	0
	Shim twice,. -	0	1	4
	Double mould-board ditto,	0	2	4
		15	14 · 0

Experiment, No 17.

Nine other acres of the fame foil were alfo planted at the fame time · this is the fecond crop of madder . the firft is regiftred in Experiment, No. 9.—The rows, culture, expences, the fame as No. 16.

Experiment, No 18.

Two other acres were also planted at the same time as No. 16 they yielded pease in 1768 only podded, the land very clean; the tillage and planting the same one half of it was manured like them, with 25 loads of rich yard dung, and the other half with 20 loads of sheep dung taken from the sheep pen

It is on this crop very observable, that although the manuring, planting, &c. are the same with the above-mentioned 7 acres, yet is not the appearance of the crop near so good; this Mr. *Arbuthnot* can attribute only to the land not having received that extraordinary good and deep tillage, which the other had done by taking up the preceding crop. a striking proof of the expediency of planting land with successive crops of madder.

Experiment, No 19.

Six acres of a rich, deep, black loam, were sown with rye at *Michaelmas* 1768; but the crop failed In *April* 1769, it was ploughed up; harrowed once; and planted by drawing furrows, double rows at 14 inches,

inches, with intervals of 2 feet 10 inches. The following summer hand-hoed the rows thrice. and horse-hoed the intervals with shim and double mould-board thrice; covering by the last operation 15 sacks an acre of rabbits dung: after which the furrows were struck deep.

1770.

This year two hand-hoeings were given, and one weeding; and the intervals twice ploughed with shim and double mould-board.———

The appearance of this crop very great. The expences as follow.

		£.	s.	d.
1769.	Ploughing, -	0	7	6
	Harrowing, -	0	0	6
	Planting, - -	1	0	0
	Three hand-hoeings,	1	10	0
	Shim thrice, -	0	2	0
	Double mould-board ditto,	0	3	6
	15 Sacks rabbit dung,			
	1s. 4d. - -	1	0	0
	Striking furrows, -	0	2	6
1770.	Two hand-hoeings,	1	0	0
	One weeding, -	0	7	0
	Shim twice, - -	0	1	4
	Double mould-board ditto,	0	2	4
		5	16	8

Experiment, No. 20.

The nine acres regiftered in Experiment, No. 10 were again planted.

The land remained, after taking up, under a winter fallow. In ploughing up the crop a quickfand was cut into, from which the water arofe this induced Mr. *Arbuthnot* to drain it very deep with covered drains . he carried ten through the field, 4 feet deep; the length was 600 rods; and the expence 30*l*

It was dunged in the fpring with 25 loads an acre of rotten yard dung, which were ploughed in, and afterwards the land crofs ploughed . it was then flit down flat; rolled with the fpiky roller; and with the large common one to break the fmall clods left by the other. As the land was drained, it was planted flat; double rows at 14 inches, and 9 inches in the rows, with intervals of 2 feet 4 inches: executed by drawing furrows as before, laying the plants in them, and covering them with hoes. They were twice hand-hoed · fhimmed twice; and the furrows twice ploughed with the double mould-board. The expences as follow.

		£.		
1770.	Draining, -	3	6	8
	Manuring, -	7	10	0
	Ploughing three times with *Rotherham*, -	0	15	0
	Rolling with fpiky roller,	0	2	0
	Ditto with large common ditto, - -	0	1	6
	Planting, - -	1	0	0
	Two hand-hoeings, -	1	0	0
	Shim twice, -	0	1	4
	Double mould-board ditto,	0	2	4
	Filling vacancies, -	0	15	0
		14	13	10

Experiment, No. 21.

Four acres planted with madder in 1767 (See Experiment, No. 11.) and deftroyed by the fod worm, were again planted. The turnips were fed on the ground by fheep in the fpring; but finding it much baked, Mr. *Arbuthnot* ordered it to be broken up with a plough with 2 coulters. It was then worked with fpiky roller, and fown with barley; the ftubble of which, was manured with 25 large loads an acre of purchafed dung; fo rotten, that it appeared

peared like black butter; it was ploughed in 12 inches deep, laying it at the fame time in large round lands. In which manner it remained the winter.

1770.

In the fpring, ploughed it in the gathering way, beginning in the middle, and ending in the old furrows, which deepened them for the purpofe of draining: a point of confequence as the foil is fpringy. It turned up whole furrow; it was therefore worked with a fpiky roller; and after a fhower of rain harrowed, and rolled with common roller; after which it was harrowed again: upon which operation it was planted, by drawing furrows as before. It has been horfe-hoed twice with the fhim, and as often with double mould-board.

Expences.

1769.	Manuring,	-	£.10	10	0
	Ploughing,	-	0	17	0
	Ditto a common earth *,		0	4	6
	Spiky roller,	-	0	2	0
	Carry over,	-	11	13	6

* *N. B.* Three *Rotherham* ploughs did 4 acres in a day.

	£.		
Brought over,	11	13	6
Common harrowing, -	0	0	6
Ditto rolling, -	0	0	3
Planting, - -	1	0	0
Shim twice, -	0	1	4
Double mould-board plough ditto, -	0	2	4
	12	17	11

Experiment, No. 22.

Two acres of land were cropped in 1769, one with potatoes, and the other with turnips; the latter was very much poached by drawing and carting them off. Both the turnips and potatoes were manured for, at the rate of 15 loads of good dung *per* acre. —The potatoe ridges were flit down, and fown with 2 loads of rabbit dung.

The turnip land ploughed up whole furrow; it was left till dry, and then run over with fpiky roller and manured; half the acre with 50 bufhels of lime, and the other half with 5 loads of fifted coal afhes. The whole two acres planted flat. It has been twice hand-hoed; and been horfe-hoed with fhim and double mould-board

plough

plough once. The piece has carried an
indifferent appearance; but the potatoe
half the beft.———The expences of the Potatoe acre.

		£	s	d
1770.	Ploughing, -	0	5	0
	2 Loads rabbit dung,	7	0	0
	Ploughing, -	0	5	0
	Planting, - -	1	0	0
	Two hand-hoeings, -	1	0	0
	Shim once, -	0	0	8
	Double mould-board ditto,	0	1	2
		9	11	10

Of the Turnip acre.

Ploughing, -	0	7	6
Spiky roller, -	0	2	0
50 Bufhels lime, at 9d.	1	17	6
5 Loads coal afhes, -	3	0	0
Ploughing, -	0	5	0
Planting, - -	1	0	0
Hand and horfe-hoeing,	1	1	10
	7	13	10

Experiment, No. 23.

One acre of good mellow loam was ploughed up in autumn 1769, being part of a mad-

X 3   der

der crop. The lands 8 feet broad, and 2 feet higher in the center than in the furrows; in which manner it was left till spring.

1770.

In *May*, two small furrows were turned from the beds, and the land then manured with 2 loads of rabbit dung harrowed in. It was then planted in double rows, at 14 inches, in the old furrows of the 8 feet beds: This was done with an intention to manure the large intervals, and plough them gradually to the rows; but the intervals were so high, and the weather wet, that the carts could not go on, which prevented the intended earthing of the rows; but they were twice hand-hoed; and the whole interval shimmed once. The appearance of the crop very dwindling, owing, as believed, to its being planted too late.

The expences.

1770. Manuring,	-	£.7	0	0
Harrowing,	-	0	0	6
Planting,	-	0	10	0
Hand-hoeing,	-	0	15	0
Shim once,	-	0	1	6
		8	7	0

Upon

Upon this experiment it fhould be obferved, that our very ingenious cultivator
having difcovered a peculiarity in the
growth of madder, formed this trial to afcertain the fact in large · He obferved,
from an experiment made on a plant in
the garden, that by earthing up the rows,
the ftalk was converted to the richeft part
of the root: this uncommon circumftance
gave him the hint of planting in the furrows, inftead of on the tops of the ridges,
with intention of forming the ridge int·
a rich compoft, and turn it gradually to
the rows, until the furrows came to be fituated in the center of the old ridges, and the
rows growing out of new ones—in a word,
to plant and cultivate madder in the common method of managing celery. The
thought is a beautiful one; how far it will
anfwer in practice, experience can alone
determine. the only objection that appears
at firft view is, the doubt whether the rows
will fpread fufficiently to fill fuch large
fpaces: but this concerns only wide intervals; it may be found proper to adopt this
new method in furrows of two or three feet
lands, as well as thofe of 8 feet ones. It

X 4   muft

muft depend greatly on the fertility of the foil ploughed down to the rows, for as the whole depends on a vaft luxuriant ftrength of fhoots, it muft be abfolutely neceffary to force them as much as poffible. If madder was planted, literally fpeaking, in a dung-hill, this method appears to be the moft eligible; and it will probably be found *comparatively* fuccefsful, in exact proportion to the richnefs of the land.

Experiment, No. 24.

Four acres of light fandy loam were cropped with barley in 1769, and the ftubble being ploughed up directly after harveft, cabbages were planted on it; which were fed-on the land, in the fpring, by fheep; it was then ploughed into broad lands with deep furrows for draining it; this ploughing was not more than eight inches deep, the earth for the cabbages being at leaft 12 deep. It was then fpiky rolled and planted.

One acre was folded, and the reft manured with rabbit dung, about 70 facks an acre, harrowed in. The planting was performed as before, by drawing furrows. They have been twice hand-hoed; and

horfe-

horfe-hoed once more with fhim and double mould-board plough.

The appearance of the plants very good, except in the lower part of the field, which is wet.

Expences.

			£		
1770.	Ploughing,	-	£ 0	7	6
	Spiky rolling,	-	0	2	0
	Rabbits dung,	-	4	4	0
	Planting,	- -	1	0	0
	Hand-hoeing twice,	-	1	0	0
	Shim,	- -	0	0	8
	Double mould-board,		0	1	2
			6	15	4

Experiment, No. 25.

Seven acres of a dark rich mould on brick eaith, were manured with 25 loads an acre of purchafed dung, that had laid three years without turning; quite black butter. It was ploughed in 14 inches deep in broad lands with great wheel plough; the furrows left deep. Mr *Arbuthnot* remarked that the worms worked the dung quite through all the furrows, from whence he juftly

concludes

concludes that there is no danger of burying dung; an idea common among the farmers.

On diffecting many of the tubes made by the worms, he found them from top to bottom full of folid dung; from whence it is evident, that they mix the dung more immediately with the foil than could be performed by any tool.

1770.

In the fpring of this year the lands were arched up by a gathering earth, and harrowed and rolled; alfo ox-harrowed. Planted in double rows, 14 inches afunder, on 4 feet lands. They have been hand-weeded twice; and ploughed with fhim and double mould-board plough twice.

The appearance of the crop is remarkably great.

The expences.

1769. Manuring,	-	£.10	10	0
Ploughing,	-	0	14	0
1770. Gathering,	-	0	5	0
Harrowing twice,	-	0	1	0
Rolling,	- -	0	0	6
Harrowing,	-	0	1	0
Carry over,	-	11	11	6

Brought over,	£.11	11	6
Planting, - -	1	0	0
Hand-hoeing, -	1	0	0
Shim, - -	0	1	4
Double mould-board			
plough, - -	0	2	4
	13	15	2

Experiment, No. 26.

Five acres of a deep, black, rich, loamy foil were cropped with turnips in 1769, the crop eaten on the land by sheep; ploughed early in the spring. It was then manured with 8 loads an acre of night foil from *London*, which were ploughed in, and the land harrowed flat; upon this harrowing the fets were planted as in the preceding trials. The crop has been once hand-hoed; once weeded; and horfe-hoed twice with double mould-board plough, which earths up the plants, and once with the fhim. The appearance of the crop very great.

Expences.

1770. First ploughing, -	£.0	5	0
8 Loads, at 11 s. -	4	8	0
Carry over, -	4	13	0

	£.		
Brought over,	4	13	0
Second earth, -	0	5	0
Harrowing, -	0	1	0
Planting, - -	1	0	0
Hand-hoeing, -	0	10	0
Weeding, - -	0	6	0
Shim, - -	0	0	8
Double mould-board,	0	2	4
	6	18	0

Experiment, No. 27.

In 1766, Mr. *Arbuthnot* set one plant of madder in his garden. A hole was dug of 3 feet diameter, and filled with the rotten mould of a melon bed; as it grew it was regularly earthed up with the same mould, the vines of the plant being spread, and the earth laid on them, leaving out the points; continued this earthing during that year, and in autumn covered the whole with the melon mould. The two following years the same management was observed in every respect. In autumn 1768, dug it up; the plants and roots were washed clean and drained from water; the weight green, 42 *lb.*; dryed ready for grinding, it
weighed

weighed 7 ¼ *lb.*; the dry weight, there-fore, is rather better than a fixth of that green.

He has alfo another plant, now growing, which was fet the fame day, and treated in the fame manner on a black foil near the furface of water, to determine how far it will prejudice the root.

Obfervations.

A fingle plant of madder coming in three years to 7 ¼ *lb.* is a moft extraordinary growth. But it is obfervable that this plant did not diminifh above 6-7ths, whereas the general run of plants diminifh 7-8ths. This muft be attributed to the folidity of the plant from its extraordinary fize. This evidently fhews that ground cannot be made too rich. And though the treatment was not fuch as could be imitated in a field, yet it fhould be confidered as a leffon to madder planters, never to fear exceffive richnefs of foil or manure it is evident that no manuring is too much for this vegetable; and in all probability this fact will be found fo extenfively true, that it may anfwer to contract the attention and

expence

expence of ten acres to a single one. Suppose an acre planted in the same manner as in the above experiment, there would be 4840 plants, which at 7 ¼ *lb.* amount to 15 tons 13 *C. wt.* and at 4*l.* 10*s. per C. wt.* to 1408*l.* If you cover an acre a yard deep with dung or rotten compost, it will take 4840 loads, of 30 bushels each, which may be called 3500 farmers loads, and at 8*s.* come to 1400*l.* It is clear the experiment on an acre of land would be a losing one; but it is at the same time astonishing to think how near the first crop would come towards paying such an immense expence. But suppose the land, in the taking up such a crop, to be dug 4 feet deep from the surface, 1 foot of the old mould would then be mixed with the new addition of 3 feet, and on this a new plantation of madder for three years more; the probability of a vast profit would then be great—and the land would for ever bear the richest crops.

GENERAL OBSERVATIONS.

The culture of this valuable plant has been so great a novelty in *England*, that not one farmer in five hundred knows that such

a vegea vegetable exifts; even the endeavours, fpirited as they have been, of a very patrio- tic fociety, have not done much in extending the culture through this kingdom: a pre- mium of *5 l. per* acre on all planted, was a meafure that feemed to infure fuccefs, and to promife us the lafting benefit of raifing as much of this dye as our manufactures require. But this appearance has been fomewhat deceitful: very many claimants for the premium have difcontinued the culture from its proving difadvantageous; and the general idea has been, that we cannot rival the *Dutch* in this branch of agriculture. The failures that have hap- pened, probably have arifen from a want of knowledge in the nature of the plant, and the proper method of treating it—and doubtlefs much mifchief was done by an elaborate publication under a celebrated name, which interdicted the ufe of dung. But to whatever caufe it has been owing, certain it is that this branch of cultivation has made no progrefs the Society's pre- miums raifed a temporary purfuit, which has of late fubfided, and left this important article in a fair way to as total a neglect as

ever

ever it was in through the firſt half of the
preſent century.

In this ſituation there was little hope of
reviving the attention of the public to madder, unleſs ſome very ſpirited experiments
were made, which ſhould prove how far
the culture is beneficial—what ſoil is proper
for it—and what treatment requiſite in
planting, cleaning, &c   Reports concerning it were ſo vague, that no dependance
could be placed in them ; nothing could be
liſtened to but real proof—and not only
real, but *diſintereſted* proof ; for perſons
intereſted in the *trade* of madder, had pro-
miſed ſuch mountains of profit, that every
aſſertion began to be ſuſpected ; until many
people treated the idea of it as a profitable
article of *Engliſh* culture, as a chimera.

In this critical juncture Mr. *Arbuthnot*
gave his attention to cultivating madder,
and from the moment he began, has proſe-
cuted it with a ſpirit that does honour, not
to himſelf alone, but I will venture to add,
even To HIS COUNTRY.   The unremitted
attention which he has given to every minutiæ of the culture, and the ſteady perſe-
verance with which he has attacked every
difficulty

difficulty as it arofe; have been nobly calculated for commanding fuccefs.

He has fhewn the world that madder
may be profitably cultivated on foils not of
extraordinary natural fertility—that thorough
good hufbandry, with rich manuring, will
prove fufficient; confequently, that our
madder culture need not be confined to
fpots unufually rich, but extended over moft
parts of the kingdom, except on very poor,
ftoney, or clayey foils.

The patriotic ideas of a private indivi-
dual fo fpiritedly exerted, deferves the
utmoft commendation, but the teftimony
of many hundred perfons to whom this
gentleman has fhewn and explained (with
the utmoft freedom and candour) all his
experiments, renders any eulogy unneceffary.

It fhould be obferved, that the preceding
experiments, which are complete, include
only the beginning of his culture; many
variations are made, not from experience
having proved them right, (for there has
not been time for the completion of fuch)
but to difcover from the event the moft advantageous. They include feveral trials
which fuffered from a want of that know-

ledge which he now poffeffes; and I fhould further add, that none of them nearly equalled, in appearance, moft of his crops at prefent on the ground.

By throwing the particulars into one view, a clearer idea will be formed of them.

Experiment, No. 7. The firft

crop, lofs on one acre,	£.31	9	0
No. 13. Ditto on 6 acres,	68	14	0
	100	3	0

This fum being the amount of lofs in the preceding trials, is the price of the plants when not purchafed; when they were bought, the amount is charged in the refpective account. 98 Acres have been planted; it may therefore be called 20s. an acre, as there is no probability of the crops on the ground turning out unprofitable. The fum of 20s. an acre is therefore to be deducted from each crop.

Experiment, No.

8. Profit on						
7 acres,	£.165	0	6			
Deduct for plants,	7	0	0			
				158	0	6
No. 9. Profit on						
9 acres, -	245	1	0			
Deduct, -	9	0	0			
				236	1	0
Profit on 17 acres in 3 years,				394	1	6

No. 10. Half an

acre,	-	£. 15	2	1			
Six acres,	-	72	17	0			
Two and half ditto,		54	16	3			
		142	15	4			
Deduct,		9	0	0			
					133	15	4

No. 12. Profit on

4 acres,	-	97	19	4			
Deduct,	-	4	0	0			
					93	19	4

No. 14. Profit on

7 acres,	-	245	17	6			
Deduct,	-	7	0	0			
					238	17	6

No. 14. Profit on

3 acres,	-	86	18	6			
Deduct,	-	3	0	0			
					83	18	6

No. 15. Profit on

3 acres,	-	105	7	6			
Deduct,	-	3	0	0			
					102	7	6
Profit on 26 acres in 4 years,		652	18	2			
Which is *per* acre,	-	-	25	2	2		
And *per annum*,		-	6	5	6		

394 *l.* 1 *s.* 6 *d.* on 17 acres, in
3 years, are *per* acre,   £.23 3 0

And *per annum,* -   -   7 14 4
Ditto on the 4 years,   -   6   5 6

Superiority,   -   1 8 10

I need not here be particular in obferving, that the profit made by an application of the land during three years, being
fuperior to that of four, is a circumftance
decifive in favour of the fhorter time, as
the land, it is to be fuppofed, might have
been applied in the extra year to other
advantage : the profit of three years equal-
ling four, fhews that the ground, in the
latter, was in a ftate that required the previous fallow, and which it muft have had
for any other crop.

It fhould here be obferved, that Mr.
Arbuthnot is clearly of opinion, that no
crop requires *cleaner* ground, from the
great difficulty of extracting root-weeds
from among the fibres of the plants, which
confequently would, in three years, get
entire poffeffion of the ground.

The average profit *per* acre *per ann.* on
all

all the crops taken up, amounting to above
7*l* 7*s.* is, upon the whole, a degree of
advantage, that fpeaks greatly in favour
of the culture. It is in itfelf very confiderable, and much exceeds any thing
that common hufbandry can execute; but
there are attendant circumftances, which
fhould, on no account, be overlooked :
this average is drawn from the firft 'crops
raifed. Mr. *Arbuthnot* had no guides to
follow, but fuch as led him much aftray.
he found no directions in books, but fuch
as loft him confiderable fums of money.
Under thefe difadvantages, with that univerfally acting one, the want of experience, it is aftonifhing, that the crops here
minuted fhould turn out profitable on the
whole, and is, I think, a much greater
proof of the advantages of the culture,
than much fuperior fuccefs hereafter may
turn out. If the difficulties attending new
undertakings be confidered, this will not
be thought an extravagant idea. Notwithftanding thefe unfavourable circumftances, yet, had the foil been naturally
rich, fuch as old hop-grounds for inftance,
the profit would certainly have been con-
fiderably greater, probably double.

A clear

A clear profit of 7*l.* 7*s.* *per* acre *per annum,* on a plant, whose culture ameliorates and cleans the foil in a great degree, deferves no flight attention. It will be difficult to find a well-managed farm that pays 40*s.* an acre clear profit; but thefe beginnings in the madder culture return more than thrice as much. It muft be the very perfection of common hufbandry to pay two or three pounds *per* acre; but madder does it even under very unfavourable circumftances, unavoidable at firft fetting out: the one cleans the land, the other fills it with weeds. All thefe crops receive 20*s. per* acre *per ann.* in hand-hoeing alone, befides numerous horfe-hoeings! And the extraordinary tillage the ground receives, by taking up the roots, is fuch as no other hufbandry will admit of, except the fimilar culture of licquorice. It is known about *Pomfret,* that, by this tillage, they are able to repeat the fame crop *ad infinitum:* a practice, which, Mr. *Arbuthnot* is very clear, may be purfued in madder; which, indeed, is confirmed by experiment, No. 8 and 16. Nor is it to be believed, that this plant, notwithftanding the great luxuriance

of

of the growth, can impoverifh the land,
as it is well known, that all green fmothering crops, to which this is fimilar, are
great improvers, provided they are not
fuffered to perfect their feed, which madder
rarely does in this country. The crops
now on the ground look, beyond all comparifon, better than thofe which have been
taken up; from which it is extremely evident, that the products will be vaftly larger,
although the expences are encreafed but little.
Upon the whole, the advantages of madder are fo great, that no perfon need to
fear a vaft profit, if he poffeffes the proper
foil, and will follow the improved practice
of this gentleman.

Thefe experiments are not only very
confiderable in their extent, but the conclufions to be drawn from them are uncommonly important; for we not only
find what practice is beft, but we alfo
difcover *why* it is beft, from the experience
of contrary meafures.

The importance of very rich manuring,
and the great mifchief done to the crops by
drawing plants from them, are points that
have hitherto been totally unknown, but
are here proved in the cleareft manner.

It fhould be obferved, that Mr *Arbuth-not* has conftantly found the roots of madder to bear exact proportion to the luxuriance of the branches and leaves : a circum-ftance, which is not allowed to be the cafe by fome, who have written on the fubject·

From a converfation he has had with Mr. *Crowe* of *Feverfham*, he is deter-mined once more to try winter plants, as the uncertainty of the feafon, when fpring plants can only be put into the ground, renders that practice very ha-zardous.

IV. EXPERIMENTS IN THE DRILL CULTURE OF SEVE-RAL CROPS.

There is not a part of agriculture, which has been more the fubject of diverfity of opinion, than the comparative merit of the old and new hufbandry. Every experi-menter has tried the practice of drilling; almoft every one has given a different idea of it; yet, in fuch variety, we have not hitherto met with any regular feries of trials, that have indifputably decided the degree of advantage to be attributed to it. The very ingenious and accurate cultivator, whofe

I

whofe experiments I have now the fatif-
faction of laying before the public, has
not overlooked this part of hufbandry; but
has formed a variety of trials, upon a very
different plan from any yet known.

Wheat, cultivated in this manner, is
the object in general moft attended to. it
will be neceffary here to unite it with
beans, as fome of the chief of Mr. *Arbuthnot*'s experiments in drilling wheat,
are in fucceffion with drilled beans.

Experiment, No. 28.

*Culture, expences, and produce, of eight
acres of drilled beans,*

1767.

Culture.

The foil of this field is a ftrong, dark-
coloured loam, tending to clay, on a clay
bottom. In 1766, it yielded wheat, the,
ftubble of which was very foul with numerous weeds. It was ploughed once in
the fpring, and on that earth dibled with
beans, part tick, and part horfe-beans · of
the firft 2 ½ bufhels *per* acre, of the latter
2 bufhels. the rows equally diftant, 16
inches afunder: they were hand-hoed
twice; the crops 3 ½ quarters *per* acre.

Expences

Expences per acre.

One ploughing,	-	-	£. 0 10 0
Seed,	-	-	0 8 0
Dibling,	-	-	0 6 0
Two hand-hoeings,	-		0 12 0
Reaping,	-	-	0 7 0
Harvesting,	-	-	0 5 0
Thrashing, 3 ½ quarters,	-		0 4 6
Carrying ditto out,	-		0 5 0
Rent, &c. &c.	-		1 2 0
Total,	-		3 19 6

Produce.

Three quarters and a half,* at 26 s.	4 11 0
Straw,	-	1 10 0
	6 1 0
Expences,	3 19 6
Clear Profit,	2 1 6
And on the 8 acres,	-	16 12 0

Near two guineas an acre profit on a crop, that is to be confidered as a preparative for corn, and a fubftitute for a fallow, is very confiderable. It is a ftrong proof, that

* N B. The meafure is nine gallons for this and all the enfuing experiments.

that drilled beans, even on a fingle ploughing, may be depended on for cleaning a
foul piece of land, and, at the fame time,
yielding a very beneficial produce.

Experiment, No. 29.

*Culture, expences, and produce, of eight
acres of drilled wheat.*

1768.

Culture.

The bean ftubble of the preceding experiment was ploughed directly after harveft,
throwing down the lands. The field was
then crofs ploughed with little *Suffolk*
fwing ploughs. Five of them did the
8 acres in a day; after which it was
ridged up again : the ridges two bout
lands, 3 ½ feet over. They were harrowed once and drilled ; two rows of wheat
on each, at ten inches afunder : the quantity of feed three pecks *per* acre After
the drilling, the furrows were ftruck with
the double mould-board plough, and the
land left well water-furrowed. In the
fpring, ten facks an acre of malt-duft were
fown on the corn ; the ten-inch partition
was once horfe-hoed with the fhim, and
the intervals five times with the fame inftrument, being followed each time by the
double

double mould-board plough. The laft
horfe-hoeing was after the bloffoming of
the corn, the horfes being muzzled. the
rows were once hand hoed with five-inch
hoes. The product 4 quarters *per* acre.

Expences.

		£	s	d
1768. First ploughing,	-	0	8	6
Second ditto,	-	0	4	6
Third ditto,	- -	0	4	6
Harrowing,	- -	0	0	6
Three pecks of feed,		0	5	0
Drilling,	- -	0	1	6
Striking furrows,	-	0	1	2
Water-furrowing,	-	0	1	0
Two facks of malt-duft, at 1s. 4d.	-	1	6	8
Shim fix times,	-	0	4	0
Double mould-board, 5 dit.		0	5	10
Once hand-hoeing,		0	4	0
Reaping,	- -	0	8	0

This is a great price ; but
the men would not do
it for lefs, on account of
its being fprawled about.

		£	s	d
Harvefting,	- -	0	3	0
Thrafhing and binding the ftraw,	-	0	13	6
Carrying out,	-	0	2	0
Rent, &c. &c.	-	1	2	0
Total,	- -	5	15	8

Produce.

4 Quarters, at 52*s.* 6*d.* £.10	10	0
1 ¼ Load ftraw, -	1	10	0
	12	0	0
Expences, -	5	15	8
Clear profit, - -	6	4	4
And on the 8 acres,	49	14	8

Obfervations

This crop reflects no flight honour on the drill culture of wheat; and much exceeds what is conceived of it in nine tenths of the kingdom. The profit of more than 6*l. per* acre is not the only object; the hoeings, amounting to thirteen operations, could not fail being of great fervice to the land, both in ameliorating and cleaning it. The efficacy of fuch means of cleaning can never be doubted: for here was a wheat ftubble taken out of the hands of a wretched farmer, as foul as poffible; by one hoeing crop of beans it is prepared for wheat; that wheat kept as clean as a garden, and yet pays 6*l.* an acre profit: In product, many broad-caft crops exceed it, but then the land is left in a very different ftate.

It

It will not be improper to remark, that this mode of drilling leaves an interval of 2 feet 8 inches wide, which is much narrower than the space recommended by *Tull*, and so regularly persisted in by M. *de Chateauvieux*. It is evident that such a space is sufficient for every purpose of keeping the land clean. The horse-hoeing in the 10 inch partition was with a small share in the shim on purpose for such a breadth.

Experiment, No. 30.

Culture, expences, and produce of eight acres of drilled beans.

1769.

Culture.

The wheat stubble of the last experiment was ploughed up the beginning of *December*; the ridges on which the wheat grew being reversed: they were then drilled with beans, double rows on each, at 14 inches; consequently the intervals were 2 feet 4 inches. The seed, 2 bushels an acre. Five acres were the mazagan sort, and three the tick. The culture bestowed on them while growing, consisted of two hand-hoeings, and six horse-hoeings; three with the shim, and as many with the double

mould

mould-board plough. The product was 3 quarters *per* acre.

Account of the mazagan.

Expences.

		£	s	d
1769.	Ploughing, -	0	4	6
	Harrowing, -	0	0	6
	Drilling, - -	0	1	6
	Seed, - -	0	10	0
	Striking furrows, -	0	1	2
	Water-furrowing, -	0	1	0
	Two hand-hoeings, -	0	10	0
	Shim thrice, -	0	2	0
	Double mould-board ditto,	0	3	6
	Reaping, - -	0	8	0
	Harvesting, - -	0	3	0
	Thrashing 3 quarters, 1 s. 2 d. - -	0	3	6
	Rent, &c. - -	1	2	0
		3	10	8

Produce.

	£	s	d
3 Quarters beans, at 40 s.	6	0	0
Straw, - -	0	10	0
	6	10	0
Expences,	3	10	8
Profit,	2	19	4
On the 5 acres,	14	16	8

Account of the ticks.

Expences.

As above, except feed,	-	3	0	8
Seed, 2 bufhels, at 3*s.* 6*d.*		0	7	0
		3	7	8

Produce.

3 Quarters, at 28*s.*	-	4	4	0
Straw,	-	1	0	0
		5	4	0
Expences,	-	3	7	8
Profit,	-	1	16	4
On the three acres,	-	5	9	0
Ditto the five,	-	14	16	8
Total,	-	20	5	8
Average,	-	2	10	8

Obfervations.

The difference in the profit between the two forts is great, and fhews how much, in many cafes, depends on chufing the fort of feed with judgment. Mr. *Arbuthnot* has remarked, that the great advantage of the mazagan bean, is its being harvefted a month before the tick, and fix weeks be-

fore

fore the common horfe-bean, which in many inftances is a moft valuable circum-ftance · and if a perfon chufes to fow tur-nips among his beans, to be covered by the laft hoeing, this fort, by coming off fo early, muft fuit much the beft The meal is far whiter, and the bean fuller of it than any other fort.

Experiment, No. 31.
Culture, expences, and produce of eight acres of drilled wheat.

1770.

Culture.

The fame field. The bean ridges ploughed down directly after harveft, and then crofs ploughed; upon which earth it was ox-harrowed; that is, with the great harrows drawn by horfes. Next it was ridged up again into 3 ½ feet lands, and harrowed with one horfe,* In *October* it was drilled with wheat; 4 rows on each land, 8 inches afunder, with 1 bufhel *per acre.* After which the furrows were ftruck as ufual with a double mould-board plough, and the field water-furrowed.

The 14th of *November*, one land was manured with rabbit dung, at the rate of

* This is done with one horfe walking in the fur-row, drawing two fmall harrows, each covering a land.

18 facks *per* acre, at 1 *s* 2 *d.* a fack. Another land with poultry dung, at the rate
of 72 bufhels *per* acre, at 6 *d.* And a third
with wood afhes, the fame quantity, at 4 *d.*
The poultry dung turned out much the beft;
the rabbit next; and the afhes laft. In
March all the reft of the field was manured
with 20 facks an acre of rabbit dung. It
was hand-weeded once between the rows;
and fhimmed twice in the intervals of 1 foot
6 inches, and once with the double mould-
board. The product 3 quarters *per* acre.

Expences.

Firft ploughing, - -	£.0	12	0
N. B. The land very dry.			
Second ditto, - -	0	10	0
Harrowing twice, 6 horfes,	0	3	0
Ridging up, - - -	0	4	6
Harrowing, - - -	0	0	3
Drilling, - - -	0	1	6
Seed, - - - -	0	6	0
Striking furrows, - -	0	1	2
Water-furrowing, - -	0	1	0
20 Sacks rabbit dung, at 1 *s.* 2 *d.*	1	3	4
Hand-hoeing, - -	0	4	0
Shim, - -	0	1	4
Double mould-board, -	0	1	2
Reaping, - -	0	8	6
Carry over, - -	3	17	9

		£.		
Brought over,	-	3	17	9
Harvesting,	- -	0	5	0
Thrashing,	- -	0	9	0
Carrying out,	- -	0	1	6
Rent, &c.	- -	1	2	0
		5	15	3

Produce.

3 Quarters, at 50 s.	- -	7	10	0
1¼ Load straw, at 25 s.	- -	1	17	6
		9	7	6
Expences,	- -	5	15	3
Profit,	- -	3	12	3
On the 8 acres,	-	28	18	0

Observations.

Here ends a course of 4 years drilling
on the same land; it includes, therefore,
all the circumstances that could affect
common methods—whether favourable or
unfavourable. The land was received in
foul order—no other fallow was given to
clean it than drilled crops; that material
end was answered, and the products at the
same time profitable. But the merit of the
culture will best appear from throwing the
whole into one view.

	Expences £ s d	Product £ s d	Profit £ s d
1767. Beans.	3 19 6	6 1 0	2 1 6
1768. Wheat.	5 15 8	12 0 0	6 4 4
1769. Beans.	3 9 6	6 0 3	2 10 8
1770. Wheat.	5 15 3	9 7 6	3 12 3
Totals *per* acre,	18 19 11	33 8 9	14 8 9
Ditto of the 8 acres,	151 19 4	267 10 0	115 10 0
Average *per* acre *per ann.*	4 14 11	8 7 2	3 12 2
Per 100 acres *per ann.*	474 11 8	835 16 8	360 16 8

This table shews the exact degree of the advantage of the drill culture. The point to be most attended to, is the profit of 3 *l.* 12 *s.* 2 *d. per* acre *per ann.*, upon which it may be observed, that there is not the least reason to suppose the common method would have equalled it. One summer fallow at a dead expence would have been included; and in all probability without producing better successive crops. The farmers course here is, 1. Fallow; 2. Wheat; 3. Oats; 4. Clover; 5. Wheat; 6. Oats. Now it muſt be at once apparent to the moſt common apprehenſion, that this courſe cannot poſſibly equal the profit of 3 *l.* 12 *s.* 2 *d. per* acre.

But without recurring to an ideal compariſon, is it not a noble anecdote in the hiſtory of drilling, that an annual *clear* profit of 360 *l.* 16 *s.* 8 *d.* may be made from 100 acres of ploughed land? — by no means of ſuperior goodneſs If ſuch a fact, deduced from the experience of four years, and not on a ſmall patch of land, but over a large field, does not abſolutely prove the benefit of this mode of drilling, nothing can, noi is there a fact in all huſbandry.

, Reſpecting the probability of a farmer's ſucceſs in it; it is to be obſerved, that what a gentleman profitably executes *in large,* may undoubtedly be advantageouſly practiſed by a farmer; but if he curtails the expences, (which are high) or deviates from the directed path, it certainly is no fault of the huſbandry, but of the huſbandman. The drill plough with which theſe crops were drilled, admits of many variations, and yet is ſcarcely ever out of order; as any one may judge from the circumſtance of its

Z 3

having

having drilled fome hundreds of acres without the leaft repair.

This fucceffion of drilled beans and
wheat, fhews plainly that thofe vegetables
may follow one another for any number of
years without any fallow—and this on land,
as I before obferved, not of the beft quality.

Experiment, No. 32.
Culture, expences, and produce of feven acres
of drilled beans.

1768.
Culture.

The foil of this field is the fame as that
of the four preceding trials. In 1766, it
yielded oats; the ftubble of which, very foul
with twitch, was ploughed up early in the
fpring of 1767. It was fown with hemp,
with a defign to clean it, by the advice of
Dr. *Solander*, but it did not fucceed; either
from the poverty of the foil, from dry weather, or fome other circumftances. It came
to nothing; was therefore ploughed up in
June, and afterwards crofs ploughed.
Next it was dragged with the great ox-
drag, drawn by 6 horfes, going thrice in a
place. After this it was ploughed flat,
and cut up whole furrow, though the furface of the ground was like duft: this was

I   owing

owing to the exceffive weight of the draught.
It then remained in this condition till dry
enough to be made fine by harrowing and
rolling; ridged up, into 3 ½ feet lands, the
beginning of *September* After this, fo
much rain came that it was impoffible to
drill wheat as intended; it was therefore
water-furrowed and left till the winter.

It is here to be obferved, that this difap-
pointment was very much owing to the
dragging · the draft and the preffure of the
tines abfolutely ruined the feafon; which
is no uncommon effect with this prepofterous machine, fo much exceeded in utility
on ftrong land by the fpiky roller. The
ploughing up whole furrow after this
operation fufficiently proves it.

In *February*, 1768, the ridges were harrowed and drilled with horfe-beans, double
rows, at 14 inches on each, 1 bufhel feed
per acre. After which the water-furrows were ploughed and dug. In *April*
the rows hand-hoed; and the beginning
of *May* the 14 inch partition was horfe-
hoed with a 9 inch fhim, and the intervals
with a 17 inch one: one horfe did 5 acres
a day. The furrows were then ftruck with
a double mould-board plough. The begin-

ring

ning of *June* hand-hoed again; after which it was again horse-hoed by shim and double mould-board. When ripe they were pulled by women. The product 3 ½ quarters *per* acre.

Expences.

		£	s	d
1767.	First ploughing, -	0	10	0
	Second ditto, -	0	7	6
	Third ditto, -	0	7	6
	Dragging, - -	0	4	6
	Fourth ploughing, -	0	7	6
	Harrowing, -	0	1	0
	Fifth ploughing, -	0	4	6
	Water-furrowing, -	0	1	6
1768	Harrowing, - -	0	0	6
	Drilling, - -	0	1	6
	Seed, - - -	0	3	6
	Water-furrows,	0	1	6
	Two hand-hoeings, -	0	7	0
	Shim twice, -	0	1	4
	Double mould-board ditto,	0	2	4
	Pulling, - -	0	6	0
	Binding, - -	0	1	0
	Harvesting, - -	0	4	0
	Thrashing, 3 ½ quarters, at 1 s. 4 d.	0	4	8
	Two years rent, &c.	2	4	0
		6	1	4

Expences, - - £.6 1 4

Product.

3 ½ Quarters, at 28s £.4 18 0
1 Load ftraw, - 1 0 0
—————— 5 18 0

Lofs, - - - 0 3 4

Obfervations.

Mr *Arbuthnct*'s plan of culture for thefe fields, was to clean and bring them into heart by drilling the lofs of the firft year, with accumulated expences, was wholly owing to his adopting a hint of an ingenious foreigner. the fcheme of hemp on land run out of heart and full of weeds was a bad one hemp fo far deftroys weeds as to require no hand-hoeing or weeding; but then it muft be fown on land in heart, fufficient to pufh it on to a vigorous luxuriant growth. Inftead of hempen fallow, beans were to have been drilled, which would, as in the preceding field, have cleaned the land, and paid above 40s. an acre profit; and then wheat with much greater advantage This lofs is therefore no effect of drilling.

There is another obfervation to be made here that may have its ufe; which is the

crop

crop not being the better for fucceeding a fummer fallow. Poffibly it may be a bufhel or two fuperior, but nothing comparable to the expence · this fhould be a leffon to all farmers to make their drilled beans the fallow; and never beftow a preparatory one.

Experiment, No. 33.

Culture, expences, and produce of feven acres of drilled wheat.

1769.
Culture.

The bean ftubble of Experiment, No. 32. was ploughed up directly after harveft; the ridges being reverfed, and harrowed once. It was then begun to be drilled; 8 lands were done with double rows, at 14 inc. 3 pecks feed; but fuch a deluge of rain then came, that the reft of the field was afterwards forced to be fown broad-caft, and the feed covered by arching up the lands with a double plough, an invention of Mr. *Arbuthnst*'s, going once in a place; a man, a boy, and two horfes, did 5 acres a day: the quantity of feed ufed, 1½ bufhel *per* acre. 15 Sacks an acre of rabbit dung were

were fown over the whole field, except the 8 ridges. The double mould-board plough followed the double plough in the furrows and ftruck them.

In *March* the 8 ridges were manured, at the rate of 15 facks an acre of rabbit dung. In *April* they were hand-hoed, and the intervals horfe-hoed with fhim and double mould-board plough. In *May* all thefe operations were repeated; and the two laft once more in *June*. The broad-caft was hand-weeded once. Product *per* acre, of the broad-caft, 18 bufhels; of the drilled, 17¾ bufhels. A load and half of ftraw to the firft, and a load to the fecond.

Account of the broad-caft per acre.

Expences.

	£.		
Firft ploughing, - -	0	7	6
Harrowing, - - -	0	1	0
Seed, - - - -	0	9	0
Sowing, - - -	0	0	3
Second ploughing with double plough, - -	0	1	3
15 Sacks rabbit dung, -	0	19	0
Striking furrows with 3 horfes,	0	2	0
Water-furrowing, -	0	1	6
Carry over, ꝛ	2	1	6

Brought over,	£.2	1	6
Hand-weeding,	0	6	0
Reaping,	0	9	0
Harvesting,	0	4	0
Thrashing 18 bush. at 4 d. ½,	0	6	9
Carrying out,	0	1	6
Rent, &c. &c.	1	2	0
	4	10	9

Produce.

2 Quarters 2 bushels, at 40 s.	4	10	0
1 ½ Load straw, at 25 s	1	17	6
	6	7	6
Expences,	4	10	9
Profit,	1	16	9

Account of the drilled per acre.

Expences.

Ploughing,	0	7	6
Harrowing,	0	1	0
Drilling,	0	1	6
Seed,	0	4	6
Striking furrows,	0	2	0
Water-furrowing,	0	1	6
15 Sacks rabbit dung,	0	19	0
Two hand-hoeings,	0	7	0
Carry over,	2	4	0

		£	s	d
Brought over,	-	2	4	0
Shim thrice, - - -		0	2	0
Double mould-board plough ditto,		0	3	6
Reaping, - - -		0	7	6
Harvesting, - - -		0	3	9
Thrashing, 17 ½, at 4 d. ½, -		0	6	7
Carrying out, - -		0	1	6
Rent, &c. - - -		1	2	0
		4	10	10

Produce.

		£	s	d
2 Quarters 1 bushel 2 pecks, at 40 s. - - -		4	7	6
1 Load straw, - -		1	5	0
		5	12	6
Expences, - -		4	10	10
Profit, - -		1	1	8
Profit by the broad-cast,		1	16	9
Ditto by the drilled, -		1	1	8
Superiority of the former,		0	15	1

Observations.

The balance of this account is not a clear superiority to that amount, because the land in one case must certainly be left in better order than in the other—probably to

5   the

the amount of this balance. As to products, the drill has the advantage, for the
saving in seed exceeds the superiority of
product by one peck: this may however
be called an equality.

Experiment, No. 34.

Culture, expences, and produce of seven acres
of drilled beans.

1770.

Culture.

In *October* the wheat stubble was thrown
down and water-furrowed. In *November*
5 acres were drilled with mazagan beans,
3 bushels *per* acre, in double rows, at 14
inches; and again water-furrowed. In
February the remaining two acres were
dibbled in the same manner with the same
bean. They were hand-hoed once in *April*;
and horse-hoed with shim and double
mould-board. The crop found on a trial
of thrashing to be 3 ½ quarters *per* acre on
an average of the whole: but the *February*
season not equal to *November* by 4 bushels.

Expences.

Ploughing,	-	-	£.0	7 6
Water-furrowing,			0	1 0
Carry over,			0	8 6

Brought over,	-	£.0	8	6
Drilling,	-	-	0	1	6
Seed,	-	-	-	0	12	0
Water-furrowing,	-	0	1	0
Hand-hoeing,	-	-	0	5	0
Shim,	-	-	-	-	0	0	8
Double mould-board	-	0	1	2
Pulling and binding,	-	0	10	6
Harvesting,	-	-	0	4	0
Thrashing, at 1 s. 4 d.	-	0	4	8
Rent,	-	-	-	1	2	0
			3	10	6

Produce.

3 ½ Quarters, at 40 s.	-	7	0	0
1 Load of straw,	-	1	0	0
		8	0	0
Expences,	-	-	3	10	6
Profit,	-	-	4	9	6
On the 7 acres,	-	31	6	6

Observations.

The register of this seven acred field during four years, has not, on the whole, turned out near so advantageous as the preceding field of 8 acres. This will appear from throwing the whole into one view, as I before practised with the field above-mentioned.

	Expenses	Product	Loss / Profit
1767 and 8. Beans.	Expences, £.6 1 4	Product, £ 5 18 0	Lofs, £ 0 3 4
1769. Wheat.	4 10 10	5 12 6	Profit, 1 1 8
1770. Beans.	3 10 6	8 0 0	4 9 6
Totals,	14 2 8	19 10 6	5 11 2 / 0 3 4 / 5 7 10
Ditto of the 7 acres,	98 18 8	136 13 6	30 14 10
Average *per* acre *per ann.*	3 10 8	4 17 7	1 1 11

The deficiency of a greater profit here, is not to be fo much wondered at as the exiftence of any. The heavy expence of a fallow inftead of a profitable crop, which reduced the wheat years to one, changed the account from the very beginning .—under such difadvantages the clear annual piofit of a guinea is by no means inconfiderable;

indeed, it is more ¬han one farmer in an hundred makes. If two profitable crops be fubftituted in the room of the unprofitable one of the two firſt years, which would have been the cafe, had not the hemp been fown, the account would, on the whole, have been very advantageous.

General obfervations on experiments 28, 29, 30, 31, 32, 33, and 34.

Mr. *Arbuthnot* threw thefe two fields into the alternate hufbandry of beans and wheat, to difcover if the land could profitably be kept clean without a fallow: the affirmative is proved very ſtrongly in thefe trials; for the fields are both much cleaner than any farmer's ſtubbles in the country, and the bean one again ready for wheat, if it was thought proper to fow that grain; but having conducted the trial through a courfe of four years, the conclufions are as clear, as if it was extended to fourteen: for the difadvantages, which have occurred in the laſt regiſtered field, are greater, in all probability, than would happen in any fucceeding four. That land may be kept clean, therefore, by the courfe of beans and wheat alternately, both being drilled, and the profit arising confiderable, cannot for a moment be doubted.

But, at the fame time that this gentleman is well convinced of the fact, yet he is of opinion, that it would be more profitable to crop fuch land in a different manner. He purpofes throwing one of thefe fields into the following round: 1. Cabbages. 2. Windfor beans. 3. Oats. 4. Clover. 5. Wheat. Which he apprehends will turn out more advantageous; and in this he is certainly right: for the quantity of manure arifing from the cattle, which are maintained by the cabbages and the clover, will enrich the land to a very great degree; and in the conduct of fuch a courfe, if all the dung arifing from the field was duly returned to it, the exact advantage of it would be found, which otherwife cannot be.

Experiment, No. 35.
Culture, expences, and produce, of five acres of drilled wheat.

1768.

Culture.

The foil of this field is a light loam, but not light enough for feeding turnips on.

In

In 1767 it yielded peafe, the ftubble of which was ploughed up in *September*, and then thrown on to lands 3½ feet wide: harrowed in 3 quarters *per* acre of fheep trotters, and drilled each land with double rows of wheat, at 14 inches, ufing one bufhel *per* acre of feed. The rows were once hand-hoed, and twice horfe-hoed with fhim and double mould-board plough. the product 2¼ quarters *per* acre.

Expences.

	£.	s.	d.
Firft ploughing, -	0	8	6
Second ditto, -	0	7	6
Harrowing, - -	0	1	0
Three quarters of trotters,	1	7	0
Carriage ditto, -	0	3	0
Sowing ditto, - -	0	1	6
Drilling, -	0	1	6
Seed, - -	0	5	6
Water-furrowing, - -	0	1	0
Hand-hoeing, -	0	4	0
Shim twice, - -	0	1	4
Double mould-board, -	0	2	4
Reaping, - -	0	8	0
Harvefting, -	0	3	6
Thrafhing 2¼ quarters, -	0	7	6
Carrying, - -	0	2	6
Rent, &c. - -	1	2	0
A a 3 Total,	5	7	8

Produce.

	£	s.	d.
Two qrs. and a half, at 52s. 6d.	6	11	3
Straw, one load, -	1	5	0
Total, -	7	16	3
Expences, - -	5	7	8
Profit, - -	2	8	7
Ditto on the five, -	12	2	11

Experiment, No. 36.

Culture, expences, and produce, of five acres of drilled wheat.

1768.

Culture.

The soil a strong loam, tending to clay, the tillage, seed, hoeing, &c. the same as No. 35. The product 3 quarters *per* acre.

Expences.

	£	s.	d.
As before, except thrashing,	5	0	2
Thrashing, - -	0	8	9
Total, -	5	8	11

Produce.

	£	s.	d.
Three quarters, at 52s. 6d.	7	17	6
Straw, one load, -	1	5	0
Total, -	9	2	6
Expences, - -	5	8	11
Profit, - -	3	13	7

Experiment, No. 37.

Culture, expences, and produce, of seven acres and three roods of drilled wheat.

1770.

Culture.

The soil of this field is a strong loam, on a brick earth. In 1768, it yielded tares, the stubble of which was ploughed up in *September*, twelve inches deep. In *May*, 1769, it was hunted, and soon after cross-ploughed, and rolled with spiky roller. Ridged up half the field in *August*, in 3½ feet lands, and harrowed the other half with ox-harrows twice. Drilled the ridged half with a bushel an acre of wheat, 4 rows on each land; and, as soon as it was finished, the furrows were struck with the double mould-board plough. The other half was sown broad-cast, 2 bushels *per* acre, and ploughed in, after which the whole was water-furrowed.

In *February*, 16 facks an acre of rabbit dung spread over the whole. The drilled half was once hand-hoed, and the broad-cast hand-weeded. The products — the drilled, three quarters, seven bushels, one peck and ½ *per* acre; and the broad-cast 4 quarters.

Account

Account of the drilled.
Expences.

First ploughing, -	£. 0 12	0
Water-furrowing, -	0 1	0
Second ditto, - -	0 7	6
Third ditto, twelve inch, -	0 12	0
Spiky roller, -	0 2	0
Fourth earth, -	0 5	0
Drilling, - -	0 1	6
Seed, -	0 6	6
Striking furrows, -	0 1	2
Water-furrowing, -	0 1	0
Rabbit dung and sowing,	1 2	10
Hand-hoeing, -	0 5	0
Reaping, - -	0 10	0
Harvesting, -	0 3	6
Thrashing, - -	0 12	0
Carrying, - -	0 2	0
Rent, &c. &c. -	2 4	0
Total, - -	7 9	0

Produce.

3 qrs. 7 b. 1½ p. at 50s.	9 16	0
Straw, two loads, at 25s.	2 10	0
Total, -	12 6	0
Expences, -	7 9	0
Profit, - -	4 17	0

Account of the broad-caſt.

Expences.

Firſt ploughing, - £. 0	12	0
Water-furrowing, - 0	1	0
Second earth, - 0	7	6
Third ditto, - 0	12	0
Spiky roller, - 0	2	0
Harrowing, - 0	3	0
Sowing, - 0	0	3
Seed, - 0	13	0
Fourth earth, - 0	5	0
Water-furrowing, - 0	1	0
Rabbit dung, - 1	2	10
Weeding, - 0	5	0
Reaping, - 0	10	0
Harveſting, - 0	3	6
Thraſhing, - 0	12	0
Carrying out, - 0	2	0
Rent, - 2	4	0
Total, - 7	16	1

Produce.

Four quarters, at 50 s. - 10	0	0
Straw, two loads, - 2	10	0
Total, - 12	10	0
Expences, - 7	16	1
Profit, - 4	13	11

I

Profit by the drilled, -	£.4	17	0
————— broad-caſt,	4	13	11
Superiority, - -	0	3	1

The equality of the two methods is here very remarkable; but the ſuperiority may be fairly, according to this account, given the drill, on account not only of the 3 s but alſo the ſuperior tillage the land receives in it. A hand-hoeing is far more beneficial than a weeding.

Obſervations on the preceding crops of drilled wheat.

Theſe experiments in drilled wheat include ſeveral ſeaſons, various ſoils, and ſome difference in the methods of culture. hence they cannot fail diſcovering nearly the merit of this huſbandry for wheat. I ſhall throw the trials into one view, that a clearer idea may be formed of the reſult.

Experiment,

	l.	s.	d.		q.	b.	p.		l.	s.	d.
Experiment, No. 29. Expences,	5	15	8	Product, 4	0	0	Profit,	6	4	4
31.	5	15	3		3	0	0		3	12	3
33.	4	10	10		2	1	2		1	1	8
35.	5	7	8		2	4	0		2	8	7
36.	5	8	11		3	0	0		3	13	7
37.	7	9	0		3	7	1 ½		4	17	0
Totals,	34	7	4		18	4	3 ¼		21	17	5
Averages,	5	14	6		3	0	3		3	12	10

This table exhibits the cleareſt circumſtances in favour of drilling wheat, that I remember to have heard of; for here is not one unprofitable crop, not one but was manured, nor one that was not well cleaned by horſe and hand-hoeing:

notwith-

notwithstanding these expences, which all tend much to enriching the land for following crops, yet is the neat profit so great as 3*l.* 12*s.* 10*d. per* acre; which certainly proves, in the clearest manner, that the methods of drilling here pursued are truly advantageous, and may be practised with as great a certainty of profit, as any part of the old husbandry. It has been common with many persons to declare against drilling from experience; but such, it is presumed, have practised Mr. *Tull's* method of wide intervals, for drilling the same land every year with wheat. Mr. *Arbuthnot's* plan has been totally different: he has set his rows so close together, in several of his trials, that the field presently resembles a broad-cast one. The utility of drilling lies, first, in his being able, with one man, two horses, and a boy, to put in five or six acres in a day; whereas, in the common method of sowing under furrow on a fallow, one plough can finish but one acre after the seedsman. Secondly, it consists in the easy admission of a hand-hoe between the rows, and the horse-hoes in the intervals; both which operations must be performed while the corn is young,

and

and are done with much greater eafe and expedition, than is poffible with broad-caft crops; though many farmers, in fome parts of *England*, find it highly advan_tageous to hand-hoe all their wheat. The great fuccefs of this method is the beft proof of its propriety; for drilling, that will pay fo confiderable a profit on the average of the above trials, ought to be efteemed decifively advantageous. The degree of benefit, which, in a long courfe, would refult from keeping the land always clean while under wheat, cannot be accurately calculated: every crop would pof-fefs a fhare of it, and, beyond all doubt, every one would be regularly the better.

But Mr. *Arbuthnot* here obferves, that however advantageous thefe trials may appear, no perfon fhould think of prac-tifing the drill culture of wheat, unlefs he abfolutely determines to keep the land as clean as a garden: the fuccefs depends on keeping this refolution. Under a more imperfect fyftem, drilling would probably turn out worfe than the common mode.

He further remarks, that thefe trials have been manured for often, but mode-rately; a conduct, which he finds much

more

more beneficial than laying on a large quantity once in four or five years.

Thefe trials are, upon the whole, decifive in favour of the mode of drilling here purfued, and will, for the future, prevent thofe general expreffions of praife or condemnation, which we have fo long heard in every thing that concerns the new hufbandry.

BEANS.

Befides the trials already regiftered on drilled beans among the preceding crops of wheat, Mr. *Arbuthnot* has formed fome others much deferving attention.

Experiment, No. 38.

Culture, expences, and produce, of five acres of drilled beans.

1767.

Culture.

The foil a ftrong loam, on a clay bottom, not manured for many years. In 1766, it yielded oats, the ftubble of which was ploughed twelve inches deep in *December*, and fo left till *April*, when it was

harrowed

harrowed thrice, and drilled with tick beans, two bufhels *per* acre, in double rows, at fourteen inches, with twenty-inch intervals. The end of *May* they were hand-hoed, and horfe-hoed with fhim and double mould-board plough. In *June*, all thefe operations were repeated. After the bloffoming, t he fhoots above the flowers were cut off with a peafe hook, at the length of about twelve inches · this was done to forward the ripening. The product three quarters *per* acre.

Expences.

	£.		
Firft ploughing,	0	12	0
Harrowing,	0	3	0
Drilling,	0	1	6
Seed,	0	7	0
Two hand-hoeings,	0	12	0
Shim twice,	0	1	4
Double mould-board ditto,	0	2	8
Cutting tops,	0	0	6
Reaping,	0	7	0
Harvefting,	0	4	0
Thrafhing,	0	3	6
Rent, &c.	1	2	0
Total,	3	16	6

Produce.

Three quarters, at 25s.	£. 3 15	0
Straw, one load,	*1 0	0
Total, -	4 15	0
Expences, - -	3 16	6
Profit, - - -	0 18	6

Experiment, No. 39.
Culture, expences, and produce, of six acres of drilled beans.
1768.
Culture.

The foil of this field is a strong clay, summer-fallowed in 1767, receiving, in all, three earths and one harrowing. In *February*, it was drilled with a bushel and half *per* acre of horse-beans, in double rows, at fourteen inches, with twenty-eight inch intervals. They were hand-hoed once, and horse-hoed with shim and double mould-board once. The produce three quarters *per* acre.

Expences.

Three earths, - -	1 10	0
Harrowing, -	0 1	0
Drilling, - -	0 1	6
Carry over,	1 12	6

* It is to be observed, that for cart-horses bean-straw, when well got in, is as good as middling hay.

		£.		
Brought over,		1	12	6
Seed,	-	0	5	0
Water-furrowing,	-	0	0	6
Hand-hoeing,	-	0	4	0
Shim,	-	0	0	8
Double mould-board plough,		0	1	2
Reaping,	-	0	7	0
Harvesting,	-	0	5	0
Thrashing, at 1s. 4d.	-	0	4	0
Rent, &c.	-	2	4	0
Total,	-	5	3	10

Produce.

Three quarters, at 28 s.	-	4	4	0
Straw, one load,	-	1	0	0
Total,	-	5	4	0
Expences,	-	5	3	10
Profit,	-	0	0	2

This is a fresh instance, that beans must always be made the fallow, and not have the expences of a preparatory one to pay; for the crop does not appear to be the better: a circumstance fully sufficient to decide the matter.

Experiment, No. 40.

Culture, expences, and produce, of five acres of drilled beans.

1769.

Culture.

The five acres of experiment, No. 38, were this year again drilled with beans: the wheat ftubble that intervened ploughed at *Michaelmas,* and again in *January.* In *February* harrowed it, and drilled with two bufhels *per* acre of tick beans, in double rows of fourteen inches, with intervals of two feet. In *April,* fhimmed the rows, and then harrowed the land acrofs. In *May,* hand-hoed the rows, and then horfe-hoed with fhim and double mould-board plough. The crop three quarters *per* acre.

Expences.

	£.		
Firft ploughing, - -	0	7	6
Water-furrowing, -	0	0	3
Second earth, - -	0	7	6
Harrowing, -	0	0	6
Drilling, - -	0	1	6
Seed, - -	0	6	0
Hand-hoeing, -	0	6	0
Shim twice, - - -	0	1	4
Double mould-board once,	0	1	4
Reaping, - -	0	6	0
Carry over,	1	16	11

		£.		
Brought over,		1	16	11
Harvefting,	— —	0	4	0
Thrafhing,	— —	0	4	0
Rent, &c.	—	1	2	0
Total,	—	3	6	11

Produce.

Three quarters, at 25 s.	— —	3	15	0
Straw, 1 ¼ load,	— —	1	5	0
Total,	—	5	0	0
Expences,	—	3	6	11
Profit,	—	1	13	1

Experiment, No. 41.

Culture, expences, and produce, of five acres of drilled beans.

1769.
Culture.

The foil the fame as No. 40; alfo the culture. The produce three quarters and a half *per* acre.

Expences.

Sundries, as before,	—	3	6	11

Produce.

3 ½ quarters, at 25s.	-	£.4	7	6
Straw, 1 ¼ load,	- -	1	5	0
		5	12	6
Expences, -	-	3	6	11
Profit, -	-	2	5	7

Experiment, No. 42.

Culture, expences, and produce of three acres of drilled beans.

1770.

Culture.

The foil a ftrong yellow loam on a clay bottom; yielded wheat in 1769. The ftubble was ploughed in *November*; and in *February* drilled with mazagan beans in double rows, 14 inches, with intervals of 2 feet 4 inches; 3 bufhels of feed *per* acre. In *May* they were horfe-hoed with fhim and double mould-board plough; and in *June* hand-hoed. Pro-duct 4 ½ quarters *per* acre.

Expences.

Ploughing,	-	£.0	7	6
Water-furrowing,	-	0	1	0
Drilling,	- -	0	1	3
Carry over,	-	0	9	9

	£.		
Brought over -	0	9	9
Seed, - - -	0	12	0
Shim, - - -	0	6	8
Double mould-board, -	0	1	2
Hand-hoeing, - -	0	6	0
Pulling and binding, -	0	10	0
Harvesting, - - -	0	3	0
Thrashing, - - -	0	5	0
Rent, - - -	1	2	0
	3	9	7

Produce.

4 ¼ Quarters, at 32 *s.* -	7	4	0
Straw, 1 ½ load, - -	1	10	0
	8	14	0
Expences, - -	3	9	7
Profit, -	5	4	5

Experiment, No. 43.

*Culture, expences, and produce of three acres
of drilled beans.*

1770.

Culture.

The foil a very ftiff yellow clay; cropped with wheat in 1769; the ftubble
ploughed at *Chriftmas* and harrowed. In

February

February it was set with mazagan beans, 3 ½ bushels *per* acre   It was hand-hoed once, and horse-hoed with shim and double mould-board once. Produce, 4 ½ quarters *per* acre.

Expences.

Ploughing,	-	-	£. 0	7	6
Harrowing,			0	1	0
Setting,	-		0	7	0
Seed,	-	-	0	14	0
Hand-hoeing,	-	-	0	10	0
Shim,	-	-	0	0	8
Double mould-board,			0	1	2
Pulling and binding,			0	10	0
Harvesting,	-	-	0	10	0
Thrashing,	-		0	5	0
Rent, &c.			1	2	0
			4	8	4

Produce.

4 ½ Quarters, at 32 s.	-		7	4	0
Straw, one load,	-		1	0	0
			8	4	0
Expences,			4	8	4
Profit,			3	15	8

Experiment, No. 44.

*Culture, expences, and produce of four acres
of drilled beans.*

1770.

Culture.

The foil a good fandy loam on clay:
cropped with wheat in 1769; the ftubble
trench ploughed with *Ducket's* plough, 10
inches deep, in *October*. In *November* it
was harrowed, and drilled with mazagan
beans in double rows, 14 inches afunder,
with 18 inch intervals 4 bufhels of feed.
In *April* they were hand-hoed, and then
fhimmed; and the beginning of *June*
hand-hoed and fhimmed again. Produce,
4 ½ quarters *per* acre.

Expences.

Ploughing,	-	-	£.0	12	0
Harrowing,	-	-	0	1	0
Drilling,	-	-	-	0	1	6
Seed,	-	-	-	-	0	16	0
Water-furrowing,	-	-	0	1	3
Twice hand-hoeing,	-	0	8	6
Shim twice,	-	-	-	0	1	4
Pulling and binding,	-	0	10	0
Harvefting,	-	-	-	0	4	0

Carry over,   -   2 15 7

Brought over,	-	£. 2	15	7
Thrashing,	- - -	0	5	0
Rent,	- - -	1	2	0
		4	2	7

Produce,

4 ¼ Quarters, at 32 s.	-	7	4	0
Straw, 1 ¼ load,	- -	1	5	0
		8	9	0
Expences,	- -	4	2	7
Profit,	- -	4	6	5

General obfervations.

Thefe experiments on beans including
many variations of foil, culture, and fort,
the conclufions to be drawn from them will
appear with the greater clearnefs, by forming a table of averages as before done with
the wheat crops.

		l.	s.	d.		q.	b.	p.
To 28.	Expences,	3	19	6	Product,	3	4	0
30		3	10	8		3	0	0
32.		6	1	4		3	4	0
34.		3	10	6		3	4	0
38.		3	16	6		3	0	0
39.		5	3	10		3	0	0
40.		3	6	11		3	0	0
41.		3	6	11		3	4	0
42.		3	9	7		4	4	0
43.		4	8	4		4	4	0
44.		4	2	7		4	4	0
s,		44	16	8		39	4	0
:s,		4	1	6		3	4	2

The clear profit of 2*l.* 10*s.* an acre on fuch a variety of crops, moft of which are mere fallows for wheat, is much more confiderable than attends the bean culture throughout nine tenths of the kingdom. This great fuperiority is owing to the uncommon attention to keeping them perfectly clean by hand and horfe-hoeing; drilling gives a fair opportunity for exerting culture of this fort; and it is evident from the crops, how much benefit they reap by this conduct. Common farmers do not make near fuch a profit by wheat. What therefore can thofe counties fay to this, who continue in the abfurd courfe of, 1. Fallow; 2. Wheat; 3. Beans? Let them perufe thefe experiments with candor: Let them try the refult: It is impoffible but they muft acknowledge the infinite fuperiority.

PEASE.

Experiment, No. 45.

Culture, expences, and produce of five acres of drilled peafe.

1767.

Culture.

The foil of this field is a poor fandy loam. It yielded wheat in 1766; the ftub-

2   ble

ble of which was ploughed 12 inches deep in *December*. In *April* ox-harrowed and crofs ploughed, and then harrowed twice more; after which it was ridged up in 3 ½ feet lands; and being harrowed once were drilled in double rows, at 14 inches; the interval 2 feet 4 inches, with 1 ½ bufhel *per* acre of dwarf marrowfat peafe. In *May* they were hand-hoed, and horfe-hoed with fhim and double mould-board plough. In *June* thefe three operations were repeated. The crop 14 bufhels *per* acre,

Expences.

Firft ploughing,	-	£ 0	12	0
Harrowing,	-	0	2	0
Second ploughing,	-	0	7	6
Harrowing,	-	0	1	0
Third ploughing,	-	0	6	0
Harrowing,	-	0	0	6
Drilling,	-	0	1	6
1 ½ Bufhel feed,	-	0	12	0
Two hand-hoeings,	-	0	10	0
Fhim twice,	-	0	1	4
Double mould-board plough ditto,		0	2	8
Hooking,	-	0	6	0
Harvefting,	-	0	4	0
Thrafhing,	-	0	2	4
Carry over,		3	8	10

Brought over,	-	£.3	8	10
Carrying out,	-	0	1	0
Rent, &c.	-	1	2	0
		4	11	10

Produce.

14 Bushels, at 6 s. 6 d.	-	4	11	0
⅓ Load straw, at 15 s.	-	0	7	6
		4	18	6
Expences,		4	11	10
Profit,		0	6	8

Experiment, No. 46.

Culture, expences, and produce of two acres of drilled peafe.

1767.

Culture.

The foil a fandy loam on a brick earth; fummer fallowed in 1766, when it received four ploughings and two ox-harrowings; being left on the 4 foot ridge by the laft earth in autumn. It would not have been fummer fallowed, but was defigned for madder, only the plants fell fhort. In *April* the ridges were reverfed by a ploughing, 10 inches deep. It was then harrowed; and
about

about the end of *May* drilled with 2 bushels an acre of blue union peafe, in double rows, of 14 inches, and 2 feet 10 inch intervals. They were once hand-hoed, and horfe-hoed with fhim and double mould-board once. They were fold green in *September*. The product 10 facks *per* acre, at 7*s.* a fack.

Expences.

			£.	*s.*	*d.*
1766.	Four ploughings,	-	1	12	6
	Two ox-harrowings,		0	2	0
1767.	Ploughing,	-	0	10	0
	Harrowing,	-	0	0	6
	Drilling,	-	0	1	6
	2 Bufhels feed,	-	0	14	0
	Hand-hoeing,	-	0	6	0
	Shim,	- -	0	0	8
	Double mould-board,		0	1	2
	Rent,	- -	2	4	0
			5	12	4

Produce.

		£.	*s.*	*d.*			
10 Sacks, at 7*s.*		3	10	0			
Straw,	- -	1	0	0			
					4	10	0
Lofs,	- -				1	2	4

Experiment, No. 47.

Culture, expences, and produce of four acres
of drilled peafe.

1768.

Culture.

Soil, a fandy loam, was cropped with oats in 1767; the ftubble of which was ploughed up in *January*. Crofs ploughed the beginning of *April*, and harrowed twice. Manured it with 10 loads an acre of *London* dung, which were ploughed in and the land harrowed. It was then landed up on to 3 ½ feet ridges, harrowed, and drilled with dwarf marrowfat peafe, 1 ½ bufhel an acre, in double rows, at 14 inches, with intervals of 2 feet 4 inches. They were once hand-hoed, and horfe-hoed twice with fhim, and once with the double mould-board plough. The crop was fold on the land for pods, at 3 l. an acre, but extremely blighted.

Expences.

Firft ploughing, - - £. 0	7	6
Second ditto, - - 0	7	6
Harrowing, - - 0	2	0
10 Loads dung, (54 bufhels each)		
at 10 s. - - 5	0	0
Third ploughing, - 0	4	6
Carry over, 6	1	6

		£.		
Brought over,	-	6	1	6
Harrowing,	-	0	0	6
Fourth ploughing,	-	0	4	6
Harrowing,	-	0	0	6
Drilling,	-	0	1	6
1 ½ Bushel feed,	-	0	10	6
Hand-hoeing,	-	0	5	0
Shim,	-	0	1	4
Double mould-board plough,		0	1	2
Rent, &c.	-	1	2	0
		8	8	6

Produce.

		£.		
Crop,	-	3	0	0
Straw,	-	0	15	0
		3	15	0
Loss,	-	4	13	6

General observations.

The success of drilling peafe has proved very bad in thefe trials, and yet the attention given the crops was by no means deficient. The moft proper fields in the farm were chofen, and no omiffions were made in the cleaning them while growing. The event does not condemn the drill culture of this vegetable, becaufe the trials are not numerous, and were confined to two forts

of

of pea only; neither of which is much cultivated any where, except in the neighbourhood of *London*.

Experiment, No. 46.	Lofs,	£.	1	2	4
47.	Ditto,		4	13	6
			5	15	10
45.	Profit,		0	6	8
Total lofs,	-		5	9	2
Average,	-	-	1	16	4

It would be prepofterous to affert, from the above experiments, that thefe peafe cannot be profitably cultivated: at the fame time it fhould be remarked, that the great advantages to be expected depend on accidental circumftances, particularly on the price being high at market. But even in that cafe, the gentleman, who cannot attend the fale, muft not expect the profit of gardeners. This laft circumftance, attended with the uncertainties of the crop, has made Mr. *Arbuthnot* determine to leave it out of his courfe, and fubftitute beans, which he can confume himfelf, or always find a ready market for.

He entertains no doubts concerning the
propriety

propriety of drilling peafe from the preceding ill fuccefs; on the contrary, in cafe he cultivates them in future, he is fully determined never to fow them in any other manner; not only from the conviction of his reafon, but alfo from various obfervations. He recommends for fmall peafe, double rows, at 14 inches, with 2 feet intervals; the two rows fhould, while young, be thrown fo much together by the double mould-board plough, as to feem to form but one row: but great care muft be taken to do it early enough to avoid breaking the haulm. The weeds had better get up, than the vine be difturbed when of any growth.

TURNIPS.

Experiment, No. 48.

Culture, expences, and produce of four acres of drilled turnips.

1768.

Culture.

The pea ftubble of Experiment, No. 47. was ploughed up immediately after gathering: the whole was then dunged again with 10 loads an acre from the farm yard; which was then turned in by another ploughing, throwing it on to 4 feet lands; after harrowing they were part drilled; one acre with common turnips broad-caft, and 3 acres drilled with *Reynold's* turnip; double rows, at 14 inches, with 2 feet 4 inch interval; both the beginning of *Auguft.* They were once hand-hoed, but horfe-hoeing was prevented by wet. The common turnips were confumed by ewes and lambs, and were worth 3 *l.* The others were fed off in *April*; the 3 acres kept 140 ewes and 140 lambs a fortnight; worth 3*d.* a couple *per* week. They eat them greedily; when pared down to the ground they were taken up with turnip hooks, and the fheep eat them clean. The weight of the plants did not exceed ¼ of a *lb.* tops and all: The fhoots were 2 feet high the middle of *April.*

Account of the turnips.
Expences.

	£.		
Furrowing,	0	3	0
Manuring, 10 loads, at 6*s.*	3	0	0
Ploughing,	0	7	6
Harrowing,	0	1	0
Sowing and feed,	0	1	0
Hand-hoeing,	0	6	0
	3	18	6

Brought over, total expences, £. 3 18 6

Produce.

Value of the crop,	- -	3	0	0

Lofs,	- - -	0	18	6

Account of *Reynolds*'s turnips.

Expences.

Furrowing,	- -	0	3	0
Manuring,	- - -	3	0	0
Ploughing,	- -	0	7	6
Harrowing,	- -	0	1	0
Drilling,	- - -	0	1	6
Seed,	- - -	0	1	6
Hand-hoeing,	- -	0	7	0
		4	1	6

Produce.

By keeping 140 fheep 2 weeks, at 3 d. 3 l. 10 s.; the third of which is, - -	1	3	4

Lofs, - -	2	18	2
Ditto by common turnips,	0	18	6

Excefs of the former, -	1	19	8

Observations.

This experiment is not offered as a full comparison between the two plants, because *August* is too late for either, and particularly so for the cabbage turnip, which is directed to be sown in *March*, and planted in *June*; it had not therefore a fair trial; but it is of no slight consequence to know that the common turnip will yield so large a produce as 3*l.* an acre from so late a sowing; and at the same time that the other plant will then produce but a trifling crop: this is evidently proved: a crop of turnips of 3*l.* after pease of the same year, is highly beneficial.

Experiment, No. 49.
Culture, expences, and produce, of two acres of drilled turnips.
1768.
Culture.

Two acres of strong loam, on brick earth, yielded drilled pease in 1767; the stubble ploughed in *October*, and the land water-furrowed. In *April* it was stirred again and harrowed. After this, it was

left

left till *June*, when it received another ploughing and harrowing. the 30th, drilled it in double rows, at fourteen inches, with two feet ten inch intervals. As foon as the plants came up, fix facks *per* acre of wood afhes were fown over them, not only as a manure, but to pre- ferve them from the fly. They were hand- hoed twice, and horfe-hoed with fhim and double mould-board plough as often. The confumption of the crop was as fol- lows: an high head-land on one fide the field was ploughed twelve inches deep, and the fheep folded on it, after being well littered with ftraw: the turnips were then given in cribs: the two acres kept 164 fheep and lambs fix weeks and two days; they were turned out of the pen at noon. the value of the keeping 2 *d.* a week.

Expences.

	£.		
Firft ploughing, -	0	7	6
Water-furrowing, -	0	0	3
Second ploughing, -	0	6	0
Harrowing, - -	0	1	0
Third ploughing, -	0	6	0
Carry over, -	1	0	9

	£.		
Brought over, -	1	0	9
Drilling, - -	0	1	6
Seed, - -	0	0	4
Wood afhes and fowing, -	0	6	0
Hand-hoeing twice, -	0	8	0
Shim twice, - -	0	1	4
Double mould-board plough ditto,	0	2	0
Carting to the fold, -	0	15	4
Rent, - -	1	2	0
Total, -	3	18	3

Produce.

Keeping 164 fheep fix weeks and two days, at 2d. 4l. 2s.; the half is - -	2	1	0
Lofs, - -	1	17	3

Experiment, No. 50.

Culture, expences, and produce, of three acres of drilled turnips.

1770.

Culture.

This piece yielded turnips in 1769, and was defigned for madder; but plants were wanting: trench-ploughed it in *June*, and drilled it the 10th of *July*; part in rows, equally

equally diftant, three feet, with rows of lucerne between. They were twice hand-hoed, and fhimmed three times : the lucerne was deftroyed by the fly, before they began the turnips, the latter being faved by burning weeds. The rows, at 18 inches, were attacked by a grey grub; foot was fown to kill them ; but had no effect. Part of this piece is a gravelly foil ; and it is remarkable, that the grub eat only thofe parts ; this was probably owing to the more luxuriant growth of the reft of the field. The eighteen-inch rows were only hand-hoed, as thefe intervals would not admit the horfe-hoe, without danger of burying the plants.

Expences.

Ploughing,	-	£. 0	10	0
Harrowing,	-	0	1	0
Drilling,	-	0	0	6
Seed,	-	0	0	2
Hand-hoeing twice,	-	0	9	0
Shim twice,	-	0	1	4
Rent, &c.	-	1	2	0
Total,	-	2	4	0

One square perch, the best that could
be found among the eighteen-
inch rows, was pulled and
weighed, - - 210 *lb*,
One square perch of three-feet rows
weighed, - - - 244
_____
Superiority, - - 34
_____

N. B. The perch of the three-feet rows
was not near so good as what had been
drawn for the sheep before this experiment was made.

Experiment, No. 51.

Culture, expences, and produce, of one acre of drilled turnips.

1770.

Culture.

The soil of this acre is a rich, deep
black mould : it was summer fallowed in
1769, when it received two earths. In
May it was ploughed again, and well harrowed : in *June* another earth was given,
and fresh harrowing. It was then manured
with nine loads an acre of fresh yard dung,
which was ploughed in, and the land
again

again harrowed. It was then drilled with turnips, in rows equally diftant, two feet afunder, and twice hand-hoed. Thefe are to be tranfplanted, to ftand for feed: they are to be planted in equidiftant rows, three feet and an half afunder, and are to be at two feet diftance in the rows.

Expences.

1769.	Two ploughings,	o	12	o
1770.	Third earth, -	o	6	o
	Harrowing, -	o	1	o
	Fourth earth, -	o	4	6
	Harrowing, -	o	1	o
	Manuring, -	2	14	o
	Fifth earth, -	o	4	6
	Harrowing, -	o	1	o
	Drilling, - -	o	2	o
	Seed, - -	o	o	6
	Twice hand-hoeing,	o	10	o
	Rent, &c. -	2	4	o
	Total, -	7	o	6

Obfervations.

The experiment, No. 50, fhews the great advantage of horfe-hoeing turnips, which could not be performed in the eigh-

teen-inch

teen-inch rows without danger of burying the plants; but Mr. *Arbuthnot* is of opinion, that two-feet rows will admit of sufficient culture with the horfe-hoe, and produce a larger crop than in rows at three feet diftance.

PREVENTING THE FLY.

Mr. *Arbuthnot* has tried various receipts to deftroy the turnip fly; but none of them have anfwered, except the following.

He collects all forts of green weeds from hedges, hedge-rows, &c. mixes them with ftraw, and lays them on heaps on the windward fide of the field: they are then fet on fire, fo that the wind may blow the fmoak over the whole field. But it fhould be obferved, that the weeds muft not be withered too much, as it is the fmothering of the flame that produces the fmoak, which is expected to have the defired effect. This drives away the fly at once, and faves the crop: he this year preferved ten acres, on which the fly had begun, by purfuing this method: they were fafe in three or four days. This hint he received from Mr. *Booth*, of *Glendon*, in *Northamptonfhire*.

CAB-

CABBAGES.

Experiment, No. 52.
Culture, expences, and produce, of four acres of cabbages.
1769.
Culture.

The foil a fandy loam, on brick earth. In 1768 it yielded barley, the ftubble of which was ploughed up the 12th of *September*, 14 inches deep, with the great wheel plough, and twice harrowed. It was then planted with various forts of gardeners cabbages: the rows equally diftant, at 18 inches and two feet, and the plants one foot afunder in the rows: they were once hand-hoed: three acres were fed off with ewes and lambs: they maintained 270 ewes, and 70 lambs, a fortnight, in *April* and *May*, at 3*d.* a week. N. B. A very mild winter from *Michaelmas* to *Chriftmas*. The other acre was fold to *Covent-Garden* by the bunch; from fix to twelve in a bunch, at 3*d.* At two feet by one, there are 21780 plants on an acre, which, at ten for 3*d.* come to 27*l.* 4*s.* 6*d.*

I

Expences

Expences.

Ploughing,	-	£. 0	14	0
Harrowing,	- -	0	1	0
Planting,	- -	0	12	0
Seed, and feed-bed, &c.	-	0	7	0
Hand-hoeing,	-	0	7	0
Water-furrowing,	-	0	0	6
Rent, &c.	- -	1	2	0
Total,	-	3	3	6

Produce.

Keeping 350 fheep, at 3*d.* is 8*l.* 15*s.* 8*d.* or *per* acre,	2	18	6
Lofs, - -	0	5	0

Experiment, No. 53.
Culture, expences, and produce of a rood of cabbages.
1770.
Culture.

The foil ftrong loam on clay, fallowed in 1769; manured with twelve loads an acre of yard dung; in *October* ridged into four feet lands; harrowed the beginning of *May*, and the 8th planted, two rows, equally diftant, one foot from plant to plant. They have been twice hand-hoed, once with fhim, and once with the double mould-board plough.

Expences.

		£.		
1769.	Three ploughings,	1	2	6
1770.	Manuring, -	3	12	0
	Harrowing, -	0	1	0
	Fourth ploughing,	0	6	0
	Harrowing, -	0	1	0
	Planting, -	0	5	0
	Two hand-hoeings,	0	7	0
	Shim, -	0	0	8
	Double mould-board plough	0	1	2
	Rent, &c. -	2	4	0
	Total, - -	8	0	4

Experiment, No. 54.

Culture and expences of a rood of cabbages.

1770.

Culture.

The proportion and management of this rood the fame as the preceding, only it was drilled when the ridges of the other were planted; the great *Scotch* cabbage feed, double rows on each ridge. Some rows planted. Other lands were at the fame time drilled with a cabbage from *Northamptonfhire*, a fugar-loaf fort, foft, and of

a pale

a pale green. *May* 29, hand-hoed, but did not set them out. *June* 6, the plants were pricked out from the drills, leaving the remainder two feet apart : then all were hand-hoed. *June* 28, the drilled beds were horse-hoed, and the furrows struck with double mould-board plough. *July* 16, the plants that were pricked ou t were transplanted for good. *August* 2, the transplanted were hand and horse-hoed, and the drills the same. The 24th, both were horse-hoed, and earthed up, with double mould-board plough. *November* 5, the best *Scotch* was picked out of the drilled : he weighed,   -   20½ *lb.*
A *Northampton* ditto,   - - 13½

A *Scotch* transplanted,   -   10½
A *Northampton* ditto,   -   8

The drilled being in a distant field, many were stolen : they were therefore obliged to be consumed : it could not therefore be known how long they would stand the winter.

The *Northampton* sort much the forwardest : a proof that they will not last so well.

Expences.

Expences.

		£.		
1769.	Three ploughings,	3	12	0
	Harrowing, -	0	1	0
	Fourth ploughing,	0	6	0
	Harrowing, -	0	1	0
	Drilling, -	0	1	0
	Seed, - -	0	2	0
	Thrice hand-hoeing,	0	10	0
	Shim, - -	0	1	4
	Double mould-board,	0	2	4
	Rent, &c.	2	4	0
	Total, -	7	0	8

Experiment, No. 55.

Culture and expences of three roods of cabbages.

1770.

Culture.

The land a rich turnip foil. In 1769, it yielded madder, which was taken up in the fpring of 1770, ploughed in *April,* and harrowed; then drew futrows four feet afunder, in which madder was planted, on a dreffing of rabbit dung, 60 facks *per* acre. The beginning of *June* it was taken up again, the plants being wanted for another place: the 16th of *July*, *Scotch* and

North-

Northamptonshire cabbage-plants were set in the furrows after being new drawn; the rows four feet by two from plant to plant. they have been horse-hoed, with the shim thrice, and with the double mould-board twice, besides two hand-hoeings: the last was for drawing in the earth, after the double mould-board, to the plants.

Expences.

	£.		
First ploughing,	0	7	0
Harrowing,	0	1	0
Manuring,	3	10	0
Drawing furrows,	0	0	6
Planting,	0	5	0
Shim thrice,	0	2	0
Double mould-board twice,	0	2	4
Two hand-hoeings,	0	6	0
Rent, &c.	1	2	0
Total,	5	15	10

Experiment, No. 56.

Culture and expences of one acre of cabbages.

1770.

Culture.

The soil a deep black mould, fallowed in 1769, being ploughed five times; again

in *April*, 1770, when it was alſo ox-
harrowed four times in a place; ſtirred
again in *May*, and again harrowed, another ploughing in *June*, and two harrowings, manured with nine loads an acre
of yard dung; ploughed it in, and harrowed again; ſtruck the furrows, and
planted with cabbages three feet by two.
They have been twice hand-hoed, and
ſhimmed once.

Expences.

		£.		
1769.	Five earths, -	1	10	0
1770.	Sixth ditto, -	0	6	0
	Harrowing, -	0	4	0
	Seventh earth, -	0	6	0
	Harrowing, -	0	4	0
	Eighth earth, -	0	5	0
	Harrowing, -	0	1	0
	Manuring, -	2	15	6
	Ninth earth, -	0	5	0
	Harrowing, -	0	1	0
	Striking furrows,	0	1	6
	Planting, -	0	8	0
	Hand-hoeing, -	0	6	0
	Shim, -	0	0	8
	Rent, &c. -	2	4	0
	Total,	8	17	8

BARLEY.

Experiment, No. 57.

*Culture, expences, and produce of four acres
and a half of drilled barley.*

1767.

Culture.

The foil of this field is a very ftrong clayey loam: it was cropped with wheat in 1766, the ftubble of which was ploughed up at *Michaelmas*. In *April* it was flit down and harrowed, after which it was landed up in four-feet ridges, and drilled, double rows, at fourteen inches, on each ridge; one bufhel and a half of feed *per* acre. It was twice horfe-hoed with fhim, and thrice with the double mould-board plough. The produ&t two quarters and a half *per* acre.

Expences.

Firft ploughing,	-	£. 0	8	6
Second ditto,	-	0	6	0
Harrowing,	-	-	0	1	0
Third ploughing,	-	0	4	6
Drilling,	-	-	0	1	6
Seed,	-	-	0	4	6
	Carry over,	-	1	6	0

	£.		
Brought over, -	1	6	0
Shim twice, -	0	1	4
Double mould-board thrice,	0	3	6
Reaping, - -	0	5	0
Harvesting, -	0	3	6
Thrashing, - -	0	4	2
Rent, &c. - -	1	2	0
Carrying out, -	0	0	6
Total, -	3	7	0

Produce.

Two quarters and a half, at 26 s.	3	5	0
Straw, one load, - -	0	16	0
Total, -	4	1	0
Expences, -	3	7	0
Profit, - -	0	14	0

Experiment, No. 58.
Culture, expences, and produce of two acres.
1767.
Culture.

The soil a strong loam; yielded oats in 1766; the stubble ploughed in lands in autumn; in the spring the lands were reversed, and one acre drilled, double

rows, on three feet ridges, using one
bushel of seed; the other acre was sown
broad-cast, three bushels *per* acre; the
drilled was once hand-hoed, once weeded,
and horse-hoed twice, with shim, and as
often with double mould-board. Product
of the broad-cast twelve bushels; of the
drilled ten.

Account of the broad-cast.
Expences.

	£	s	d
First ploughing,	0	10	0
Water-furrowing,	0	1	0
Second earth,	0	7	6
Sowing,	0	0	3
Seed,	0	9	0
Mowing,	0	2	0
Harvesting,	0	4	0
Thrashing,	0	2	3
Carrying out,	0	1	0
Rent,	1	2	0
Total,	2	19	0

Produce.

	£	s	d
Twelve bushels, at 30 s.	2	5	0
Straw, one load,	0	16	0
Total,	3	1	0
Expences,	2	19	0
Profit,	0	2	0

Account of the drilled.

Expences.

First and second earth, and water- furrowing, - £. 0	18	6
Drilling, - - 0	1	6
Seed, - - 0	3	0
Hand-hoeing, - 0	4	0
Weeding, - 0	4	0
Shim twice, - - 0	1	4
Double mould-board ditto, 0	2	4
Reaping, - - 0	4	0
Harvesting, - - 0	3	0
Thrashing, - 0	1	10
Carrying out, - 0	0	10
Rent, - - 1	2	0
Total, - - 3	6	4

Produce.

10 Bushels, - - 1	17	6
Straw ¼ load, - - 0	12	0
Total, - 2	9	6
Expences, - - 3	6	4
Produce, - - 2	9	6
Lofs, - - 0	16	10
Profit by broad-caft, - 0	2	0
Superiority, - - 0	18	10

Observations

This is a very fair comparison of the two methods in the culture of barley, and the result clearly decisive in favour of the broad-cast, but the extreme poverty of the produce not exceeding 12 bushels an acre, which for barley is a paltry crop, shews that drilling at these distances will by no means answer. Instead of 12, the common husbandry ought to have yielded three times 12 bushels If barley is drilled, it certainly must be in very close rows, or it cannot answer This crop was in the proportion of single rows at 18 inches, a width perhaps sufficient for beans The profit of No. 58, at a wider distance, is somewhat an exception to this remark; but 14s. an acre bears no proportion to the advantage of a good broad-cast crop.

Experiment, No 60.

Culture, expences and produce, of five acres of drilled barley.

1767

Culture.

The soil a strong loam on clay; summer fallowed in 1766, receiving five ploughings. In *April,* 1767, stirred again, and after twice harrowing, drilled with

barley

barley, double rows, at 14 inches, on 5 ½ feet lands, ufing one bufhel of feed *per* acre It was once hand-hoed, once weeded, and horfe-hoed with fhim and double mould-board four times; product two quarters an acre.

Expences.

		£	s	d
1766. Five earths,	-	1	17	6
1767. Sixth,	- -	0	7	6
Harrowing,	-	0	1	0
Drilling,	- -	0	1	6
Seed,	- -	0	3	0
Water-furrowing,		0	0	6
Hand-hoeing,	-	0	5	0
Weeding,	-	0	5	0
Shim four times,	-	0	2	8
Double mould-board ditto,		0	4	8
Reaping,	- -	0	5	0
Harvefting,	-	0	3	0
Thrafhing,	-	0	3	0
Carrying out,	-	0	1	0
Rent,	- -	2	4	0
Total,	-	6	4	4

Produce.

		£	s	d
2 Quarters, at 32s	-	3	4	0
Straw 3 quarters of a load,		0	12	0
Total,	- -	3	16	0

Expences,	-	-	£.6	4	4
Produce,	-	-	3	16	o
Lofs,	-	-	-	2	8	4

Obfervations.

Every perfon muft be fenfible, that fuch excellent tillage as this field received, would, in the broad-caft method, have yielded a very confiderable crop of barley; but all thefe advantages are unable to do it with drilling at wide intervals. It is fufficiently evident, that this mode of culture is improper for barley, unlefs the rows are very near each other. Mr. *Arbuthnot* concludes from thefe trials, that barley muft be excluded from the lift of drill crops, unlefs in very narrow intervals, which will juft admit the hand-hoe.

POTATOES.

Experiment, No. 61.

Culture, expences and produce, of three roods of potatoes.

1769.

Culture.

The foil a ftrong loam on clay; yielded beans in 1768, on land 3 ½ feet wide. Slit them

them down in *October* very deep; the end of *March* ploughed them back again, and harrowed and dunged the furrows with 15 loads an acre of yard dung. The land would have been planted early, but Mr. *Arbuthnot* could not get the *Howard* potatoe till the beginning of *May*; he then had a sack of them from Mr. *Howard* of *Greyflock*. The sets were laid on the dung, one row in a furrow, and one foot asunder; covered them with the double plough, turning a furrow from each side the land, which was suffered to remain till the shoots appeared. When a few inches above ground, the land was ploughed down to them, which was repeated till the centers of the old ridges became the furrows. After this they were once hand-hoed, horse-hoed thrice with the shim, and thrice with the double mould-board plough. In *October* they were dug up with prongs; product 102 bushels, each 80*lb*. Many of them were very large, and the size in general improved. They were sent to *Covent-Garden* and other markets; but nobody would purchase them. It was asserted, that the fort had been tried, and they would not boil well. Some were

however

however fold at laft for fets, the reft given
to cows and hogs. the cows had them
inftead of hay, and eat them very greedily
Porkers were fattened on fome, boiled and
mafhed, with a little barley meal mixed
In ftating the proportions *per* acre, I fhall
fuppofe a value for feeding cattle; for
inftance, 2*s.* 6*d.* a bufhel.

Expences.

	£.	s.	d.
Firft ploughing, -	0	8	6
Second ditto, - -	0	4	6
Harrowing, - -	0	1	0
Manuring, - -	4	10	0
Five bufhels fets, -	0	12	6
Slicing and planting, -	0	5	0
Covering, - -	0	2	6
Earthing twice, -	0	5	0
Hand-hoeing, - -	0	4	0
Shim thrice, - - -	0	2	0
Double mould-board ditto,	0	3	6
Digging up, - -	0	8	0
Carting home, &c. -	0	5	0
Total, - -	7	11	6
Rent, &c. - -	1	2	0
	8	13	6

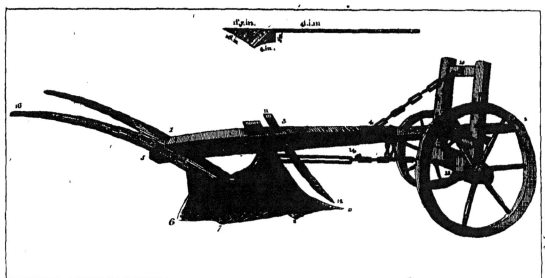

Plate IX page 199

Produce.

136 Bufhels, at 2 *s.* 6 *d.*   -   £. 17   0   0

Expences,   -   8   13   6

Profit,   -   -   -   8   6   6

Obfervations.

There can be little doubt but potatoes
are worth 2 *s.* 6 *d.* a bufhel, of 80 *lb.* for
feeding cattle; and at that rate, the profit
of this experiment is very confiderable.
The expences run high from the manuring
and fuch repeated cleaning; which are circumftances very advantageous to the fucceeding crops; and yet the balance is 8 *l.*
6 *s.* 6 *d.*; far more than could have been
gained by any corn crop. But there is
another circumftance much worthy of noting, which is, the crop being planted fo
late as *May*; a feafon utterly improper for
planting potatoes: this was undoubtedly a
great drawback from the product, which
from an earlier planting would certainly
have been more confiderable. As to the
root not being fo marketable as other forts,
(fuppofing it true) I efteem it a matter of
fmall confequence: the great object in cultivating potatoes is not *Covent Garden*, but
the food of cattle   the firft is very confined, but the latter is univerfal,

V. EXPERIMENTS TO ASCER-
TAIN THE BEST COURSE
OF CROPS.

In the range of experimental hufbandry, there is nothing demands greater attention than the courfe of crops · the adapting a proper fucceffion to each foil, is the great object of rural œconomics. It is of very little confequence to be able to cultivate any crop fingly, ever fo well, unlefs it unites properly with others to form a courfe beneficial upon the whole. When many fields have been cropped extremely different, and regifters kept of them ; there muft appear from a general view, ftrong reafons for concluding fome courfes much more beneficial than others.

To affert that the arranging of crops muft be a matter of chance, accident, or caprice, would be abfolutely abfurd : It is true, no man can fay, I will, in fpite of feafons, fow a field with fuch or fuch grain ; but in thirty nine inftances out of forty, he has it in his power to chufe. A field is fowing with barley—fhall I throw in clover, or let it alone ? A field has yielded wheat ; fhall I take a crop of barley, or

4   turnips ?

turnips? If a man knows not which courſe is moſt advantageous, what egregious blunders will he commit? We ſee theſe blunders committed every day through whole counties; and all for a want of poſ-ſeſſing the requiſite knowledge in this ma-terial point. They who ſow four or five ſucceſſive crops of white corn, know not this part of huſbandry; but ſurely we may aſſert that there are fixed and determined courſes, not a little worthy the attention of ſuch men; inſtead of ſuppoſing that the whole is a matter in which farmers will neceſſarily judge right.

The method here purſued, is to ſtate the crops yielded by certain fields; and after ſtriking a balance of profit and loſs, to com-pare them together, to diſcover which fields have been moſt profitable, and in what degree owing to variations of crops.

Experiment, No. 62.

Courſe—Graſs ploughed for

1. Peaſe	3. Fallow
2. Winter tares	4. Wheat.

Three acres: the ſoil a ſtrong loam on clay.

1767.

Ploughed up the lay for peafe; the crop 10 bufhels an acre.

Expences.

		£		
Ploughing,	- -	0	8	6
3 Bufhels feed,	- -	0	9	0
Sowing,	- -	0	0	3
Harrowing,	- -	0	1	6
Water-furrowing,	-	0	1	0
Topping thiftles,	-	0	0	6
Cutting,	- -	0	3	0
Harvefting,	- -	0	2	0
Thrafhing 10 bufhels,	-	0	3	4
Rent, &c.	- -	1	2	0
		2	11	1

Produce.

		£		
10 Bufhels, at 30s.	£.1	17	6	
Straw,	- -	0	12	0
		2	9	6
Lofs,	- -	0	1	7

1768.

Sowed winter tares; eaten by horfes in foiling in the ftable, began in *June*. the three acres kept 10 horfes 6 weeks, at 7s. *per* horfe *per* week; which 7s. was calcu-lated by the faving in oats and hay.

	£	s	d
1 Bufhel of oats, —	0	2	6
3 ½ Trufs of hay, — —	0	4	8
	0	7	2

Expences.

	£	s	d
Ploughing with 4 horfes, —	0	9	0
Sowing, — — —	0	0	3
Seed, 2 bufhels, — —	0	10	0
Harrowing, — —	0	1	6
Striking furrows, — —	0	0	9
Water-furrowing, —	0	1	0
Mowing and carrying. N. B This was done by the carter, therefore coft nothing; but as he might be employed about other work, where the food dry meat, I charge — —	0	5	0
Rent, — — —	1	2	0
	2	9	6

Produce.

	£	s	d
Keeping 10 horfes 6 weeks, at 7s. — 21 l. the three acres, or per acre, —	7	0	0
Expences, — —	2	9	6
Profit, — —	4	10	6

1769.

It was then intended for wheat, but the black bent came fo thick after ploughing, that it was ridged up for fome other crop. From the middle of *April* till *June*, the black bent was fed with fheep, by lodging them in it from a common. After this it was fallowed, and in *October* fown with wheat; the crop 4 quarters an acre.

Expences.

Firft ploughing,	o	7	6
Harrowing,	o	1	o
Landing up with double mould-board plough,	o	2	1
Water-furrows,	o	1	o
Second ploughing 12 inches deep,	o	12	o
Third, hunting down,	o	7	6
Fourth, crofs ploughing,	o	9	o
Ox-harrowing twice,	o	2	o
Fifth ploughing,	o	7	6
Landing up the fixth,	o	3	9
2 Bufhels feed,	o	12	o
Sowing,	o	3	o
Sixth earth ploughing,	o	3	9
Water-furrowing,	o	1	o
Reaping,	o	10	o
Harvefting,	o	3	6
Carry over,	4	6	7

		£ s d
Brought over, -	£.	4 6 7
Thrashing, at 3 s. 4 d. -		0 12 4
Carrying out, - -		0 2 0
Rent, - - -		2 4 0
		7 4 11

Produce.

4 Quarters, at 5 s. 6 d. -		10 10 0
Straw, 2 loads, at 21 s. -		2 2 0
		12 12 0
Expences, - -		7 4 11
Profit, - -		5 7 1

Recapitulation.

1768. Winter tares . profit,		4 10 6
1769. Fallow, - -		
1770. Wheat ditto, -		5 7 1
		9 17 7
1767. Peafe : lofs, -		0 1 7
Profit, - - -		9 16 0
Or *per ann.* - -		2 9 0

Obfervations.

This courfe is by no means an advantageous one. The pea crop not advifable by

any

any means. Had oats been harrowed in, probably the balance would have been a confiderable profit inftead of lofs; and the fallow year, in all probability, might have yielded a profitable crop of beans, fucceeded by wheat; but this is uncertain. However, the profit of 2*l* 9*s*. an acre clear, is by no means to be defpifed. It much exceeds what the farmers in general make.

Experiment, No. 63.

Courfe—1. Fallow   3. Wheat
      2. Spring tares   4. Oats.

Three acres: foil, a ftrong loam on clay, but not deep.

1767.

Fallowed for fpring tares; the crop mown and given to fheep in a pen. The three acres kept 80 ewes a month, at 2*d*. a week. During which time they made 20 loads of dung from 2 loads of ftraw.

Expences.

	£.		
Two ploughings, - - -	0	9	0
Third ditto, - -	0	9	0
Part of it 12 inches deep.			
Landing it up into 3 bout lands,	0	7	6
Water-furrowing, - -	0	1	0
Gathering 2 into one in *May*,	0	7	6
Carry over, •	1	14	0

	£		
Brought over, -	1	14	0
Sowing, - -	0	0	3
2 Bushels of tares, - -	0	9	0
Harrowing, - - -	0	1	6
Striking furrows, - -	0	0	9
Mowing and giving the sheep, &c.	0	5	0
Rent, &c. - - -	2	4	0
	4	14	6

Produce.

Keeping 80 Sheep 4 weeks, at 2 *d.* a sheep, 2 *l.* 13 *s.* 4 *d.* the third of which is, -	0	17	9
Loss, - -	3	16	9

1769.

After the tares wheat was sown; the product 2 quarters *per* acre.

Expences.

	£		
Ploughing, - - -	0	7	6
Harrowing, - - -	0	1	6
Seed, 2 bushels - -	0	11	0
Sowing, - - -	0	0	3
15 Sacks *per* acre of rabbit dung, and sowing, -	0	19	0
Carriage ditto, - -	0	2	6
Striking furrows, - -	0	0	9
Carry over, -	2	2	6

		£.		
Brought over,	-	2	2	6
Water-furrowing,	-	0	1	0
Weeding,	-	0	6	0
Reaping,	-	0	8	0
Harvesting,	-	0	3	6
Thrashing,	-	0	6	0
Carrying out,	-	0	1	0
Rent, &c.	-	1	2	0
		4	10	0

Produce.

2 Quarters, at 44 s.	-	4	8	0
Straw, 1 ½ load,	-	1	10	0
		5	18	0
Expences,	-	4	10	0
Profit,	-	1	8	0

1770.

Ploughing,	-	0	5	0
Harrowing,	-	0	1	6
3 Bushels oats,	-	0	8	6
Sowing,	-	0	0	3
Striking furrows with double mould-board plough,	-	0	1	2
Water-furrowing,	-	0	1	0
Mowing,	-	0	1	8
Carry over,	-	0	19	1

Brought over,	-	£.0	19	1
Harvesting,	- -	0	4	6
Thrashing,	- -	0	4	6
Rent,	- -	1	2	0
Total,	- -	2	10	1

Produce.

3 Quarters of oats,	-	3	0	0
Straw 1½ load,	-	1	10	0
Total,	-	4	10	0
Expences,	- -	2	10	1
Profit,	- -	1	19	11

Recapitulation.

1768. Tares, lofs,	-		3	16	9
1769. Wheat, profit, £.1	8	0			
1770. Oats ditto,	1	19	11		
				3	7	11
Lofs,	-	-		0	8	10
Or *per annum,*	-		0	2	2

Observations.

This courfe is as difadvantageous, as can well be imagined. To give a complete fallow for a crop of fpring tares, is what no perfon would willingly do, unlefs he fore-

fees

fees a great want of food for his ftock:
this occafioned the firft lofs, and a poor
crop of wheat fucceeding, rendered the
whole uncommonly difadvantageous. The
principal profit here, is reaped from fowing
oats after wheat; bad hufbandry in general,
but clover was fown with this wheat, which
mifcarried, and that was the reafon of fowing the oats.

Experiment, No. 64.
Courfe.

1. Barley   3 Clover
2. Clover   4 Wheat.

Three acres; the foil a ftrong loam on
clay,

1767.

Sown with barley; the produce 2 quarters and a half *per* acre.

Expences.

	£	s	d
Firft ploughing, 12 inches deep in winter, 1766, -	0	12	0
Slitting down in *April*, -	0	7	6
Two bufhels barley, -	0	6	0
Sowing, -	0	0	3
Harrowing, -	0	1	6
Striking furrows, -	0	0	9
Water-furrowing, -	0	1	0
Carry over, -	1	9	0

Brought over,	-	£ 1	9	0
Mowing,	-	0	1	6
Harvesting,	-	0	4	6
Thrashing,	-	0	4	6
Carrying out,	-	0	2	6
Rent,	-	1	2	0
Total,	-	3	4	0

Produce.

2 ¼ quarters, at 30s.	-	3	15	0
Straw one load,	-	1	0	0
Total,	-	4	15	0
Expences,	-	3	4	0
Profit,	-	1	11	0

1768.

Clover was sown with the barley; it was mown twice for hay, and yielded 3 ½ loads: the first mowing the 10th of *June,* to cut off the black bent, that it might not shed . the second was the beginning of *August.*

Expences.

10 *lb.* Seed clover,	-	0	3	4
Sowing,	-	0	0	3
Manuring in *January* 12 loads an acre yard dung and coal ashes, at 7s.	-	4	4	0
Carry over,	-	4	7	7

E e 3

	£.		
Brought over, -	4	7	7
Spreading, - -	0	1	6
Mowing twice, -	0	4	9
Making twice, - -	0	12	0
Carting and ſtacking ditto,	0	10	0
Rent, - -	1	2	0
Total, -	6	17	10

Produce.

3 ¼ Loads, at 3 *l.* -	10	10	0
Sheep feed, - -	0	5	0
Total, -	10	15	0
Expences, -	6	17	10
Profit, - -	3	17	2

1769.

Mown once; produce 1 ¼ load.

Expences.

Mowing, - -	0	2	6
Making, - -	0	6	0
Carting and ſtacking, -	0	5	0
Rent, - -	1	2	0
Total, - -	1	15	6

Produce.

Produce.

1 ½ Load hay, at 3 *l.* —	£.4	10	0
After-grafs, — —	0	15	0

Total, —	5	5	0
Expences, —	1	15	6

Profit, — —	3	9	6

1770.

Wheat harrowed in on one trench-ploughing; produce 3 ½ quarters *per* acre.

Expences.

Trench-ploughing with *Ducket's* plough in *September*, —	0	13	0
Seven pecks feed, —	0	9	0
Sowing, — —	0	0	3
Harrowing, —	0	3	0
Water-furrowing, —	0	1	0
Striking furrows, — —	0	0	6
Weeding, — —	0	7	0
Reaping, — —	0	10	0
Harvefting, —	0	4	0
Thrafhing, — —	0	10	6
Carrying out, — —	0	1	9
Rent, — —	1	2	0

Total, —	4	2	0

Produce.

		£.		
3 ½ quarters, at 50s.	-	8	15	0
Straw, 2 loads, at 24s.		2	8	0
Total,	-	11	3	0
Expences,	- -	4	2	0
Profit,	- -	7	1	0

Recapitulation.

1767. Barley, profit,	-	1	11	0
1768. Clover, ditto,	-	3	17	2
1769. Ditto,	-	3	9	6
1770. Wheat, ditto,	-	7	1	0
Total,	- -	15	18	8
Or per ann.	-	3	19	8

Observations.

This course is perfectly confiftent with the beft ideas of modern hufbandry, and we accordingly find it very profitable: there cannot well be a ftronger argument for adopting a beneficial courfe of crops, than the refult of this. Near 4l. per acre clear profit per ann. fhews what the foil is capable of when properly managed. The material point, which calls for a particular remark, is the leaving the clover two

years

years on the land. It is here evidently
moſt excellent huſbandry, notwithſtanding
the black bent appeared in it ſo early. A
clear profit of 3*l* 9*s*. *per* acre, on the ſecond crop is an object of no trifling
magnitude; and the great produce of
wheat following ſhews plainly, that that
crop did not ſuffer the leaſt from the clover
lying two years inſtead of one.

Another point, which I ſhall beg leave
to obſerve, is the ſucceſs which here attends trench-ploughing the clover-lay for
wheat. This is an uncommon practice,
but it is evidently an excellent one· it is
what the farmers are fearful of, tho' plainly
without reaſon

Experiment, No. 65.
Courſe.

1. Tares and flax   3 Tares
2. Fallow   4. Wheat.

Six acres, the ſoil a good mellow loam
on brick earth.

1767.

In 1766, it yielded wheat, and one half
ploughed afterwards for tares: they were
cut for horſes, and kept eight a month.
Flax was ſown on the other half, which
was pulled in *Auguſt,* and came to 4*l. per*
acre.

Account of the tares.

Expences.

Ploughed 12 inches deep,	£.	o	12	o
In *April* a second earth,	–	o	7	6
2 Bushels tares,	–	o	9	o
Sowing,	–	o	o	3
Harrowing,	–	o	1	6
Mowing and carting,	–	o	5	o
Rent,	–	1	2	o
Total,	–	2	17	3

Produce.

Keeping 8 horses a month, at 7*s.*				
11 *l.* 4*s.* the 3d of which is		3	14	8
Expences,	–	2	17	3
Profit,	–	o	17	5

Account of the flax.
Expences.

Ploughing,	–	o	12	o
2 Bushels flax feed,	–	o	9	o
Sowing,	–	o	o	3
Harrowing,	–	o	2	o
Pulling,	–	o	8	o
Binding and bringing home,	o	5	o
Watering,	–	o	3	o
Carry over,	–	1	19	3

	£.		
Brought over, —	1	19	3
Sodding and unsodding,	0	3	0
Spreading on grafs, —	0	5	0
Turning, — —	0	2	6
Gathering, binding and carting,	0	8	0
Rent, — — —	1	2	0
Total, —	3	19	9

Produce.

Yielded *per* acre, —	4	0	0
Expences, — —	3	19	1
Profit, — —	0	0	11

1768.

Ploughing 12 inches deep in autumn, —	0	12	0
Water-furrowing, —	0	1	0
Hunting down in *May*, —	0	7	6
In *June* crofs ploughing, —	0	7	6
Fourth earth in *July*, ftirring,	0	5	0
Ox-harrowed in *Auguft*,	0	3	0
Defigned for wheat; but fuch a deluge of rain in *September*, that could not go on; but furrows were drawn in the low places, — —	0	0	6
Water-furrowing, —	0	1	0
Carry over, —	1	17	6

Brought over,	-	£. 1	17	6
In *May* trench-ploughed,		0	13	0
2 Bushels tares,	-	0	9	0
Harrowing, -	-	0	1	0
Rent, -	-	1	2	0
Total, -	-	4	2	6

Produce.

Sheep fed. worth *per* acre,		0	5	0
Loss, -	-	3	17	0

1770.

Trench-ploughed it in *August*,		0	13	0
Ox-harrowing, -	-	0	3	0
Landing-up in *September*,		0	5	0
Harrowing, -	-	0	1	0
2 Bushels wheat, -	-	0	10	6
Sowing, -	-	0	0	3
Ploughing in, -	-	0	5	0
Water-furrowing,	-	0	1	0
15 Sacks rabbits dung,	-	1	0	0
Sowing, -	-	0	1	6
Weeding, -	-	0	6	0
Reaping, -	-	0	8	0
Harvesting, -	-	0	3	6
Carrying, -	-	0	1	3
Thrashing, -	-	0	7	6
Rent, -	-	1	2	0
Total, -		5	8	6

Produce.

2 ½ quarters, at 48 s.	-	£.6	0	0
Straw, 1 ½ load, at 25 s.		1	17	6
Total,	- -	7	17	6
Expences,	- -	5	8	6
Profit,	- -	2	9	0

Recapitulation.

1768,9. Tares, lofs,	-	3	17	0
1767. Tares, profit, £.0 17 5			
1770 Wheat, ditto, 2 9 0			
		3	6	5
Lofs,	- -	0	10	7
Or *per ann.*	- -	0	2	7

1768,9. Tares, lofs,	-	3	17	0
1767. Flax, profit, 0 0 11			
1770. Wheat, ditto, 2 9 0			
		2	9	11
Lofs,	- -	1	7	1
Or *per ann.*	-	0	6	9

Obfervations

An unfortunate feafon in preventing the wheat fowing, rendered this courfe almoft

3   as

as bad a one as could have happened. Tares here paid nothing for an extraordinary expence beſtowed on them. Had beans been ſown inſtead of the ſecond crop of tares, the account would have been very different.

Flax anſwers very badly in this trial; the crop is not large, but the expences run very high. It is here however to be obſerved, that this field is exceſſive poor, and had not received a load of dung of 20 years.

Experiment, No. 66,

Courſe.

1. Oats   3. Fallow
2. Peaſe   4. Wheat.

Three acres; the ſoil the ſame as No. 65.

1767.

In 1766 it yielded clover, ploughed up, and harrowed in oats; the crop 4¼ quarters an acre.

Expences.

	£	s	d
Ploughing, - -	0	9	0
3 Buſhels oats, -	0	6	9
Harrowing, - -	0	1	6
Water-furrowing, - -	0	1	0
Mowing, - -	0	1	8
Harveſting, - -	0	4	6
Carry over, -	1	4	5

5

	£.		
Brought over,	1	4	5
Thrashing, - -	0	6	9
Rent, - - -	1	2	0
Total, -	2	13	2

Produce.

4 ½ Quarters, at 17*s.* -	3	16	6
Straw 1 ½ load, at 16*s.* -	1	4	0
Total, - -	5	0	6
Expences, - -	2	13	2
Profit, - -	2	7	4

1768.

Ploughed up the oat stubble in *January*, - -	0	7	6
2 Bushels 1 peck pease, at 5*s.* 6*d.*	0	12	3
Sowing, - -	0	0	3
Harrowing in in *February*,	0	1	6
Also 10 sacks kiln dust, -	1	0	0
Carriage of ditto, - -	0	2	6
Sowing, - -	0	1	6
Striking furrows, -	0	0	9
Topping thistles, -	0	0	4
Cutting, - -	0	1	8
Harvesting, - -	0	3	0
Thrashing, - -	0	3	0
Carry over, -	2	14	3

		£.	s.	d.
Brought over,	-	2	14	3
Carrying out,	-	0	0	9
Rent,	-	1	2	0
Total,	-	3	17	6

Produce.

	£.	s.	d.
12 Bushels, at 36s.	2	14	0
Straw, 3 quarters load,	0	15	0
	3	9	0
Lofs, - -	0	8	6

1769.

		£.	s.	d.
Ploughed in autumn,	-	0	7	6
Water-furrowed,	-	0	1	0
In the spring the black bent came thick; it was fed by sheep till the middle of *May*, then hunted down,	-	0	5	0
Crofs ploughing,	-	0	7	6
Stirring,	-	0	5	0
Ox-harrowing,	-	0	3	0
Landing up in *Auguft*,	-	0	5	0
2 Bushels wheat,	-	0	11	0
Sowing in *October*,	-	0	0	3
Harrowing,	-	0	0	6
Water-furrowing,	-	0	1	0
In *February* 15 facks of rabbit dung,	-	1	0	0
Carry over,	-	3	6	9

		£.	s.	d.
Brought over,	-	3	6	9
Sowing,	- -	0	1	6
Reaping,	- -	0	8	0
Harvesting,	- -	0	4	0
Thrashing,	- -	0	10	6
Carrying out,	-	0	1	9
Rent,	- - -	2	4	0
Total,	-	6	16	6

Produce.

3½ quarters, at 48 s.	-	8	8	0
Straw 2 loads, at 25 s.	-	2	10	0
Total,	- -	10	18	0
Expences,	-	6	16	6
Profit,	- -	4	1	6

Recapitulation.

1767. Oats, profit,	-	2	7	4
1770 Wheat ditto,	-	4	1	6
Total,	- -	6	8	10
1768. Pease, lofs,	-	0	8	6
Profit,	- -	6	0	4
Or *per ann.*	-	1	10	1

Observations.

A pea crop to prove unprofitable is not uncommon; but to be neceffitated to fucceed it with a fallow, was a circumſtance that could not fail of making this courſe indifferent; yet the profit amounts to 1 *l.* 10 *s. per* acre *per ann.* which is vaſtly more than one would at firſt ſight imagine: indeed it is ſo much, that it is difficult to allow the courſe to be ſo bad as it appears. Probably it would have proved more advantageous, had not the whole field been peſtered with the running ſow-thiſtle, an extreme bad weed.

Experiment, No. 67.
Courſe.

1. Beans.   2. Wheat.   3. Tares.

One acre and three roods; the ſoil a ſtrong yellow loam on brick earth. In 1766 it was a very bad old weedy lay.

1767

Dibbled with beans; the product five and a half quarters an acre.

Expences.

	£.		
Ploughing in *January,* -	0	11	0
Harrowing, - -	0	1	0
Dibbling, - - -	0	5	6
2 ¼ Buſhels tick beans, -	0	8	9
Harrowing, - -	0	1	0
Striking furrows, -	0	0	9
Twice hand-hoeing, -	1	0	0
Carry over,	2	8	0

		£.	s.	d.
Brought over,	-	2	8	0
Topping,	-	0	0	6
Reaping,	-	0	8	0
Harvesting,	-	0	3	6
Thrashing,	-	0	6	5
Rent, &c.	-	1	2	0
Total,	-	4	8	5

Produce.

5 ½ quarters, at 25 s.	-	6	17	6
Straw 2 loads, at 25 s.	-	2	10	0
Total,	-	9	7	6
Expences,		4	8	5
Profit,	-	4	19	1

1768.

Ploughed the stubble once, and harrowed in wheat : the crop 4 quarters an acre.

Expences.

Ploughing,	-	0	9	0
Harrowing,	-	0	1	6
Two bushels feed,	-	0	12	0
Sowing,	-	0	0	3
Water-furrowing,	-	0	1	0
Reaping,	-	0	9	0
Harvesting,	-	0	3	6
Thrashing,	-	0	12	0
Carrying,	-	0	2	0
Rent,	-	1	2	0
Total,		3	12	3

Produce.

			£.			
4 Quarters, at 52s. 6d.			£.	10	10	0
Straw 2 loads, at 25s.	-			2	10	0
Total,	-	-		13	0	0
Expences,		-		3	12	3
Profit,	-	-		9	7	9

1769.

Ploughed the wheat ſtubble once, and harrowed in winter tares; cut green for ſoiling horſes; they kept eight four weeks.

Expences.

Ploughing,	-	-	0	9	0
Two buſhels tares,		-	0	10	0
Sowing,	-	-	0	0	3
Harrowing,	-	-	0	1	6
Striking furrows with double mould-board plough,		-	0	1	2
Water-furrowing,		-	0	1	0
Mowing and carrying,			0	5	0
Rent,	-	-	1	2	0
Total,	-	-	2	9	11

Produce.

The acre and ¼ kept 8 horſes 4 weeks, at 7s. which is *per* acre,	-	-	6	8	0
Expences,	-		2	9	11
Profit,	-	-	3	18	1

1770.

Ploughed up the tare ftubble in *September*, and harrowed in rye; the beginning of *March*, and in part of *April*, eat off the rye with fheep. It kept 20 couple five weeks; it was then ploughed four times, and planted in *Auguft* with cabbages, in equally-diftant rows, 2 ½ feet afunder.

Expences.

	£.	s.	d.
Ploughing, - -	0	7	6
Two bufhels rye, -	0	7	0
Sowing, - -	0	0	3
Harrowing, - -	0	1	6
Striking furrows with double mould-board plough,	0	1	2
Water-furrowing, -	0	1	0
Ploughing ten inches deep,	0	10	0
Crofs ditto, - -	0	9	0
Stirring, - -	0	7	6
Rolling with fpiky roller,	0	2	0
Manuring with night foil, 7 loads *per* acre, -	3	17	0
Spreading, - -	0	1	3
Ox-harrowing, -	0	1	0
Ploughing, - -	0	7	6
Spiky roller, - -	0	2	0
Harrowing, -	0	1	0
Planting, - -	0	10	0
Horfe-hoeing, fhim twice,	0	1	4
Hand-hoeing once, -	0	4	0
Rent, - -	1	2	0
Total, -	8	14	0

Recapitulation.

		£.	s.	d.
1767. Beans, profit,		4	19	1
1768. Wheat ditto,	-	9	7	9
1769. Tares ditto,	-	3	18	1
Total,	-	18	4	11
Average,	-	6	1	7

Experiment, No. 68.

Course.

1. Drilled beans 3. Drilled beans
2. Drilled wheat 4. Winter tares.

Five acres; the foil good; a ftrong loam on clay.

1767.

This crop of drilled beans is minuted in *Experiment*, No. 38.

			£	s.	d.
Product, 3 quarters, at 25 s.			3	15	0
Straw,	-	-	1	0	0
Total,	-	-	4	15	0
Expences,	-	-	3	16	6
Profit,	-	-	0	18	6

1768.

This drilled wheat is that of *Experiment*, No. 36.

			£	s.	d.
Product, 3 quarters, 52 s. 6 d.			7	17	6
Straw,	-	-	1	5	0
			9	2	6

I

			£.		
Product,	-	-	9	2	6
Expences,		-	5	8	11

Profit,	-	-	3	13	7

1769.

Thefe drilled beans regiftered in *Experiment*, No. 40.

Produce, 3 quarters,		-	3	15	0
Straw,	-	-	1	5	0

Total,	-	-	5	0	0
Expences,		-	3	6	11

Profit,	-	-	1	13	1

1770.

In *October* the bean ftubble was ploughed up with 2 horfes, 8 or 9 inches deep, and 2 bufhels *per* acre of winter tares harrowed in the crop mown for foiling horfes, and kept 12 two months.

Expences.

Ploughing,	-	-	0	5	0
Seed,	-	-	0	10	0
Sowing,	-		0	0	3
Harrowing,	-	-	0	1	6
Striking furrows,		-	1	2	0
Water-furrowing,		-	0	0	3
Mowing and carrying,		-	0	5	0
Rent, &c.	-	-	1	2	0
Total,	-	-	2	5	2

Produce.

Keeping 12 horses 8 weeks, at
7s. 6d.—36l.; the fifth is £.7 4 0
    Expences,   -   2 5 2
    _____

    Profit,   -   -   4 18 10
    _____

Recapitulation.

	£	s	d
1767. Drilled beans, profit,	0	18	6
1768. Ditto wheat, ditto, -	3	13	7
1769. Ditto beans, ditto,	1	13	1
1770. Winter tares, ditto,	4	18	10
Total, - -	11	4	0
Which is *per ann.* -	2	16	0

Observations.

Both the drill husbandry, and that of
winter tares, figure very advantageously in
this course, which is upon the whole unexceptionable: the vast produce of a good
crop of winter tares renders them remarkably profitable.

Experiment, No. 69.
Course.

1. Oats, stubble left   3 Drilled wheat
2. Fallow   4. Drilled beans.

Three acres; the soil a strong loam on
clay.   3

1768.

In autumn, 1767, the old ftubble was ploughed up, 12 inches deep, and tilled through this year, and in autumn following.

1769.

Drilled with wheat, double rows on three-feet lands, three pecks of feed *per* acre. In the fpring it was manured with twenty facks *per* acre of rabbits dung; it was hand-hoed once, weeded once, and horfe-hoed twice, once with fhim, and once with the double mould-board plough . the crop two quarters *per* acre.

Expences.

Ploughing,	-	-	£.0	12	0
Hunting,	-	-	0	7	6
Crofs ditto,	-		0	7	6
Stirring,	-	-	0	7	6
Ox-harrowing,	-		0	4	6
Landing up with double mould- board plough,	-		0	2	1
Drilling,	-	-	0	1	6
Seed,	-	-	-	0	2	6
Striking,	-	-	0	1	2
Water-furrowing,	-		0	1	0
Rabbit dung,	-		1	8	6
Hand-hoeing,	-	-	0	6	0
Shim,	-	-	0	0	8
Double mould-board plough,		0	1	2

Carry over,	-		4	3	7

		£.		
Brought over,	-	4	3	7
Weeding,	-	0	6	0
Reaping,	-	0	8	0
Harvesting,	-	0	3	6
Thrashing,	-	0	6	0
Three years rent, &c.	-	3	6	0
Total,	-	8	13	1

Produce.

2 Quarters, at 44s.	4	8	0
Straw,	1	0	0
	5	8	0
Lofs,	3	5	1

From this crop it is extremely evident, that the mere resting land is of no benefit without tillage; the crop could scarcely fail being unprofitable with such an accumulation of expences. It should however be remarked, that this field, when first Mr. *Arbuthnot* had it, was remarkably foul and poor.

1770.

These beans are minuted in *Experiment*, No. 43.

The profit *per* acre 4*l.* 11*s.* 8*d.*

Recapitulation.

1770. Drilled beans, profit,	4	11	8
1769. Wheat, lofs, -	3	5	1
Profit, - -	1	6	7
Or *per ann.* -	0	6	7

This field is now drilled with wheat.

Experiment, No. 70.
Courfe.

1. Fallow   3. Wheat
2 Drilled beans   4. Drilled beans.

Three acres; the foil a ftrong clay; taken in miferable order, quite foul and poor.

1767.

In 1766, yielded oats, the ftubble of which was ploughed up in *May*, 1767, and hemp fown; but the crop mifcarried: it was then landed up for the winter.

1768.

In the fpring, drilled with horfe-beans, kept clean by hand and horfe-hocing, the crop 3 quarters *per* acre.

Expences.

	£.		
Firft ploughing, -	0	9	0
Harrowing, - -	0	1	6
Crofs ploughing, -	0	7	6
Landing up, - -	0	7	6
Water-furrowing, -	0	1	0
Drilling, - -	0	1	6
Harrowing, - -	0	0	6
1 Bufhel and a half feed, -	0	5	3
Water-furrowing, - -	0	1	0
Hand-hoeing, - -	0	5	0
Shim, - -	0	0	8
Double mould-board plough,	0	1	2
Carry over, -	2	1	7

	£.		
Brought over, -	2	1	7
Ditto both again, -	0	1	10
Pulling, -	0	7	0
Harvesting, -	0	3	0
Thrashing, -	0	4	6
Rent, -	2	4	0
Total, -	5	1	11

Produce.

3 Quarters, at 30*s.* -	4	10	0
1 Load straw, -	1	0	0
Total, -	5	10	0
Expences, -	5	1	11
Profit, -	0	8	1

1769.

Ploughed up the bean stubble in autumn; ploughed it again in *November*; in *January* landed up, and in *March* sowed with wheat, and with it 20 sacks an acre of rabbit dung. It was weeded; the crop 2 quarters and a half *per* acre.

Expences.

First ploughing, -	0	7	6
Second ditto, -	0	7	6
Water-furrowing, -	0	1	0
Two bushels seed, -	0	13	0
Sowing, -	0	0	3
Carry over, -	1	9	3

	£.		
Brought over, -	1	9	3
Rabbit dung, &c. -	1	8	2
Weeding, -	0	6	0
Reaping, -	0	8	0
Harvesting, -	0	3	6
Thrashing, -	0	3	9
Rent, &c. - -	1	2	0
Total, - -	5	0	8

Produce.

Two quarters and a half, at 44 s.	5	10	0
Straw 1 load and a half, at 25 s.	1	17	6
Total, - -	7	7	6
Expences, -	5	0	8
Profit, - -	2	6	10

1770.

This crop of drilled beans is that of *Experiment*, No. 42.

Profit *per* acre 6 *l.* 0 *s.* 5 *d*

Recapitulation.

1767. Fallow.			
1768. Drilled beans, profit,	0	8	1
1769. Wheat ditto, -	2	6	10
1770. Drilled beans ditto,	6	0	5
Total, - -	8	15	4
Or *per ann.* - -	2	3	10

Experiment, No. 71.
Course.

1. Drilled peafe   3. Beans
2. Wheat   4. Wheat.

Five acres; the foil a fandy loam.

1767.

This is the crop regiftered in *Experiment*, No. 45. Profit 6*s*. 8*d*.

1768.

This drilled wheat is minuted under *Experiment*, No. 35. The profit 2*l*. 8*s*. 7*d*. *per* acre.

1769.

Drilled beans. See *Experiment*, No. 41. Profit 2*l*. 5*s*. 7*d*.

1770.

The bean ftubble ploughed directly after harveft, and after harrowing, and hunting, fown broad-caft with wheat. In *February* manured with rabbit dung. Product 2 quarters *per* acre.

Expences.

		£.		
Firft ploughing,	-	0	10	0
Harrowing,	-	0	1	0
Second ploughing,	-	0	7	6
Harrowing,	- -	0	1	0
Two bufhels feed,	- -	0	12	6
Sowing,	- -	0	0	3
Carry over,	-	1	12	3

	£.		
Brought over, -	1	12	3
Ploughing in gathering up,	0	5	0
Water-furrowing, -	0	1	0
15 Sacks rabbit dung, -	1	1	6
Weeding, -	0	5	0
Reaping, -	0	8	0
Harvesting, -	0	3	6
Thrashing, -	0	6	0
Rent, - -	1	2	0
Total, -	5	4	3

Produce.

2 Quarters, at 48 s. -	4	16	0
1 Load straw, -	1	5	0
Total, -	6	1	0
Expences, -	5	4	3
Profit, -	0	16	9

Recapitulation.

1767. Drilled pease, profit,	0	6	8
1768. Ditto wheat, ditto,	2	8	7
1769. Ditto beans, ditto,	2	5	7
1770. Wheat ditto, -	0	16	9
Total, -	5	17	7
Or per ann. -	1	9	4

This field was also extremely foul and poor: it is now winter tares, succeeded by a bastard fallow.

Experiment, No. 72.

Courſe.

1. Drilled beans   3. Ditto beans
2. Ditto wheat   4. Ditto wheat.

Eight acres regiſtered in the *Experiments* 28, &c.

Average profit *per annum* of the four years, 3 *l.* 15 *s.* 2 *d.*

Experiment, No. 73.

Courſe.

1. Fallow   3 Ditto wheat
2. Drilled beans   4. Ditto beans.

See *Experiments*, No. 32, 33, and 34.

Average profit of the 4 years, 1 *l.* 1 *s.* 11 *d.*

Experiment, No. 73.*

Courſe.

1. Oats   3. Fallow
2. Tares   4. Drilled wheat

Seven acres and 3 quarters; the ſoil a ſtrong loam on brick earth.

1767.

Yielded clover in 1766, ploughed it in ſpring, and harrowed in oats; the crop 4 quarters *per* acre.

Expences.

Ploughing,	–	–	£. 0 10	0
3 Buſhels oats,		–	0 6	9
Sowing,	–		0 0	3
Carry over,		–	0 17	0

Brought over,	-	£. 0	17	0
Harrowing,	-	0	2	0
Water-furrowing,	-	0	1	0
Mowing,	-	0	2	0
Harvefting,	-	0	5	0
Thrafhing,	-	0	6	0
Rent,	-	1	2	0
Total,	-	2	15	0

Produce.

4 Quarters, at 16s.	-	3	4	0
2 Load ftraw,	-	1	12	0
Total,	-	4	16	0
Expences,	-	2	15	0
Profit,	-	2	1	0

1768.

Ploughed up in *January*, and harrowed in tares; but they nearly failed; the value not more than 8s. an acre.

Ploughing,	-	0	9	0
2 Bufhels feed,	-	0	8	0
Harrowing,	-	0	2	0
Sowing,	-	0 ,	0	3
Water-furrowing,	-	0	1	0
Rent,	-	1	2	0
Total,	-	2	2	3

Produce.

Value of food,	-	0	8	0
Lofs,	-	1	14	3

VOL. II.   G g

1770.

For this wheat, fee *Experiment*, No. 37.
Profit 4*l.* 17*s.*

Recapitulation.

1767. Oats, profit,	-	£.2	1	0
1770. Wheat ditto,	-	4	17	0
Total,	-	-	6	18	0
1768. Tares, lofs,	-	1	14	3
Profit,	-	-	5	3	9
Or *per annum*,	-	1	5	11

Experiment, No. 74.

Courfe.

1. Oats. 2. Drilled Peafe. 3. Barley.

1769

Four acres and a half; the foil a light
loam on brick earth ; the crop of oats five
quarters and a half

Expences.

Ploughing,	-	-	0	10	0
Three bufhels feed,	-	-	0	6	9
Harrowing,	-	-	0	2	0
Sowing,	-	-	0	0	3
Water-furrowing,	-	-	0	1	0
Mowing,	-	-	0	2	0
Harvefting,	-	-	0	5	0
Thrafhing,	-	-	0	8	3
Rent,	-	-	1	2	0
Total,	-	-	2	17	3

Produce.

5 Quarters and a half, at 17*s.*	£.4	13	6
Straw 2 loads,	-	-	1	12	0
Total,	-	-	6	5	6
Expences,		-	2	17	3
Profit,	-	-	3	8	3

1768.

For this crop of drilled peafe, fee *Experiment*, No. 47. Lofs 6*l.* 8*s.* 6*d.*

1769.

In *April* ploughed it with double coulters, crofs ploughed it and broke the clods, which were very rough, with the fpiky roller; after the roller ox-harrowed it with fix horfes. Without the ufe of this roller, a barley feafon could never have been made. It was fown with three bufhels an acre: after fowing and harrowing clods remaining, it was again rolled with little fpiky roller: the product 4 quarters *per* acre.

Expences.

Ploughing,	-	-	0	7	6
Crofs ditto,	-	-	0	7	6
Spiky rolling,	-	-	0	2	0
Ox-harrowing,	-	0	3	0
Carry over,	-	1	0	0

			£		
Brought over,	-		1	0	0
Three bushels feed,	-		0	9	0
Sowing,	-	-	0	0	3
Harrowing,	-	-	0	1	6
Striking furrows,	-		0	1	2
Spiky rolling,	-	-	0	0	6
Mowing,	-	-	0	2	0
Harvesting,	-		0	4	0
Thrashing,	-	-	0	6	0
Carrying,	-		0	1	0
Rent,	-	-	1	2	0
Total,	-	-	3	7	5

Produce.

			£		
4 Quarters, at 20s.	-		4	0	0
Straw 2 loads,	-	-	1	12	0
Total,	-	-	5	12	0
Expences,	-		3	7	5
Profit,	-	-	2	4	7

Recapitulation.

1768. Drilled pease, loss,			6	8	6
1767. Oats, profit, £. 3	8	3			
1769. Barley, profit, 2	4	7			
			5	12	10
Loss,	-	-	0	15	8
Average,	-	-	0	5	2

Experiment, No. 75.

Courſe.

1. Fallow   3. Madder
2. Madder   4. Madder.

Seven acres; the ſoil a ſandy loam.

Regiſtered in *Experiment*, No. 8. Profit in the four years 165*l*. 0*s*. 6*d*. or *per* acre 23*l*. 11*s*. 6*d*. *Per* acre *per ann.* 7*l*. 17*s*. 2*d*.

Experiment, No. 76.

Courſe.

1. Fallow   3. Madder
2. Madder   4. Madder.

Nine acres; regiſtered ın *Experiment*, No. 9. Profit on the nine, 245*l*. 1*s* which is *per* acre 27*l*. 9*s*. and *per* acre *per ann.* 9*l*. 3*s*.

Experiment, No. 77.

Courſe.

1. Drilled barley   3. Potatoes.
2. Ditto beans

Two acres; the ſoil a ſtrong loam.

1767.

For drilled barley, ſee *Experiment*, No. 59. Loſs 16*s*.

1768.

Drilled with tick beans, double rows, on three-feet lands; product 2 quarters 1 buſhel *per* acre.

Expences.

Ploughing in autumn,	-	£. 0	9	0
Water-furrowing,	-	0	1	0
Drilling in *March*,	-	0	1	6
Two bushels feed,	- -	0	6	0
Striking with double mould-board				
plough,	- -	0	1	2
Water-furrowing,	-	0	1	0
Two hand-hoeings,	- -	0	10	0
Shim once,	-	0	0	8
Double mould-board plough ditto,	0	1	2
Pulling,	-	0	7	0
Harvesting,	- -	0	4	0
Thrashing,	- -	0	2	7
Rent,	- -	1	2	0
Total,	-	3	7	1

Produce.

2 Quarters 2 bushels, at 25 s.	2	13	1
Straw half a load,	-	0	10	0
Total,	- -	3	3	1
Lofs,	- -	0	4	0

1769.

For the potatoes, fee *Experiment*, No. 61. Profit 8 *l.* 6 *s.* 6 *d.*

Recapitulation.

1769. Potatoes, profit,	£.	8	6	6
1767 Ditto barley, lofs,	0	16	0	
1768. Beans, ditto,	0	4	0	
		1	0	0

Profit, - -	7	6	6
Per annum, -	2	8	10

Experiment, No. 78.
Courfe.

1. Drilled barley   3. Turnips.
2. Broad-caft beans

Soil the fame as No. 77.

1767

The drilled barley the fame.

1768.

Sown with tick beans ; the crop 2 quarters *per* acre.

Expences.

Ploughing, - -	0	9	0
Water-furrowing, - -	0	1	0
Sowing, - -	0	0	3
Three bufhels feed, -	0	9	0
Harrowing, - -	0	2	0
Striking furrows, - -	0	1	2
Water-furrowing, -	0	1	0
Two hand-hoeings, -	0	10	0
Carry over, -	1	13	5

	£.		
Brought over, -	1	13	5
Pulling, - - -	0	7	0
Harvesting, -	0	4	0
Thrashing, - -	0	2	4
Rent, - -	1	2	0
Total, - -	3	8	9

Produce.

Two quarters, at 25 s.	2	10	0
Straw three quarters of a load,	0	15	0
Total, - -	3	5	0
Loss, - -	0	3	9

1769.

Well tilled and manured for turnips; the crop 3 l. 3 s. *per* acre.

Expences.

Ploughing, - -	0	9	0
Water-furrowing, -	0	1	0
Hunted in *May*, - -	0	7	6
Ox-harrowing, -	0	3	0
17 Loads yard-dung, -	5	2	0
Spreading, - - -	0	2	0
Twice ploughing, -	0	10	0
Harrowing, - -	0	1	0
Drilling with the cag-plough,	0	0	9
Seed, - - -	0	0	3
Hand-hoeing, - -	0	10	0
Rent, - - -	1	2	0
Total, -	8	8	6

			£.		
Expences,	-		8	8	6

Produce

Food,	-	-	3	3	0
			—	—	—
Lofs,	-	-	5	5	6
			—	—	—

Recapitulation.

1767. Drilled barley, lofs,		0	16	0
1768 Beans ditto,	-	0	3	9
1769. Turnips ditto,	-	5	5	6
		—	—	—
Lofs,	-	-	6	5	3
		—	—	—
Per ann.	-	-	2	1	9

Experiment, No. 79.

Courfe

1. Oats.   2. Beans.   3. Tares.

One acre and three quarters; the foil a ftrong clay. In 1766 it yielded wheat.

1767.

The ftubble of which was ploughed up in *March*, and oats harrowed in; the crop three quarters *per* acre.

Expences.

Ploughing,	-		0	10	0
Harrowing,	-	-	0	2	0
Seed three bufhels,	-	0	6	9
Sowing,	-	-	-	0	0	3
Water-furrowing,	-	0	1	0
Mowing,	-	0	1	8
		—	—	—
Carry over,	-	1	1	8

		£		
Brought over,	-	1	1	8
Harvefting,	-	0	4	0
Thrafhing,	- -	0	4	6
Rent, &c.	- -	1	2	0
Total,	- -	2	12	2

Produce.

Three quarters, at 15 s.	-	2	5	0
One load and quarter ftraw,		1	0	0
Total,	- -	3	5	0
Expences,	-	2	12	2
Profit,	- -	0	12	10

1768.

Ploughed up the oat ftubble in *January*, and harrowed in tick beans, the crop two quarters *per* acre.

Expences.

Ploughing,	- -	0	10	0
Sowing,	-	0	0	3
Three bufhels feed,	-	0	9	9
Harrowing,	- -	0	4	0
Hand-hoeing once,	-	0	7	0
Pulling,	- -	0	7	0
Harvefting,	-	0	4	0
Thrafhing,	- -	0	3	0
Rent,	- -	1	2	0
Total,	- -	3	7	0

Produce.

Two quarters, at 25 s.	-	£. 2	10	0
Straw one load.		1	0	0
Total,	- -	3	10	0
Expences,	-	3	7	0
Profit,	-	0	3	0

1769.

Ploughed the bean stubble in *March*, and harrowed in tares in *May*; the crop came but to little, not worth more than 5 s. an acre.

Expences.

Ploughing,	- -	0	10	0
Sowing,	-	0	0	3
Seed two bushels,	-	0	10	0
Harrowing,	- -	0	1	6
Rent,	- -	1	2	0
Total,	- -	2	3	9
Produce,	-	0	5	0
Lofs,	- -	1	18	9

Recapitulation.

1769. Tares, lofs,	-	1	18	0
1767. Oats, profit, £. 0 12 10				
1768. Beans ditto, 0 3 0				
		0	15	10
Lofs,	- -	1	2	11
Which is *per ann.*	-	0	7	7

Obfervations

Mr. *Arbuthnot* has had fuch a variety of undertakings in the hufbandry way, that all his fields could not poffibly receive equal attention. The lofs on this field has been firft fowing oats after wheat, and afterwards always fowing it on one earth, which on a ftiff clay cannot be right. It is a proof, that the common management of thefe lands yield a very poor advantage at beft.

Experiment, No. 80.

Courfe.

1. Fallow
2. Drilled barley
3. Tares
4. Wheat
5. Oats.

Five acres; foil a ftrong loam on clay, fallowed in 1766, and in 1767 drilled with barley; for which crop fee *Experiment*, No. 60. Lofs 2*l*. 8*s*. 4*d*.

1768.

Harrowed in tares on two earths; mown for foiling horfes; kept ten three weeks, and yielded thirty fhillings worth of fheep feed befides.

Expences.

	£		
Firſt ploughing, -	0	7	6
Water-furrowing, -	0	0	6
Second ploughing, -	0	7	6
Harrowing, - -	0	1	6
Two buſhels tares, -	0	10	0
Mowing and carting, -	0	5	0
Rent, - - -	1	2	0
Total, - -	2	14	0

Produce.

Keeping ten horſes four weeks, at 7s. 6d.—15l.; the fifth is	3	0	0
Sheep feed 30s.; the fifth is	0	6	0
Total, - -	3	6	0
Expences, -	2	14	0
Profit, - -	0	12	0

1769.

Harrowed in wheat on one ploughing; produce three quarters *per* acre.

Expences.

Ploughing, - -	0	7	6
Harrowing, -	0	1	6
Two buſhels feed, -	0	13	0
Striking furrows, -	0	0	9
Water-furrowing, -	0	1	0
Reaping, - -	0	8	6
Harveſting, - -	0	4	0
Carry over, -	1	16	3

			£.	s.	d.
Brought over,	–		1	16	3
Thrashing,	–	–	0	9	0
Carrying,	–	–	0	1	6
Rent,	–		1	2	0
Total,	–		3	8	9

Produce.

Three quarters, at 44 s	–		6	12	0
One load straw,	–		1	5	0
Total,	–	–	7	17	0
Expences,	–	–	3	8	9
Profit,	–	–	4	8	3

1770.

Harrowed in oats on one earth : clover was sown on the wheat, but it miscarried, which was the reason of sowing oats; for clover was wanting, under which crop it now is, and very fine. Product 3 quarters *per* acre.

Expences.

Ploughing,	–	–	0	5	0
Harrowing,	–	–	0	2	0
Three bushels feed,	–		0	7	6
Sowing,	–	–	0	0	3
Water-furrowing,	–		0	1	0
Striking water-furrows,	–		0	0	2
Mowing,	–	–	0	2	0
Carry over,	–	–	0	17	11

5

	£.		
Brought over, -	0	17	11
Harvesting, - -	0	5	0
Thrashing, - -	0	4	6
Rent, - - -	1	2	0
Total, - -	2	9	5

Product.

Three quarters, -	3	0	0
Straw one load, - -	0	16	0
Total, - -	3	16	0
Expences, -	2	9	5
Profit, - -	1	6	7

Recapitulation.

1768. Tares, profit, -	0	12	0
1769 Wheat ditto. - -	4	8	3
1770. Oats ditto, - -	1	6	7
Total, - -	6	6	10
1767. Drilled barley, lofs,	2	8	4
Profit, - -	3	18	6
Per ann. -	0	15	8

Experiment, No. 81.
Course.

1. Madder. 2. Ditto. 3. Ditto. 4. Ditto.
Six acres. For the crops, fee *Experiment*, No. 13.

		£.		
Lofs,	-	68	14	0
Which is *per* acre,		11	9	0
And *per* acre *per ann*		2	17	3

This lofs is however but in appearance. fuch numbers of plants were drawn from it, that, if reckoned, as they are elfewhere, the profit would be very great.

Experiment, No. 82.

Courfe.

1. Madder.   2. Ditto.   3. Ditto

Nine acres. the crop regiftered in *Experiment*, No. 10. Profit 211 *l.* 12 *s.* 4 *d.* Per acre 23 *l.* 10 *s.* 3 *d.* Per acre *per ann.* 5 *l.* 17 *s.* 6 *d.*

Experiment, No. 83.

- *Courfe.*

1. Fallow   3. Madder
2. Madder   4. Ditto.

Ten acres. See *Experiment*, No. 14. Profit 333 *l.* 6 *s.* which is *per* acre 33 *l.* 6 *s.* 7 *d.* and *per* acre *per ann.* 8 *l.* 6 *s.* 7 *d.*

Experiment, No. 84.

· *Courfes.*

1. Fallow   3. Madder
2. Madder   4. Ditto.

Three acres. See *Experiment*, No. 15.

		£.		
Profit,	-	105	7	6
Or *per* acre,	-	35	2	6
Per acre *per ann.*	-	8	15	7

Experiment, No. 85

Course.

1. Turnips.   2. Turnips.   3. Turnips.

Two acres; the soil a black rich loam.

1767.

Trench-ploughed some lucerne, and harrowed in turnips   they were drawn for sheep, at 4*l.* an acre.

Expences.

	£.		
Trench-ploughing with *Ducket*'s			
plough, - -	0	13	0
Harrowing, -	0	2	0
Sowing, - -	0	0	3
Seed, - - -	0	0	6
Twice hand-hoeing, -	0	10	0
Rent, &c. - -	1	6	0
Total, - -	2	11	9

Product.

By sheep feed, - -	4	0	0
Expences, -	2	11	9
Profit, - -	1	8	3

1768

Trench-ploughed it again, and harrowed in turnips, fed on the land by sheep, 3*l.* an acre.

Expences.

	£.		
Ploughing, - -	0	13	0
Harrowing and fowing,	0	2	9
Seed, - - -	0	0	6
Twice hand-hoeing, -	0	10	0
Rent, &c. -	1	6	0
Total, -	2	12	3

Produce.

Sheep feed, - -	3	0	0
Expences, -	2	12	0
Profit, - -	0	8	0

1769

Trench-ploughed again for turnips, as before; fed with sheep, 3*l.* 10*s. per* acre.

Product.

Sheep feed, - -	3	10	0
Expences as before, except but one hoeing, -	2	7	3
Profit, - -	1	2	9

Recapitulation.

1767. Turnips, profit, -	1	8	3
1768. Ditto, ditto, -	0	8	0
1769. Ditto, ditto, -	1	2	9
Total, - -	2	19	0
Per annum, -	0	19	8

But in addition to this profit is that very great one of feeding on the land by sheep, which is certainly more than 19 s. 8 d. a year.

Experiment, No. 86.

Courfe.

1. Fallow   3. Madder
2. Madder   4. Madder.

Four acres; regiftered in *Experiment*, No. 12.

	£.		
Profit, -	£. 97	19	4
Per acre, - -	24	9	10
Per acre *per annum*,	6	2	5½

Experiment, No. 87.

Courfe.

1. Lucerne   4. Lucerne
2. Lucerne   5. Lucerne.
3. Lucerne

Twelve acres. See *Experiment*, No. 5. Profit *per* acre *per ann.* 6 l. 4 s. 4 d.

General Obfervations.

In order to draw thofe really ufeful con-clufions from the preceding regifter of courfes, which they certainly will afford, it is neceffary to ftate them in one complete view, retaining no other circumftances than the crops, and the clear profit or lofs.

Courses that have proved profitable.

Experi- ment,	Expended in manure			Profit per acre per annum		
No	l.	s.	d.	l.	s.	d.
62. 1 Peafe, 2 Winter tares, 3 Fallow, 4. Wheat,	0	0	0	2	9	0
64. 1 Barley, 2 Clover, 3 Clover, 4 Wheat, —	4	5	6	3	19	8
66 1 Oats, 2. Peafe, 3 Fallow, 4 Wheat, —	2	5	6	1	10	1
67 1 Beans, 2 Wheat, 3 Tares,	3	18	3	6	1	7
68 1 Drilled beans, 2 Drilled wheat, 3 Drilled beans, 4 Winter tares, —	0	0	0	2	16	0
69 1. Stubble, 2 Fallow, 3 Drilled wheat, 4 Drilled beans, —	1	8	6	0	6	7
70. 1 Fallow, 2. Drilled beans, 3 Wheat, 4 Drilled beans,	1	8	2	2	3	10
71 1 Drilled peafe, 2. Drilled wheat, 3 Beans, 4 Wheat,	2	13	0	1	9	4
72 1. Drilled beans, 2 Ditto wheat, 3 Ditto beans, 4. Ditto wheat, —	2	10	0	3	15	2
73 1 Fallow, 2 Drilled beans, 3 Ditto wheat, 4. Ditto beans, — —	0	19	0	1	1	11
73 *1. Oats, 2. Tares, 3. Fallow, 4. Drilled wheat,	1	2	10	1	5	11
75. 1. Fallow, 2 Madder, 3 Madder, 4. Madder,	3	10	0	7	17	2
76. 1 Fallow, 2. Madder, 3. Madder, 4. Madder,	7	10	0	9	3	0
77. 1. Drilled barley, 2. Ditto beans, 3 Potatoes,	4	10	0	2	8	10
80 1. Fallow, 2 Drilled barley, 3 Tares, 4 Wheat, 5 Oats,	0	0	0	0	15	8
82. 1 Madder, 2. Madder, 3 Madder, —	3	12	6	5	17	6
83. 1 Fallow, 2 Madder, 3. Madder, 4 Madder,	6	0	0	11	10	7

Courses that have proved profitable, continued.

Experiment,	Expended in manure.			Profit per acre per annum.		
No.	l	s	d.	l	s.	d.
83 1 Fallow, 2 Madder, 3. Madder, 4. Madder,	3	12	0	7	4	11
84 1 Fallow, 2 Madder, 3. Madder, 4. Madder,	6	0	0	8	15	7
85 1 Turnips, 2. Turnips, 3 Turnips, -	0	0	0	0	19	8
86 1 Fallow, 2. Madder, 3 Madder, 4 Madder,	2	4	0	6	2	5½
87. 1 Lucerne, 2. Lucerne, 3 Lucerne, 4. Lucerne, 5. Lucerne, -	0	0	0	6	4	4

Courses that have been attended with loss

	Manure			Loss.		
63 1 Fallow, 2 Spring tares, 3 Wheat, 4 Oats,	1	1	6	0	2	2
65 1. Tares and flax, 2. Fallow, 3. Tares, 4. Wheat,	1	1	6	0	6	9
74 1 Oats, 2. Drilled pease, 3. Barley, -	6	15	0	0	5	2
78. 1 Drilled barley, 2 Beans, 3 Turnips, -	5	4	0	2	1	9
79 1 Oats, 2 Beans, 3 Tares,	0	0	0	0	7	7
81 1 Madder, 2 Madder, 3. Madder, 4. Madder,	0	0	0	2	17	3

The firſt object that ſtrikes one here is, the vaſt profit attending ample manurings; by dividing the table, this will appear deciſive.

In the laſt line of the preceding page, *for* 11 *l* 10ſ 7 *d* *read* 8 *l.* 6ſ. 7 *d*

470 THE FARMER's TOUR

Courses manured for above 3 l. an acre.

Profit.

			£	s	d
No. 64,	-	-	£. 3	19	8
67,	-	-	6	1	7
75, Madder,		-	7	17	2
76, Ditto,	-	-	9	3	0
77,	-	-	2	8	10
82, Madder,		-	5	17	6
83, Ditto,		-	8	6	7
83, Ditto,	-	-	7	4	11
84, Ditto,	-	-	8	15	7
Total,	-	-	59	14	10
74, Loss, £. 0 5 2					
78, Ditto, 2 1 9					
			2	6	11
Total,	-	-	57	7	11
Average,	-	-	5	4	4

Courses manured for under 3 l. an acre.

Profit.

			£	s	d
No. 66,	-	-	1	10	1
69,	-	-	0	6	7
70,	-	-	2	3	10
71,	-	-	1	9	4
72,	-	-	3	15	2
73,	-	-	1	1	11
73 *,	-	-	1	5	11
86,	-	-	6	2	5½
Total,	-		17	15	3½
63, Loss, 0 2 2					
65, 0 6 9					
			0	8	11
Total,	-	-	17	6	4½
Average,	-	-	1	14	7

Unmanured crops.

			£		
No. 62, Profit,	-		£.2	9	0
68,	-	-	2	16	0
80,	-	-	0	15	8
85,	-	-	0	19	8
Total,	-	-	7	0	4
79, Lofs,	£.0	7 7			
81, Madder,	2	17 3			
			3	4	10
Total,	-	-	3	15	6
Average,	-		0	12	7
Lucerne profit,			6	4	4

Madder excluded the account will be thus.

Manurings above 3 l an acre.

No 64, Profit,	-	-	3	19	8
67,	-	-	6	1	7
77,	-	-	2	8	10
Total,	-		12	10	1
74, Lofs,	0	5 2			
78, Ditto,	2	1 9			
			2	6	11
Total,	-		10	3	2
Aveıage,	-	-	2	0	7

H h 4

Manurings under 3 l. an acre

Average profit, as before,	£ 1	14	7

The unmanured crops

No. 62, 68, 80, and 85,	7	0	4
79, Lofs, - -	0	7	7
Total, - -	6	12	9
Average, -	1	6	6
Manured for above 3 *l* -	2	0	7
Under 3 *l.* -	1	14	7
Superiority, -	0	6	0
Above 3 *l.* - -	2	0	7
Unmanured, - -	1	6	6
Superiority, -	0	14	1
Under 3 *l* - - -	1	14	7
Unmanured, - -	1	6	6
Superiority, -	0	8	1

Lucerne is excluded, which is fo uncommonly profitable without manuring, that it would overturn all conclufions.

From this view of the crops, with an eye to manures, it is very evident, that *profit* depends very much on *manure*, and
that

that the degree of the one is very inti-
mately connected with the other. This is
a general refult, but not fo important as a
more particular one. From examining the
courfes, it appears, that very ample manurings will be but lofing, unlefs the *courfe*
is good. thus, in 74 and 78, drilled peafe
and drilled barley are introduced, both
crops improper for this foil; fo that manuring of 6*l* 15*s* and 5*l*. 4*s*. are attended
only with lofs. No. 68, though unmanured, pays 2*l*. 16*s* profit; whereas
No. 80, unmanured, pays but 15*s* 8*d*.
This is owing to drilled beans being in one,
and drilled barley in the other.

The moft profitable courfes are ;

No. 64. 1. Barley,   2. Clover,
  3. Clover, 4. Wheat. it pays £. 3 19   8
No. 67. 1. Beans,   2 Wheat,
  3. Tares,   -   -   6   1   7
No. 72. 1. Beans, 2. Wheat,
  3. Beans, 4. Wheat: all drilled, 3 15   2

Hence it is evident, that the moft profitable method of manuring thefe foils is
to make clover, beans and tares, the fallow
crops, and to have wheat the only white coin
one. This will be further illuftrated by
felecting the next rank of profitable crops.

No. 68. 1. Drilled beans, 2. Ditto
    wheat, 3. Ditto beans, 4. Winter
    tares,   -   -   £. 2 16 0
No. 70. 1. Fallow, 2. Drilled
    beans, 3. Wheat, 4. Drilled
    beans,   -   -   2 3 10
No 77 1 Drilled barley, 2. Ditto
    beans, 3. Potatoes,   -   2 8 10

The drilled barley was unprofitable, this profit was therefore on the beans, &c. This scale of profit shews evidently the beneficial courses, as to barley, oats, and turnips, they are comparatively contemptible to the superior crops of clover, beans, tares, and wheat. Potatoes are but once tried; but they bid extremely fair for exceeding any.

Wheat appears to pay very well for a complete summer fallow.

If a hint is taken from these courses, such an one as the following may probably be found uniformly advantageous.

1. Fallow	8. Winter tares
2. Wheat	9. Beans
3. Beans drilled	10. Wheat
4. Oats	11. Potatoes
5. Clover	12. Oats
6. Clover	13. Clover
7. Wheat	14. Wheat.

It

It may be fuppofed I introduce the oats merely as an introduction to the clover, and for the fake of fome ftraw, in cafe it could not be bought. A farm thus difpofed would be,

Four	Fourteenths	in	Wheat.
Two	Ditto		Oats.
Two	Ditto		Beans.
One	Ditto		Tares.
Three	Ditto		Clover.
One	Ditto		Potatoes.
One	Ditto		Fallow.

I mention nothing of cabbages, becaufe they are not yet experienced on this farm.

Eight fourteenths, cleanfe and ameliorate.
Six ditto, foul and exhauft.

The land therefore muft always be clean and in good heart.

This for common hufbandry; but the great profit is to manure very richly, and plant madder. The clear profit of the madder courfes far exceeds the common ones; but lucerne, without any manure at all, comes nearly to madder with great quantities.

VI. MISCELLANEOUS EXPE-RIMENTS.

Mr. *Arbuthnot*'s attention to hufbandry has been in no refpect confined : fome ob-

jects,

jects, as may be easily conceived, have demanded more spirited efforts than others; but very few have been neglected. It will, for the sake of clearness, be requisite to throw those enquiries, which have not been made in so extended a manner as the rest, into a division by themselves   They will be properly arranged under the following heads.

1. Manures
2. Draining
3. Deep ploughing
4. Velvit wheat
5. Growth of wheat
6. Feeding wheat
7. Carrots
8. Destroying thistles
9 Black bent
10. Sheep
11. Planting poplars

MANURES.

This gentleman, in his culture of madder, &c. has manured various of his fields in a much richer manner than I remember any where to have seen : it has been done with farm-yard dung, raised at home, and also with large quantities purchased at *London:* this practice has been carried on in so large a scale, that the experimental register of it, unless various divisions had been made with infinite trouble, could not be decisive. His general manuring therefore is not to be gathered from the following

5

trials,

trials, which are upon a different plan. The manures tried are, trotters, wood afhes, foot, coal afhes, rabbit dung, malt duft, night foil, folding fheep.

TROTTERS.

Experiment, No. 88.

This manure was tried on both ftrong and light loam for wheat, and alfo for madder, 5 quarters *per* acre, at 9*s* befides carriage from *London* They were not attended by any vifible advantage in either crop, which he attributes to their going through the hands of the glue makers.

WOOD ASHES.

Experiment, No. 89.

Sowed them on arable lands in various fields, 25 bufhels an acre, but they yielded no fort of advantage.

Experiment, No. 90.

Tried them on grafs land; the benefit there was great. The farmers were of opinion, that dreffing would burn up the grafs, which would be the cafe if laid in heaps to be ftrewed; on which account they muft be fpread directly out of a little cart. They were collected from *Banfled* downs, at 3*d* a bufhel.

SOOT.

Experiment, No. 91.

Sowed 30 bufhels an acre on grafs land, at 7 *d.* a bufhel, befides carriage and 1 *d* fowing. From various trials, the effect was found to be very great, if done early in *February*, and equally beneficial fown on green wheat at the fame time.

COAL ASHES.

Experiment, No 92.

A comparifon was formed between coal afhes and foot, on grafs land. the afhes were fifted remarkably fine; 40 bufhels *per* acre were fown of each. At firft the foot made the greateft appearance, but there was no vifible difference in the crop of hay.

RABBIT's DUNG.

Experiment, No. 93.

This is the principal top dreffing ufed by Mr. *Arbuthnot:* he has tried it on almoft all the fields of his farm. He fows 25 facks an acre over moft of his wheat in *March*, at 1 *s.* 2 *d.* a fack, carriage included; and this is in general the only manure he ufes for his wheat: on the drilled crop it was hoed in, and on the broad-caft harrowed. The advantage in general very great.

Experiment, No 94.

In *November*, a comparison was made between rabbit's dung, chicken's dung, and wood ashes, in the proportion *per* acre of 18 sacks of each. The chicken's dung was by far the best, the rabbit's next, and the wood ashes last.

MALT DUST.

Experiment, No. 95.

Fifty bushels an acre of kiln dust were tried against 20 sacks of coal ashes on arable land, and turned out much superior.

NIGHT SOIL.

Experiment, No. 96.

Tried for cabbages and madder, 10 loads an acre. It promises greatly.

FOLDING SHEEP.

Experiment, No. 97.

Mr. *Arbuthnot* has been so well convinced of the great importance of the sheep fold, that his constant practice, when the land is not dry enough for the common one, is to pen them in a standing fold on a head land, well littered with straw every day, or every other day, as circumstances admit, so as the sheep may always be dry.

One hundred and thirty-four sheep and 30 lambs penned in this manner 6 weeks were littered with 5 loads and 40 truſs of oat ſtraw, (40 *lb.* to the truſs.) They made 28 large loads of dung. They were fed morning and evening with turnips in the pen, and let out in the middle of the day for 4 or 5 hours. In the above time eat 2 acres of turnips. The dung thus made was equal to any that can be had; full as good as what he brings from *London* at 10*s.* a load.

	£.		
Suppoſe the quantity 20 ſuch loads as brought from *London*, - -	10	0	0
Five loads and 40 truſs, at 20 *s.* at the pen, -	5	15	0
Profit by the dung, -	4	5	0
Which is *per* acre for the turnips,	2	2	6
And *per* ſcore *per* week for the ſheep, - -	0	1	9¼

This trial ſhews the advantage of ſuch folding in the cleareſt manner; it alſo proves that a very high price may be paid for ſtraw with great profit: 20*s.* a truſſed load is high; but had 30*s.* been given, there would yet have remained a conſiderable profit. It is true, there is a great

advantage

advantage by eating the turnips on the land where they grow; but that can only be done in dry foils, whereas this method is applicable to all.

DRAINING.

Experiment, No 98.

Seven acres of arable land and four of grafs were drained by covered drains. furrows were drawn by the common ploughs, 8 inches deep, to mark out the cuts; they were then dug with draining-fpades, to the depth of 20 inches, at the expence of 3 d $\frac{1}{2}$ *per* perch digging, filling, &c. They were ftruck in parallel lines diagonally acrofs the flope of the fields, at the diftance of 2 perch from each other; but Mr. *Arbuthnot* remarks, that to drain his land properly, the cuts fhould be but one rod afunder. They were filled with thorns, 2 loads of which filled the drains of an acre.

Suppofe an oblong, 40 perch long, and 12 broad, it contains 3 acres.

In the above method of draining, there will be 5 drains, each 40 perch long, or 200 perch, which at 3 $d.$ $\frac{1}{2}$ come to, for 3 acres, - - £. 2 18 4

Carry over, - 2 18 4

		£.		
Brought over,	-	2	18	4
Drawing furrows,	-	0	1	8
Three acres,	-	3	0	0
Which is *per* acre,		1	0	0
Two loads of thorns, suppose		0	15	0
Total *per* acre,	▪	1	15	0

Experiment, No. 99.

The expence of the above drains being something confiderable, and good hands ufed to the work, not being always to be had, Mr. *Arbuthnot* deferred the draining his whole farm, until he could invent a -plough that would perform the operation. In this defign he fucceeded, and with the plough drained 26 acres of grafs land, the drains 2 perch afunder, as above, 17 inches deep, 2 wide at bottom, and 8'½ at top. Filled like the others with thorns, but from the cuts being truer, and narrower at bottom than they can be dug, 1 load of thorns filled 70 perch. Twelve horfes were ufed, and the whole expence of ploughing, filling, &c. came to 1 *d.* per perch.

200 Perch, at 1 *d.* on 3 acres, £. 0 16 8

Which is *per* acre, - 0 5 6

	£.		
Brought over,	0	5	6½
One load thorns, -	0	7	6
This is fomething over the truth.			
Total *per* acre, -	0	13	0¼
Expence *per* acre with the fpade,	1	15	0
With the plough, -	0	13	0¾
Superiority, -	1	1	11¼

This prodigious faving, which, in a few acres, would at once pay the expence of the implement, fhould call the attention of all, who have any quantity of land to drain in this manner. With this noble implement the trouble and expence of covered drains are reduced to a trifle, to much lefs than one crop of any fort would pay.

But here I fhould obferve, that this experiment was made with the plough, before it was perfected by adding wheels of five feet inftead of the former ones of two feet: he has reduced the draft four horfes; fo that it is now worked with only eight, confequently will do its work cheaper than mentioned in the above calculation. For an explanation fee plate XV.

DEEP PLOUGHING.

This part of hufbandry Mr. *Arbuthnot* has practifed upon the largeft fcale, and

with

with very great fuccefs. His foil is chiefly
a ftrong loam, never ploughed before more
than five inches deep · he has ftirred it 12
inches, and the additional feven are a ftrong
brick earth. He always begins with a
winter fallow, and leaves it through the
winter for beans, on one fpring ploughing
No manuring, except fome with lime.
The beans very good crops much too good
to give the leaft reafon to fuppofe them the
worfe for the deep ploughing, efpecially as
the ground was in general very foul and
poor The beans have been followed by
various other crops, none of which have
indicated any ill effect from deep ploughing.

He makes it a rule, never to fow any
fibrous-rooted crop for the firft after this
operation. He once fowed barley on it,
and laid down to clover: the barley a poor
crop; but the clover took perfectly well·
it was dunged, and yielded a very large product; alfo one the fecond year, after which
it was fed, and trench-ploughed for wheat
The crop four quarters an acre, though it
appeared to be much hurt by the worm
and was fed bare with fheep in *March*.

VELVIT WHEAT.

Experiment, No. 100.

In 1768, Mr. *Arbuthnot* gathered fix ears of this wheat, from the down on it attracting this notice; and carrying it to market, the farmers remarked that they knew it, but had loft the fort, and called it velvit wheat. This induced him to fow it feed by feed in 1768. He took off the tillers and tranfplanted them, which operation he repeated, and planted them in the middle of a field of beans, to avoid blending the different *farina* of the wheats. In doing this he obferved, that the tranfplanted plants run away for feed before their own tillers came into ear, fo that if this method was practifed in common, there would be a fortnight difference in the ripening of the ears of the fame plant; for which reafon it is a mere matter of curiofity.

The product of the fix ears was 14 quarts, which were drilled on one acre, in four rows, eight inches afunder, on four-feet lands: fome of it in double rows, 14 inches, on the fame fize lands. they were both hand and horfe-hoed fufficiently, to keep them quite clean. In harveft, the products of the two ways of drilling were

blended

blended together through hurry; but the total was three quarters three pecks; which quantity, from lefs than two pecks of feed, he juftly efteems a very great produce, and attributes it to the fort of wheat. The land had been ploughed 14 inches deep for madder. Such a crop fhews the good effect of both deep ploughing and madder, in preparing for wheat.

He propofes fowing it all this year, after which the fort will be fully regained.

GROWTH OF WHEAT.

Experiment, No. 101.

Mr. *Arbuthnot,* receiving a hint from Dr. *Fordyce,* on the different fucceffion of the roots of plants, and finding the fame clearly laid down in a manufcript, faid to be written by Dr. *Cullen,* Profeffor of Chemiftry at *Edinburgh,* who explains the nature of the roots of all culmiferous plants in the following words. " Culmiferous plants have three fets of fibres : the firft fet is formed on the radicle, the fecond fet is formed above this, at a knot on the plumula; the third, at a knot in the plumula, above the fecond: this the difcovery of *Bennet.* Upon the due formation of thefe three knots and fets of fibres, I

judge

judge the tillering of frumentaceous plants
does entirely depend . that if thefe knots
are imperfectly formed, the plant impei-
fectly tillers." Thefe three knots are
termed by *Bennet*, the infancy, the adole-
fcence, and maturity of the plant. At the
two uppermoft knots the tillering is
formed.

Mr. *Arbuthnot* was hence induced to fow
a few grains in water, to watch the fucceffion of the roots. He cut a hole an inch
fquare in a bung-cork, in which he laid fome
wool, and upon that three grains of white
wheat, and floated on water in a glafs
tube 18 inches long. Firft there were three
fibres fhot from the radicle, which branched
into innumerable fibres; upon the wheat
fpearing frefh fibres ftruck out, as defcribed
by Dr. *Cullen*. Soon after they were eftablifhed, the three firft fibres with their
branches gradually decayed , as foon as it
was in ear, the frefh fibres made their appearance, foon after which the fecond decayed,
and the laft remained in poffeffion of the
water. The roots ftraightened, when taken
out of the water, meafured 2 ½ feet long.
It bloffomed and ripened in its regular
courfe; each ear had one grain; fowed

one

one of the grains in the open garden, and when proper to feparate the tillers, it was done, and again a fecond time, to the amount in all of 98 plants. They promifed to produce a great burthen; but being near a hedge, the birds eat them the wheat very fine.

Tried the fame experiment in another glafs, mixed with fome wood afhes the feed rotted on the furface, owing, as fuppofed, to the quantity of wood afhes being too great. The motive was to fee if it would lead to any difcoveries of the caufe of fmut; for Mr. *Arbuthnot* apprehended that difeafe to be owing to a want of proper nourifhment in the laft fucceffion of roots: the grain then being in a mucilaginous ftate, there may not be a fufficient quantity of food to carry it through that ftate. He has obferved, that part of a field, which has been full of weeds, fmutted when the reft has efcaped; and likewife, that when ftrong land has been much poached in fowing, and afterwards baked, whether on the head-lands or middle of the field, fuch parts have been moft fubject to fmut, owing, as he believes, to the furface of the earth not being pervious enough to

I   admit

admit the laft fet of fibres, which it is to be obferved firft fhoot from the pumula into the open air, and then introduce themfelves into the furface, frequently at the diftance of three quarters of an inch. This fact Mr. *Arbuthnot* has many times remarked, in examining the roots of field wheat

FEEDING WHEAT.

Experiment, No. 105.

This gentleman, from obferving the effect of feeding wheat in the fpring, apprehends it to be very beneficial to a thin crop, and as prejudicial to a thick one: the feeding makes it tiller; but then it fhould be done by turning in a flock, that will eat it down in two or three days, and not by a few, who will pick and cull the fhoots

In *March*, 1770, he turned his flock into one half of a wheat field, intending to eat that half quite down to the ground, and to leave the other untouched. Wet coming on, obliged the fheep to be removed; nor could they afterwards be put in again, as the wheat began to fpine. The fide of the field fed appeared rather the better crop of the two.

CARROTS.

Experiment, No. 106.

Sowed carrot feed in *March*. When the plants were 2 inches high, fome were transplanted; it was about the middle of *May*. In drawing them up, the ends of the tap-roots were broken off. This idea of transplanting carrots arofe from the great expence of hoeing that crop, much of which would be faved by this practice. One of the plants taken up at random in *Septembr*, weighed 3 *lb.*; the top 1 *lb.* the root 2 *lb.* The principal root for 4 inches deep was 4 in diameter; and then branched into five fine ftraight roots.

Experiment, No. 107.

Mr. *Arbuthnot* having obferved in *Eaft-Frizeland*, that it was the cuftom to fow carrots in the fpring on wheat and rye, and to harrow the feed in, he was induced to try it in 1768. The field a ftrong loam on clay. In *May* he drilled a row of carrots between two of wheat, at 14 inches, on 3½ feet lands, and alfo broad-caft over feveral acres. The feed was mixed with bran, in which manner his drill delivered it very regularly. After the wheat was reaped, they were hand-hoed; the produce 40 bufhels

bufhels *per* acre. And this practice he thinks may turn out profitable on light deep foils. In *Frizeland* it is the cuftom to plough them up and houfe, or to turn their hogs into the field, and eat them on the land.

Obfervations.

The carrot being a tap-rooted plant, in all probability the damage they do the wheat is inconfiderable, or at leaft not to be named with a product of 40 bufhels an acre. Carrots are very well worth 1*s.* a bufhel in feeding cattle; 40*s.* an acre, added to the wheat, is an object of no flight magnitude; befides, it is obfervable, that thefe were drilled fo late as *May*, which is at leaft two months too late; alfo, that the foil is very ftiff, inftead of being light, which is what the root delights in. upon the whole, it is fairly to be prefumed, that the practice may prove beneficial on many foils. Another circumftance is the ploughing, which the land gets at *Michaelmas* for raifing them, which it otherwife perhaps would not have.

DESTROYING THISTLES.

Experiment, No. 108.

In a large field laid to grafs, the land having been very foul, innumerable thiftles after-

afterwards appeared; they were repeatedly
fpudded without any effect—they were repeatedly mown with no better · after this they
were fuffered to ftand till juft going to blof-
fom; the heads only were then cut off ·
this appeared to weaken the plants. They put
out lateral fhoots only from the ftem,
whereas thofe that were fpudded put out
numberlefs tillers, but ftill they were not
deftroyed. Mr. *Arbuthnot* having remarked,
that rolling in the fpring, while the land is
wet, was fatal to the crop of grafs, determined to roll this land when very wet,
with an heavy roller: he accordingly did
it, and the effect has been fo great, that
fince this operation fcarcely a thiftle has
appeared; but he fpoiled his crop of hay.

In other fields he has mown, and then
bruifed them with the heavy roller in dry
weather, but without any effect.

BLACK BENT.

This weed, called in fome places moufe
tail, is more difficult to extirpate than
many other annuals; but Mr. *Arbuthnot* has
found the following method very effectual.

Plough up the ftubble in *September*, and
leave it for the winter: in fpring, pulverize
it as foon and as fine as poffible; fo let it

remain

remain for the bent to vegetate: then plough it up and fow fummer tares, or any thing that comes off foon enough to leave time for ploughing it well before winter. Lay it up on the ridge, to be fecure from rain; if the black bent fprings again, plough the whole furface of the land with the fhim, after which harrow and leave it for fowing wheat under furrow, fhallow, and very late This method is alfo good for the deftruction of all feed weeds, if no couch is in the land. drilled crops, by admitting the hand-hoe, are excellent in deftroying it.

SHEEP.

Experiment, No. 109.

Mr. *Arbuthnot* having 20 ewes with their lambs put to turnips in *February*, in three days the ewes fhewed the appearance of the laft ftage of the rot, though not perceptible before ; their wool quitting the fide on the leaft touch, their eyes of a yellow livid colour, not the leaft rednefs remaining in their gums, and the wax on the fide of their udders being quite dry : many of them fcarcely able to walk. They were taken from turnips and put in a pen, having nothing to eat but dry meat, hay,

ground

ground beans and bran, sprinkled with salt: they loathed their food, seemingly for want of moisture · forge water, mixed with the water out of the madder, copper, was given them, being a simple decoction of madder, and this they drank regularly

Next, they had each a dose of calomel and rhubarb, the same quantity as to a grown person: this purged them extremely, and brought away a most fetid, nauseous, slimy matter. As soon as they knit, they had soap and bark given them every other morning; upon which they began to thrive, and the symptoms of health appeared in the above-mentioned circumstances. The lambs were suffered all the time to run in and out the pen. Three ewes only died; the rest have borne lambs since, and are now fatting.

This success induced him to procure some rotten sheep from a farmer in the neighbourhood, who sent him four wethers in a cart, so bad that they could not walk; one died on the road. These had not the symptoms above mentioned so strong as the 20 ewes, but had water-bladders under the gullet; in this he put a seaton of turpentine, and treated them like the rest. All died,

4   and,

and, what is extraordinary, Mr. *Neal* (the farmer from whom he had them) faved all his flock, though many of them as bad as thefe, by giving them a fpoonful of turpentine in a gill of water, once in three days.

Refpecting the breed of fheep, Mr. *Arbuthnot* was recommended to try the *Northampton* and *Leicefter* fort; but they did not well with him: they would not thrive, owing, as he apprehends, to the pafture not being rich enough. when fat, they came to 35 *lb.* a quarter. The quality of their wool declined. He finds from experience, that the *Wiltfhire* and *Hampfhire* fuit him beft. The *Dorfets*, bought in in lamb, and kept in the inclofures, fatten their lambs well; but muft themfelves be fattened off by *Michaelmas*, as they are too delicate for the commons of this country.

PLANTING.

Experiment, No. 110.

Nine years ago planted fome black poplars, eight feet afunder; the fize about $1\frac{1}{2}$ inch diameter: meafured two of them. No. 1. The beft contains 13 feet of timber, which would fell at 10 *d.* a foot, and the

forks

forks in the top would give three rails, worth with the faggots 2 *s.* In all 12 *s.* 10 *d.*

No. 2. The worst, 12 ½ feet of timber, and the top worth 1 *s.* In all 10 *s.* 5 *d.*

Average, 11 *s.* 7 *d.*

An acre planted in squares of 8 feet would contain 680 trees, which, at 11 *s.* 7 *d.* amount to   -   -   -   £. 393 0 0

Expences.

	£.	*s.*	*d.*
Suppose the trees bought or raised at 3 *d.* each, - £.	8	10	0
Planting, - -	0	5	0
Filling vacancies by death; suppose 50, - -	0	12	6
Fencing repairs, - -	0	10	0
Nine years rent, suppose at 30 *s.*	13	10	0
Total, - -	23	7	6
Product, - -	393	0	0
Expences, - -	23	7	6
Profit, -	369	12	6
Which is *per* acre *per ann.*	41	1	4

No husbandry or gardening in the world will equal this vast profit. It is astonishing that more plantations of such quick-growing

trees

trees are not made. This foil is a black, rich, low ground, near water.

Experiment, No. 3.

Some willows planted at the fame time and diftance, meafured on an average 18 feet of timber, worth 6 *d.* a foot, and the tops 1 *s.* 6 *d.*

	£.		
680, at 10 *s.* 6 *d.* -	357	0	0
Expences as above, -	23	7	6
Profit, - -	333	12	6
Or *per* acre *per ann.*	37	1	4

From which moft confiderable return there is no flight reafon to fuppofe the common idea, that this tree fhould for profit have the head cut off, is an error; for it is a queftion, whether the product by faggots would equal half this. But in fituations, where poles fell well, Mr. *Arbuthnot* obferves, that you may cut them every fix years, and fell at an amazing price, but not for faggots. He likewife remarks, that the body of the willow tree rives into pales, which are admirable for fences, hardening in the air, and are nearly as durable as oak.

VII. IMPLEMENTS.

If a perfon, the leaft fkilled in agriculture, looks around for inftruments that deferve to be called complete, how few will
he meet with! Every day brings to light
new plans of culture, for the profitable
execution of which peculiar inftruments are
neceffary: it is often the want of thefe that
cafts a damp on beginnings, which would
otherwife turn out highly fuccefsful; but
being liable to numerous mifcarriages, and
great expences, for want of the proper
machines, the modes of culture are themfelves condemned. The new hufbandry,
among other inftances, may be quoted,
which abfolutely depends on the merit of
the implements ufed.

Mr. *Arbuthnot*, on his beginning this
courfe of trials, experienced the inconveniences here mentioned; and this induced
him to invent a great variety of moft excellent machines fubfervient to hufbandry,
with which he has been enabled to carry
feveral branches of culture to a perfection
unknown before; and, at the fame time,
at a much lower expence, than was poffible to be effected with the tools before in
ufe. I will venture to affert, that the fol-

lowing

lowing implements will do honour to their inventor.

Plate IX.

The great Wheel Plough.

References.

From				Feet	Inches
1	to	2	—	10	0
1	to	3	—	3	2
3	to	4	—	2	8
4	to	2	—	4	0
5	to	6	—	1	8
7	to	6	—	2	0
6	to	A	—	1	2
7	to	8	—	2	1
8	to	9	—	1	7
9	to	10	—	2	9
11	to	12	—	3	3
7	to	10	—	2	10
13	to	14	—	3	but variable.
4	to	15	—	3	ditto.
13	to	15	—	3	0
16	to	1	—	5	0

The gallows 17 inches wide.

The beam 6 inches fquare at the coulter hole, rounded to 3 at the end.

Diameter of the little wheel 2 feet 4 inches. Ditto of the larger 4 feet.

This is the implement, with which Mr. *Arbuthnot* performs all his operations of deep ploughing; he ftirs 18 inches deep with it, the draft 8 to 12 horfes. It performs the work in the beft manner.

Plate X. Fig. 1.

The small spiky Roller.

References.

a to b	— 10 Feet	0 Inches.
b to c	— 3	0
b to e	— 2	10
e to f	— 3	0
g to i	— 1	8
g to n	— 2	0
k to l	— 2	3
i to m	— 0	6 Inches broad at bottom, 15 above the axle.

Diameter of the cylinder 1 foot 8 inches.

This roller, being drawn through any furrows, whether those of beds in fallowing, or the intervals of drilled crops, &c. is of very great use in pulverizing them, when no horse-hoe will have any effect.

Plate X. Fig. 2.

The Berkshire Shim.

References.

a to c	— 10 Feet	0 Inches.
a to b	— 5	4
c to b	— 4	6
d to e	— 2	10
b to g	— 1	7
a to f	— 1	7
h to i	— 1	0

Diameter of the wheel 14 inches.

The

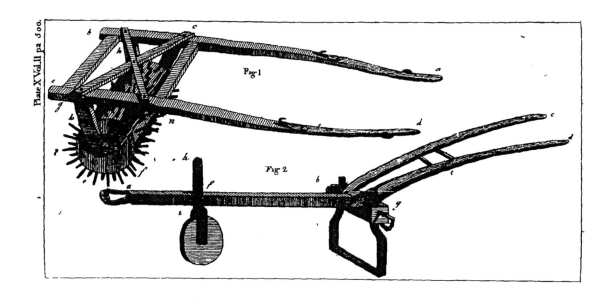

Fig. 1

Fig. 2

The fhare 14 inches long at cutting part, and 10 at top; the bottom 4 inches wide: but fhares of any fize may be fixed in it.

The block 4 inches thick by 7 inches deep.

The beam 3 inches fquare, rounded.

As the fhim is here reprefented, it is 2 feet from the top of the block to the ground, and from the top of the beam to the ground, at the wheel, 20 inches.

The fhare rifes or finks at pleafure through the block, as does the wheel through the beam.

It will not here be improper to remark, that this tool is in *Berkfhire* no longer a common one, and that feveral gentlemen, who had tried it, laid it afide as a bad inftrument; which has arifen from not attending fufficiently to the variations of the wheel. Mr. *Arbuthnot* has improved it, by fetting the fhare into the earth, inftead of leaving it flat, by which means the effect in cutting is much ftronger. He has found a fhim of incomparable ufe in anfwering the purpofe of the hand-hoe, cutting through all the weeds, and leaving them to die in the fun. It is fimple, and very expeditious. The price 2 *l.* 3 *s.*

K k 3

Plate XI page 502 Vol.II

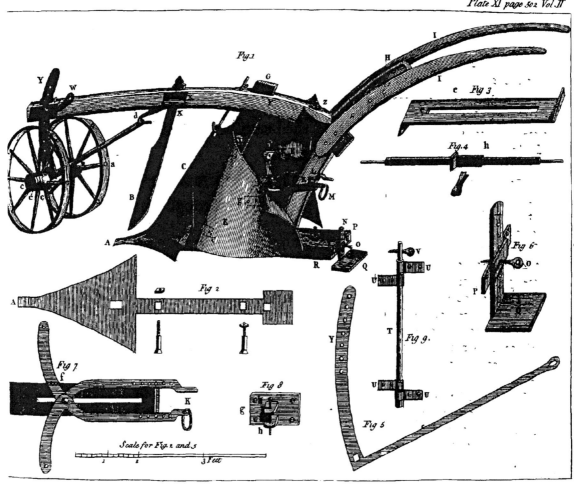

Fig.1

Fig.2

Fig.3

Fig.4

Fig.5

Fig.6

Fig.7

Fig.8

Fig.9

Scale for Fig. 2 and 5

inches by 3 ¼ at the fhoulder of its tenon, which is inferted into the beam poft H. The whole length of the plough from the fore end of the beam to the extremity of its handles is 11 feet 2 ½ inches.

G. The fheath, is 2 feet 4 inches long, 5 ½ broad, and 1 ½ thick; its back edge is 11 ¼ inches from the fhoulder of the beam, inclining to the horizon 40 degrees.

H. The hind fheath is 3 feet 2 ½ inches long, 4 ¼ inches broad, and 3 inches thick; its under end is mortifed into the chip, but the beam and handles are faftened to the hind fheath with wooden trundles, wedges, and nails.

I I. The handles of the plough, are 2 feet 8 ¼ inches diftant from each other at their points or upper ends.

K. An iron caliper, whofe fore ends are faftened with iron pins (fee fig. 8) h h, to the inner fides of the mould-boards, or bended iron wings; the outer ends of the caliper are pierced through with holes to receive the hook L, which ferves to fix the caliper, &c, to the degree of expanfion required.

L. An iron hook faftened to the hind fheath H.

M. An

M. An iron ring 3 inches diameter, which paſſes looſely through a hole in one of the arms of the caliper, and is laid over the other arm to fix the caliper, when the mould-boards are opened to their full extent.

N. The perpendicular ſhank of the gage plate.

O. A flat headed iron ſcrew, which paſſing through the ſtaple P, and perpendi-cular ſhank of the hind gage, ſcrews into the end of the chip S, and ſerves occa-ſionally to elevate or depreſs the gage.

P. A flat ſtaple, which embraces the perpendicular ſhank of the tail gage, and the flat headed ſcrew O, with which the gage is fixed as need requires.

Q. A horizontal iron plate or gage, 5 inches ſquare, and ¼ inch thick, with a perpendicular ſhank pierced through with holes to receive the iron ſcrew; with which it is ſet to a proper degree of elevation for the purpoſe intended.

R. The chip, is 3 feet 3 inches long, 5¼ broad, and 4 inches thick; the ex-treme length of the plough from the point of the ſhare A, to the end of the chip R, is 4 feet 4 inches.

S. Two ſcrews and nuts, with which the
ſhank

shank of the share is fastened to the chip.
N. B. Only one of the screws and nuts
appear in this view of the plough.

T. A round-headed iron bolt, 16 inches
long, ⅜ of an inch thick, with a hole
through its upper end, for a pin or screw
to keep it in its place; this bolt passes
through the eyes of the four iron plates
or hinges, u u u u, which are properly
fitted and rivetted to the breast plate and iron
wings or mould-boards, and serves as a
spindle for them to turn on.

U U, &c. Four iron plates or hinges,
3 inches long, 2 ¼ broad, and ¹⁄₁₆ of an
inch thick, rivetted to the breast plate and
iron wings.

V. The flat-headed iron pin or screw,
which passes through the upper end of the
bolt or spindle, to keep it to its place.

W. An iron hook, fastened to the upper
side of the beam, and is occasionally set in
the holes of the curved gage, to regulate
the depth of the furrow.

X X X. Three clamps or iron plates,
fastened to the beam, to prevent it from
splitting.

Y. An iron gage or regulator, being a
segment of a circle, pierced through with
holes;

holes; this fegment is about 2 feet 3 inches long (exclufive of its fhank) two inches broad, and ¼ of an inch thick; its fhank is 3 feet 2 inches long, and one inch fquare, with a hole at its extremity for the hook.

Z. A flat-headed iron bolt or brace, which paffes through the chip, beam, and fheath; it is faftened thereto with a nut and fcrew, to ftrengthen the plough.

a a. The carriage wheels, are two feet diameter, and two inches on their periphery.

b. An iron axle-tree, 20¼ inches long, and 1¼ of an inch fquare in the middle, with a fmall fhoulder on each face for the under end of the fegment to bear againft, to which it is faftened with a feathered bolt or wedge through the axle-tree.

c c c. Three wooden wafhers, 4 inches diameter, and one inch thick; the ufe of thefe wafhers is to fet the carriage wheels at a greater or lefs diftance from each other, as need requires.

d. An iron hook, which paffes through a hole in the end of the fhank of the gage, and ferves to fix the axle-tree, gage, &c.

to the beam, to which the hook is faftened with a ftrong wood fcrew.

e An iron plate, 14 inches long, 2⅛ broad, and ¾ of an inch thick; this plate is fixed in a horizontal pofition, clofe under the caliper; its fore end is turned down flanting, and faftened to the fheath G, and its tail end is turned up flanting, and faftened to the fheath H. In the middle of the plate there is an aperture 13 inches long; its ufe is to guide the iron pin f, and regulate the motion of the caliper, &c. This plate ferves alfo as a brace or ftay to the hind and fore fheath.

f. A round-headed iron pin, with which the caliper is connected to the directing plate e; the under end of this pin paffing through the aperture in the plate, is thereby directed fo as to procure a regular motion to the caliper, mould-boards, &c.

g g. Two iron plates, with two horizontal ears rivetted to each of them. Thefe ears embrace the fore ends of the caliper, and are connected thereto with the iron pin h h. See fig. 8. N. B. The plates are rivetted to the infide of the iron wings or curved mould-boards; but there is only one of them feen in this view of the plough;

plough; the other is indicated by the dotted lines on the outfide of the left wing.

h. An iron pin, with which the caliper is connected to the plate, &c. as before mentioned.

A. Fig. 2. The plough fhare.

e. Fig. 3. The directing iron.

h. Fig. 4. The axis of the carriage wheels.

Y. Fig. 5. The curved gage.

Q. Fig. 6. The hind gage plate; P, the flat ftaple; O, the flat-headed iron fcrew.

K. Fig. 7. The caliper; e the directing plate; f the round-headed iron pin, with which the caliper is connected to the directing plate.

g. Fig. 8. A fquare iron plate with ears, which embrace the fore end of the caliper; h an iron pin, with which the caliper is connected to the ears.

T. Fig. 9. The round-headed iron bolt or fpindle, which paffes through the hinges u u, &c. V a flat-headed fcrew, which ferves to keep the bolt in its place.

This plough Mr. *Arbuthnot* chiefly ufes for earthing up plants in rows, and ftriking furrows. It works in light or well tilled land with two horfes, on other occafions

cafions with three. The mould-boards
expand at pleafure, according to the diftance
between the rows, and have fuch a fweep,
that they will earth up a row of plants to
any degree or height required, even to
burying them on the top of an arched
ridge.

The variations of depth are equally
fimple, being by the fegment of a circle,
which goes vertically through the end of the
beam. But as the accuracy of the performance depends on this gage always
retaining its exact form, care fhould be
taken in turning on the head-lands, not
to throw the plough on one fide, as practifed with the common wheel plough.

As I have myfelf ufed this implement,
and with uncommon fuccefs, I beg leave
to hint, that in various works I have found
it of incomparable ufe. in the operations
of horfe hoeing, earthing up the rows, it
equals the exacteft hand work: another ufe,
in which it is peculiarly important, is
forming ridges out of fine tilled *flat* lands.
If furrows are drawn with a fmall fwing
plough, on a level furface at every 4 feet,
and the double mould-board goes in them,
ridges of that breadth will at once be formed,

5   arched

arched at will by the degree of expanſion in the wings. At 5 or 6 feet the ſame, only at wide diſtances it will not *arch*, but leaves a ſmall cavity along the center of the ridge: this is of excellent uſe for cabbages, &c. the ſides to be drawn to the plants by hoeing. I have alſo uſed it for drawing water-furrows on well-ploughed land, and find it executes them extremely well.

After two bout ridges are drawn out in half ploughing, with deſign to finiſh, this plough does double work in finiſhing.

The price 8 *l.* 18 *s.* 6 *d.*

The hint taken from a plough conſtructed by *William Craik*, Eſq. of *Arbigland.*

Plate XII. *The Drill Plough.*

References.

A. Is the frame of the carriage.

B. The ſhafts, which are movable on a bar, to ſuit different ſized lands, or hang on occaſionally in front, when ſowing flat.

C. The great lanthorn wheel; it is 8 inches in diameter, is immovable on the axis, and has 6 ſtaves.

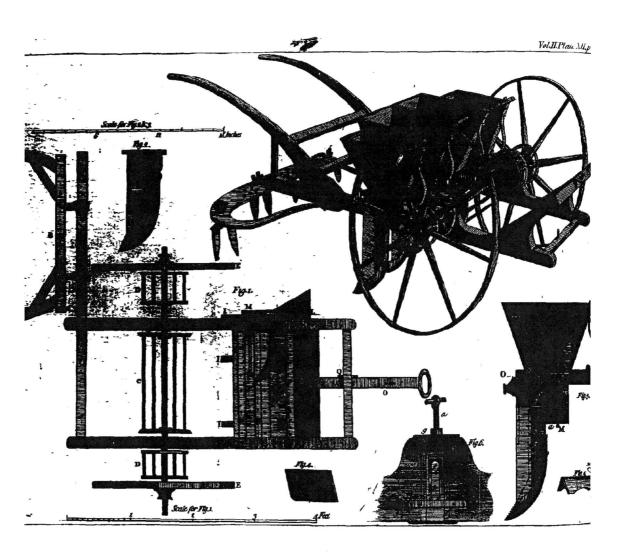

Scale for Fig.2.3

Fig.2.

Fig.1.

Fig.3.

Fig.4.

Fig.5.

Scale for Fig.1.

D D. Are two of equal diameters, which may be taken off when only two hoppers are wanted; they have likewife fix ftaves: thefe three wheels turn with the axis, and lift the ends of the levers I.

E E. Are the wheels of the carriage, which go on fquare on the axis, and may be fet at any diftance to fuit the lands.

F. Is a fquare plank, two inches thick, which flides in the two fides of the frame; there are two feed hoppers fixed on the upper fide, and on the under are the two fhares, one in its work marked G, the other reprefented by fig. 2: thefe fhares flide in the plates marked H H, in which there are holes at an inch afunder for fcrews, to fix the fhares at the required diftance; the openings at the top of the fhares are bevel, to catch the feed, which comes through the fquare holes in the plank, whichever way you move the fhare; in the center of the front plate of thefe two fhares is a hole, and another at half an inch diftance. thefe correfpond with the fcrew holes in the plate H, which are an inch afunder: this anfwers the fame purpofe, as if the holes in the plate H were

were only half an inch afunder, which would have weakened that plate.

II. Are the levers, which are fixed by a center pin in the hoppers, as reprefented in fig. 3 ; thefe ends are lifted up by the ftaves of the lanthorn wheels, which confequently lower the tongue R, to deliver the feed; thefe tongues work againft a brufh K, which is fet at the diftance fuitable to the fize of the grain.

L. Is one of the fide hoppers, to which the fhare is fixed, and which has an iron plate M fixed at the bottom, which flides in the plates N N. In the plate M, there are three holes, at an inch and a half afunder, for a fcrew to fix it at the proper diftance: thus, when each of the middle fhares is fhifted half an inch, the outward ones are fhifted an inch and half, which keeps them all at equal diftances.

O. Is an iron bar, fixed into the plank at P; it goes through the end rail of the frame, and ferves to move the plank with the hopper forward, to fet it into work, and to draw it out of work at the ends of the lands ; the fix holes are gages to afcertain the quantity of feed to be fown; a

pin

pin is fixed into either of them, which ftops againft the rail, when the fpring Q, on the other fide of the rail, catches in the correfponding notch; the further the hoppers are advanced to the wheel, the more feed is delivered, as the levers I are lifted higher by the ftaves of the lanthorn wheels.

Fig. 3. is one of the outfide hoppers, with the fhare faftened to it, all which flide together on the plate M. R is the tongue, which lets out the feed, when the end I is lifted up, and clofes the bottom of the hopper, when forced down again by the fpring S. K is the brufh, againft which the tongue works; the elafticity of the briftles prevents ftoppage or bruifing of the grain; it is fet by the gage fcrew T, according to the fize of the grain. U is a fcrew, which goes through the iron bar, that fecures the hoppers at the diftance they are fet.

Fig. 4. is an iron box, with wires faftened in it, which interfect each other; thefe are occafionally put into the fhares, when wheat is fown, to difperfe the grain, and prevent its falling in lumps.

Fig. 5. is a triangular piece of wood, hollow underneath, and on the fides; it is placed in the hopper, a little above the tongue; this fuffers the feed to fink gradually, and prevents its laying too heavy, which often makes it arch at the bottom of the hopper; and being hollow at bottom, there is room for the feed to rife by the fpring of the lever: thus the feed is kept in motion, and is delivered more equally.

Fig. 6. is a fliding box, which raifes or finks the wheels to fow deep or fhallow. *a* is a fcrew rivetted at bottom, to the top of the frame *b*, which flides up and down in two grooves *c c*. *d* is the axle of the wheel, which runs in the box *e*, and is faftened in by the pin *f*; this was neceffary to get the axle into the box, as it is fhouldered on each fide, to prevent its fliding either way the fcrew *a* works in the nut *g* to raife or fink the whole.

Plate

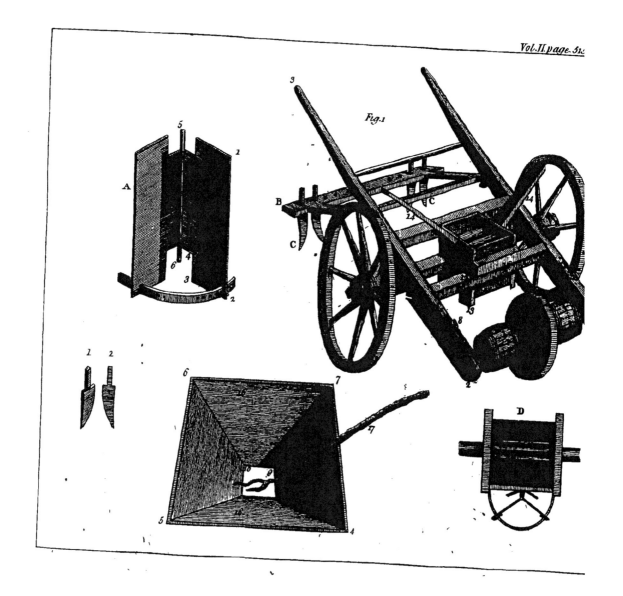

Fig. 1

Plate XIII.

The Turnip Drill, with a manure Hopper.

References.

1 to	2	—	2 Feet	6 Inches.
2 to	3	—	6	2
4 to	5	—	2	10
5 to	6	—	2	10
7 to	9	—	1	8
9 to	10	—	0	$10\frac{1}{2}$
11 to	12	—	0	4
11 to	13	—	1	0
2 to	8	—	0	11

17 A movable ſtick, with a forked end for ſtirring the manure, in caſe of choaking.

The cags, or little barrels, 9 inches long, and 6 diameter, movable on the axis 13.

The front wheels $15\frac{1}{2}$ inches diameter, and 2 inches thick.

The hopper is ſupported by the brace 14 14, and fixed by the peg 16 16.

The wheels 30 inches diameter.

The box 15 is $10\frac{1}{2}$ inches ſquare, and contains a fluted roller of wood, 8 inches diameter, turned by the axis of the wheels, and delivers the manure, which would fall perpendicularly, were it not for two ſmall boards, which expand at pleaſure by a hinge, which throws the manure over the rows. See A.

L l 2

1 to 2	—	1 Foot	$\frac{1}{2}$ Inch.
2 to 3	—	0	$4\frac{1}{2}$
3 to 4	—	0	3
5 to 6	—	0	10

This is an iron fpindle running through the hinge to fix to the bottom of the box 15.

B. Reprefents the harrow, which is hung on behind.

C. The teeth; 1 1 a front view; (2) an oblique view of one.

D. A reprefentation of the roller in profile, and A fixed for ufe.

The great ufe of this implement, which is perhaps one of the moft fimple ever invented, is to depofit the manure directly on the turnip or lucerne feed, not by way of enriching the land, but to quicken the growth while young, juft fufficient to enable the plant to efcape the fly. A fmall quantity laid directly on the feed thus, anfwers a very large dreffing in the common manner. The proper manures are foot, malt-duft, all forts of afhes, lime, dung rotted to powder, pigeon's dung, &c. *

---

* The hint of delivering the manure taken from a drill plough invented by Dr. *Gale*, of *New England*, improved only in the variation of the diftances.

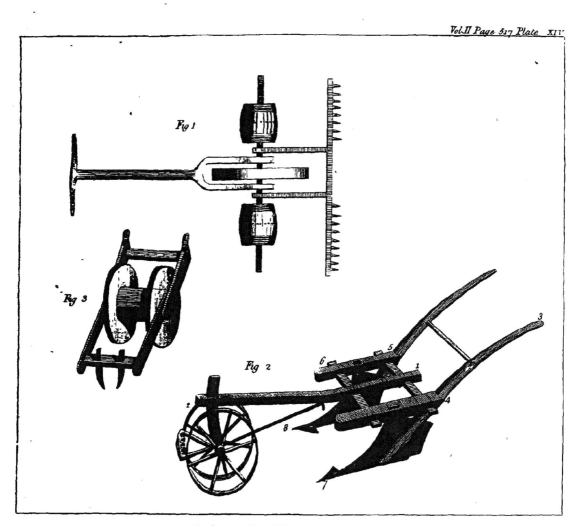

Fig 1

Fig 3

Fig 2

In the types fig 2. Reference 1 to 3 say 1 to 2

Plate XIV. Fig. 1.

The Turnip Drill.

This tool, which for fimplicity in the invention has infinite merit, is ufed on land that is worked very fine ready for turnip feed, and is drawn by a man or boy along the top of each ridge, or on the flat, at pleafure. It is unneceffary to obferve, that it is cheap, eafily repaired, or even made by a ploughman, and performs accurately and well.

Plate XIV. Fig. 2. *The Double Plough.*

References.

1 to 3	—	6 Feet	3 Inches.
3 to 4	—	3	8
4 to 5	—	2	0
6 to 2	—	3	2
7 to 8	—	2	2
9 to 10	—	2	2

From tail to tail 1 foot.

Height from the ground 18 inches.

The ufe of this plough is to head up from the flat, leaving a little fpace between each head, to be divided by the double mould-board plough. The advantage is, that the middle of thefe narrow lands, which is the beft of the field, and which ought to be in the lighteft condition, is

L l 3   trampled

trampled by the horfes in backing up the firft furrow in the common method.

Two horfes work it completely, doing double the work of common ploughs.

Plate XIV. Fig. III.

A fmall barrel drill, which fixes to the tail of any plough, and delivers turnip feed; the fimplicity of the conftruction, its cheapnefs, and other circumftances render it of more than common value.

Plate XV. *The Drain Plough.*

References.

1 to	2	—	5 Feet	0 Inches.
2 to	3	—	2	6
3 to	4	—	4	6
4 to	5	—	2	2
5 to	6	—	0	7
7 to	8	—	2	10
2 to	9	—	2	6
9 to	10	—	2	6
10 to	11	—	1	3
11 to	12	—	1	8
13 to	14	—	1	8
11 to	15	—	0	9
10 to	16	—	2	6
16 to	17	—	1	2
18 to	19	—	1	8
19 to	20	—	1	11
20 to	21	—	1	9
22 to	23	—	1	0
24 to	25	—	5	8

5 to 26 —	2	4
26 to 27 —	1	5
27 to 28 —	1	0
27 to 29 —	3	0
30 to 31 —	3	6
25 to the beam		
hole bottom	0	6
32 to 33 —	1	7
34 to 35 —	1	4

The lower fhaɪe 2 ½ inches wide; the upper one 6.

The beam at 24, is 5 inches fquare; and the fame, but rounded to 4 inches, at 4.

Standards of the gallows, 6 inches by 3.

Wheels, 5 feet diameter.

This machine cuts the drain 16 inches deep at one ftroke, on grafs or clover, and requires no cleaning after it, but accidentally; wants no furrows to be drawn out for it to work in; delivers the turf 8 inches thick on one fide of the trench, and the other 8 inches on the other fide, which of courfe facilitates the work in covering in: it requires 8 ftrong horfes, 1 holder, and 2 drivers; leaves the drain cut in a cleaner and more regular manner than poffible for a fpade, and if the ground is ftrong, brings up the bottom of the furrows in as regular a form as if caft in a mould; and the turf being

L l 4 regularly

regularly turned in one piece of equal thicknefs and dimenfions, makes the covering
particularly expeditious.

Among other trials of its performance,
fix acres were drained in 3 hours, 1 ½ rod
afunder, which amounted to 720 rods,
or 1920 in the day's work of 8 hours, with
12 horfes; but it is to be obferved, that
by giving wheels of 5 feet, Mr. *Arbuthnot*
finds 8 horfes juft as effectual as the 12.
The following fketch will fhew the expence.

Twelve horfes and 3 men, according to the price of the country, £. 1 10 0
                       ——————

The proportion of which, in 3
   hours, is,   -   -   0 11 3
   720 rods, at that price, is not a farthing
a rod.

Notwithftanding which, Mr. *Arbuthnot*
thinks this is not a tool to be generally
recommended ; becaufe it requires an accuracy in the conftruction, and reparation,
if out of order, particularly in fixing the
four coulters, not to be expected in the
generality of country workmen. That it is
alfo expenfive, coming to near 20*l.*

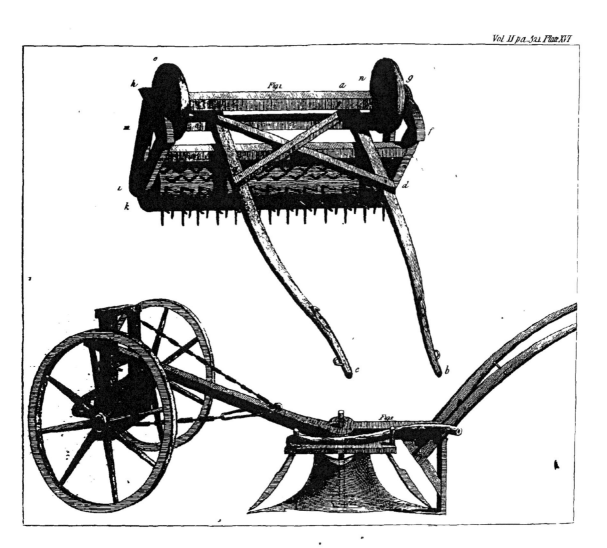

Plate XVI. Fig. 1.

The spiky Roller.

References.

a to b —	12 Feet	o Inches.
b to d —	7	3
g to f —	3	6
g to e —	2	o
n to o —	6	9
h to 1 —	2	2
c to m —	2	4
p to q —	6	10
b to c —	2	6

The square of the end braces g, h, 4 inches by 7 $\frac{1}{2}$.

Ditto of the standards e, m, 3 by 7.

Length of the cylinder, 7 feet 6 inches.

The wheel axle, 5 $\frac{1}{2}$ inches square.

Diameter of the cylinder, 18 inches.

Ditto of the wheels, 12 inches.

The shafts at q are 3 inches by 5.

The cross bars, 3 $\frac{1}{2}$ inches and 4.

256 Teeth, which weigh 512 *lb.*

However rough a fallow may be, the spiky roller will reduce it at twice going; five horses and one man do 6 acres a day, once in a place; it will be perfectly effectual when harrows or drags have no effect. Clods may be left to roast for destruction of root weeds, with certainty

I

that

that they may be at any time reduced to pulverization. The only caution to be obferved in its ufe is, that it muft never go on the ground till perfectly dry. Mr. *Arbuthnot* under that circumftance never knew an inftance of any mould adhering to it, but on the contrary, when by chance it has been carried on too foon, it immediately clogs.

Plate XVI. Fig. 2.
The Turnwreft Plough.

This is an idea of Mr. *Arbuthnot*'s it has not yet been executed, but he intends it as foon as his numerous avocations will allow him time. His objection to all the common turnwrefts is the neceffity there is of the fhare being fo narrow that it cannot cut the furrow; and the impoffibility of fixing a proper mould-board; both which objections will be here obviated.

This gentleman having, as the reader may judge from the preceding implements, given uncommon attention to the conftruction of all forts of ploughs, I was very defirous of having him lay down explicit rules for the inftruction of wheel-wrights in building a common plough; on requefting him to explain his ideas on this fubject, he was obliging enough to draw

up

up the following paper, accompanied with feveral very accurate drawings · I infert it here with the utmoft fatisfaction, under the firm conviction, that fo clear and decifive an account of the principles of conftructing a plough never yet was laid before the publick.

As different counties have adopted ploughs of different conftructions, feemingly more from chance, than the expediency of foil, or other circumftances, I fhall in the following effay endeavour to explain the principles on which the fwing and wheel-ploughs fhould be conftructed to the greateft advantage, and fhew, wherein the management of the one effentially differs from the other

Secondly, I fhall attempt to prove in which part of the plough the point of refiftance is, from which the different lines of traction muft tend to the horfes fhoulders, in different operations, and foils, and by explaining, wherein the direction of the line of draught to the wheel-plough differs from that of the fwing-plough, prove the fuperior advantage of the wheel-plough, where the nature of the foil will admit the ufe of it.

Thirdly, I fhall defcribe the form of the fhare and fweep of the breaft and mould-board, which have appeared to me moft likely to diminifh the friction and adhefion of the earth on this ufe-ful but as yet imperfect machine

Laftly, I fhall attempt to give an eafy mecha-nical rule to wheelwrights, by which they may lay down a plan for any form of a plough, which their moft inferior workmen may execute,

and

and which will likewife enable them to preferve the form and proportions of any plough they are ordered to copy, though the plough fhould be requred to be of different dimenfions

I fhall only further obferve, that what I fhall advance, is founded on experiments profecuted with the greateft attention.

I fhall begin with the fwing-plough, which is poifed by two levers, the one of which is the handle, and acts as a lever of the firft kind, the fulcrum being at the heel of the plough, between the power at the handles, and the weight on the fhare. The other lever is the beam, which is of the fecond kind, the end of the beam being the point where the power is applied, the weight being on the fhare, and the heel of the plough the fulcrum. When thefe powers are properly applied, the fwing-plough is a very good inftrument, and in the hands of ploughmen, who are ufed to obferve the proper æquilibrium, will perform its work to any reafonable depth.

As in the circumftance of the weight being on the fhare, I differ in opinion from a very ingenious author, the Rev Mr *Dickfon*, it is neceffary I fhould give my reafons, and the proofs whereon they are founded, more efpecially as the length of the beam and handles, and application of the draught, entirely depend on this propofition, as will appear hereafter fully explained, in afcertaining the line of traction.

I do not pretend to fay, that the natural center of gravity of the plough is on the fhare, but when I confider the additional weight of the part of the furrow to be lifted, though feparately the center of gravity of each is in a different point, yet when they become one body, they muft have a common center of gravity, which,

in

in my opinion, muſt be in a perpendicular line, nearer the point of the ſhare, than when the plough was a body by itſelf

And when I further conſider, that the power of coheſion in the body to be lifted is much greater than its gravity, and that the ſeparation of ſuch body is firſt to be effected by the point of the ſhare , and further, that the reſiſtance of the earth againſt the coulter, which is very conſiderable, is above the point of the ſhare; I cannot but believe, that, in proportion to the ſolidity of the body to be ſeparated, the weight and reſiſtance is advanced nearly towards, if not quite to that point. This ſeems to be confirmed by practice , for, when ploughing in loam, if the point of the ſhare touches on clay, the plough will immediately ſuck into the ground, and ſome-times require the whole weight of the plough-man on the handles to priſe it up. But to ſatisfy myſelf as to the fact, I have often (when my plough has been working to my mind) ſtopped the horſes ſuddenly, and then fixing a ſtick in the ground, to the height of the tug at the horſe's ſhoulder, and removing the earth from above the ſhare, without altering the poſition of the plough, I always found, that a line extended from the top of the ſtick to the point of the ſhare, interſected the notch of the copſe to which the draught was fixed.

But as the ſtooping of the horſe, when at his pull, will lower thoſe ends of the draught chains, and the other ends being fixed to the beam will carry the direction of the line of traction a little backward, I will not contend, that the draught is immediately from the point of the ſhare, but from a point an inch or two behind it , however, from the above mentioned

experi-

experiment, I fhould be induced to call that point, the center of refiftance, nor do I conceive that the center of gravity of a plough can be in any point of the line of traction, though I believe in the combined weights of the plough and earth, their common center of gravity is near it, at leaft on fome part of the fhare ; for as that part of the furrow, which is fupported on the mould-board, is on a much more inclined furface, than that part of the furrow, which refts on the more horizontal furface of the fhare, their centers of gravity diftinctly muft fall in different lines, and indeed the lateral furface of the board rifes fo fuddenly, that the center of gravity of that part of the mould muft foon be out of a line with the plough, confequently the medium of the weight of earth, is probably pretty forward on the fhare ; but as I mentioned before, the power of cohefion being greater than the weight, in my opinion puts it beyond a doubt.

That the length of the handle, which is the long arm of the bended lever, fhould be to the length of the bottom of the plough, which is the fhort arm, as the weight on the fhare, and tendency of the point into the ground, are to the power, which is applied at the handle, is felf-evident, and it is made fo by moft wheel-wrights But I cannot fay, that the other part of the plough, which conftitutes the lever of the fecond kind, has been fo well confidered and attended to, though it is by far the moft effential firft, as the application of it is not folely to the ftrongeft power of the horfe, which is that of drawing, but partly to his power of lifting For when the line of draught is nearly parallel to the plane whereon the horfe goes, he will draw a much greater proportion of his weight, than he

can

can carry Hence it appears, that the proper
length of this lever requires the greatest attention,
but the other, provided it is long enough, cannot
be amifs, as the whole weight of the ploughman
is the required power at the utmost.

The only rule I have been able to lay down,
is, that a line drawn from the tug at the horfe's
fhoulder to the point of the fhare, fhould interfect the notch in the copfe immediately below
the end of the beam, as that pitch admits of the
moft variations; it muft be obferved, that the
tug at the fhoulder of a full-fized horfe is about
four feet four inches from the ground, and the
length of chains neceffary for him to work freely
about nine feet; but, as I faid before, when
the horfe finks to his pull, I think it muft neceffarily carry the line of traction to a point
behind the point of the fhare, but it is fcarcely
poffible to afcertain the immediate fpot on the
fhare, from the difficulty of meafuring the
height of the tug at the horfe's fhoulder, when
he is in motion. However it is felf-evident,
that in proportion to the finking of the horfe,
as the draught chains are fixed to an inflexible
beam, the direction of the line of traction will
be carried backward, but, as the center of refiftance can lay but in one point, the ploughman will immediately be fenfible of the alteration, and if only an accidental finking of the
horfe, will remedy it by preffing on the handles,
if the natural difpofition of the horfe is to fink
to the draught, he will alter the direction of the
line of traction, by lowering the draught at the
end of the beam

I have given the above direction to my wheel-
wrights, and they find it anfwers, but, as the
different heights of horfes, and the different
applications

applications of the draught, being fingle or double, will make a great alteration in the line of traction, that is, when one horfe goes on the land, and the other in the furrow, the line of traction will be as if both horfes were on a fur-face half the depth of the furrow, and when the horfes go at length, viz one before the other, the angle of traction of the foremoft horfe with the ground will be more acute than the angle of traction from the hindmoft or thill horfe, there-fore an intermediate angle muft be found And further, as the different nature of foils, in which the plough works, will make an alteration in the above rule, it is neceffary to fix a copfe at the end of the beam to raife or lower the draught, and give the plough land or not the ule of which is fo well underftood, that a defcription of it would be needlefs, was it not in the firft place to prove, how much the cat-head ufed in *Suffolk* is fuperior to every other kind of copfe; and in the fecond place, to point out the error of many ploughmen in their application of the draught, when horfes go at length. Fig. 1, plate XVII is the cat-head, with the copfe fixed to it. Fig. 2, is the fide view of the copfe belonging to the cat-head. Fig 3, is the com-mon copfe. Fig. 4, is a copfe ufed in fome parts of *Yorkfhire* Plate XVIII fig 1, is a plough in its work, with the different lines of traction neceffary to be obferved in the appli-cation of the draught, which fhews the neceffity of afcertaining the point of refiftance, as on that depends the pofition of the beam A B is the beam of the plough, fix feet long, having a copfe extending three inches beyond it, and eight inches deep The under part of the end of the beam at B, 14 inches from the bottom of the furrow.

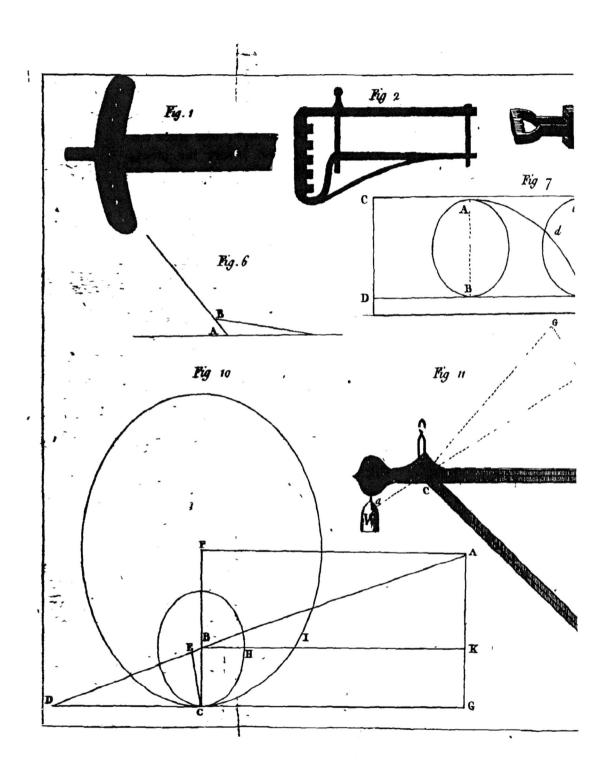

Fig. 1

Fig 2

Fig 7

Fig. 6

Fig 10

Fig 11

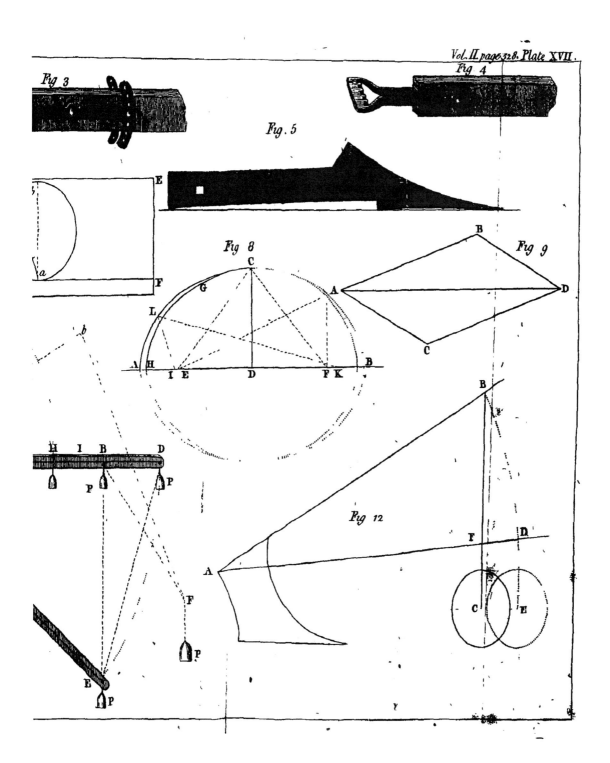

Fig. 3

Fig. 4

Fig. 5

Fig. 8

Fig. 9

Fig. 12

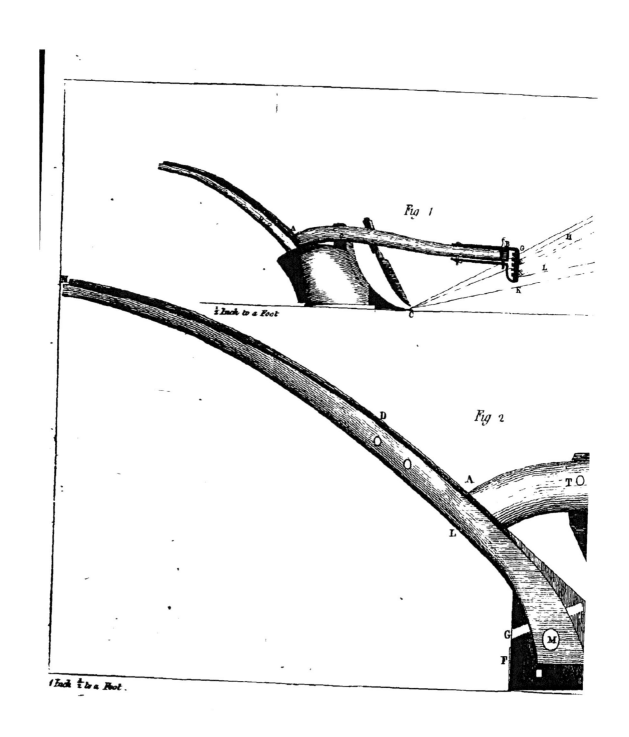

Fig 1

½ Inch to a Foot

Fig 2

1 Inch ⅛ to a Foot.

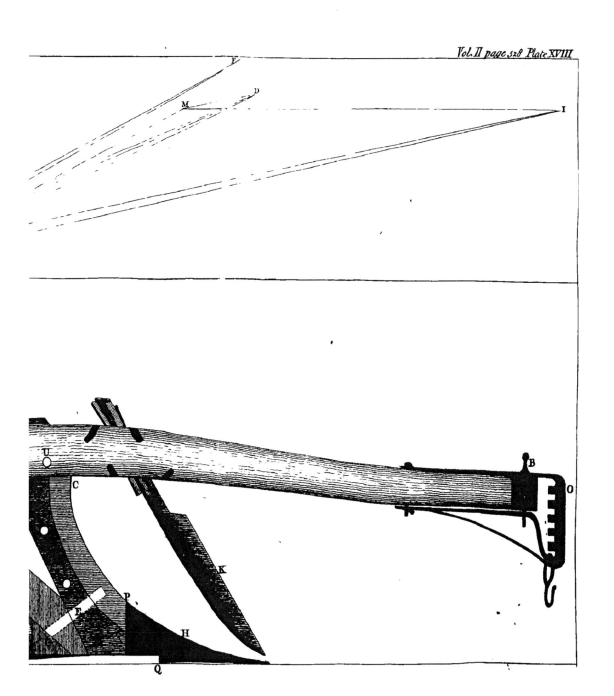

furrow. C the point of the fhare, 2 feet 10 inches diftant from the under part of the end of the beam at B D is the point of the horfe's fhoulder, about four feet four inches high, the diftance from that point to the end of the beam, for a full-fized horfe, will be about nine feet, if the horfe ftands in the furrow, the line of traction, C D, will interfect the copfe at the notch E, about two inches below the end of the beam, but if the horfe ftands on the land, his fhoulder will be at F, and the line C F will interfect at G. Thus, when horfes go abreaft, the draft muft be fixed between E G at H, but, if the horfes go one before the other, the line of traction, from the foremoft horfe's fhoulder at I, (which will be full eight feet fix inches beyond the tug of the thill-horfe) will cut below the copfe at K, confequently the lines of traction D C and I C muft be united in one draught at L, bringing the chains from the foremofthorfe to the whipping at L, the fame as from D. This is undoubtedly the method in which the draught ought to be applied but the ufual cuftom is to raife the chains of the thill-horfe up to M, level with his fhoulder, and often higher, by fhorten-ing the ridger, which is a fhort chain that goes over the horfe's back; the only ufe of which ought to be, to fupport the chains from hang-ing fo low, as that the horfe may get his legs over them; but they fhorten it to raife the beam of the plough, making the angle D M C, and letting the foremoft horfe draw from the chains of the thill-horfe, in the line I M; with-out confidering, as I faid before, that it is not only applying the power to the weakeft part of the horfe, but alfo that, by making an angle in the line of traction, the weight on the thill-horfe's

back is increafed, in proportion to the draught
of the horfes that are before him   By this method it is evident, that the whole weight of the
draft of the plough is fupported by the thill-
horfe; and though a horfe cannot continue to
work under above one third of his weight, he is
often obliged to fupport the weight of the draft
of four ftrong horfes, each of which can draw
more than one third of his weight: the confequence is, that the thill-horfes never put their
fhoulders to the collar, learning by habit, that
their fhare of the labour is to carry the weight,
and that fometimes fo intolerable a one, that
you will fee them reel in the furrow   I have
dwelled longer on this fubject, to convince gentlemen, who engage in farming, how neceffary
it is that they attend to the mechanical minutiæ
of their inftruments and labour.   Having explained the neceffity of making the alterations
of the draught at the copfe, the cat-head above
defcribed will appear much more ufeful than the
common one.   See fig. 3, plate XVII. which
moves upon a center pin at A, and is fixed to
its pitch by the movable pin B, which requiring to be keyed in, that the pin may not be
loft, it is fo much trouble to the ploughman to
make any alteration, that he always is careful
to give the plough too much depth, at the fame
time fhortening the ridger, in the manner explained above, fixing the draught as low as the
notch at N, plate XIII.   By this means, one
power counteracts the other, at the expence of
an additional horfe, almoft ufelefs in the team;
the only alteration the ploughman makes, as to
the depth, is by taking up or letting out a link
in the ridger.   Bad as this copfe is, it is ftill
preferable to the *Yorkfhire* one, (fee fig. 4,
plate

plate XVII.) which fwings up and down upon
the fixed pin A, not admitting of any alteration
as to depth, therefore anfwers no better purpofe than if the chains were faftened to the
beam at A   As to the method of notching the
plough in or out of land, the one anfwers the
purpofe as well as the other

As the perfection of the fwing plough depends
on fo great a nicety, it is continually liable to
be out of order   For example, if the point of
the fhare be made longer or fhorter by new laying, or is fet down either too deep, or not deep
enough, the plough will not go well. This
indeed a fkilful ploughman will in fome degree
rectify, by an alteration in the geers.   The beft
method is, as I have faid before, by raifing or
lowering the draught at the copfe, but if it requires fo much alteration, that the depth of the
copfe will not admit of it, the next beft is by
lengthening or fhortening the traces; which will
alter the angle of traction, and this fhews, that
the length of the traces fhould be more attended
to than I believe it generally is   When a plough
is well pitched, the fhorter the traces the better,
fo as that the horfe can but work   If the traces
will not admit of being fhortened, the only method left is to fhorten the ridger, but this is fo
very improper, that it is abfolutely neceffary,
that the plough irons fhould be kept in fuch
order, as never to require this laft operation.
The method I take to prevent my fhare being
altered from the firft form, when fent to be new
laid by the fmith, is, that the land fide of the
fhare is continued the whole length of the bottom of the plough, and when applied to the
pattern I have given him to work by, he has
the complete form of the bottom of the plough,

and can make no alteration, unlefs wilfully; neither can the ploughman fet the point up or down, or in or out of land, the whole going on at once, and fixed by a bolt at the heel See fig 5, plate XVII

The next part to be confidered is the mould-board, about which people differ much in opi-nion, as to the fhape of the breaft, and fweep of the board. I have pa d great attention to thefe, and do confefs each has its peculiar merit, in the hands of different ploughmen, in particular operations I prefer the curved board, as being moft generally ufeful The one moft common in ufe is the ftraight board, with the breaft ftraight and fharp, making an angle, fig. 6, plate XVII, A, of about 53 degrees with the bottom of the plough, and another B, of 137 with the upper plane of the fhare on the land fide. This laft angle is evidently a fault in the plough, as appears by its being filled up with earth by the time it has gone through a few furrows; which filling up proves the form it ought to be of, namely, that this angle ought to be filled up with wood or iron, as the friction or ftickage of the earth on fuch fmooth furface will be much lefs than on the earth, which has filled up the cavity.

Another evident fault in the ftraight mould-board is pointed out by the earth's wearing a hollow in the breaft, nearly fimilar to the fweep of the *Rotheram* board This fhews that *that* part is as much too full, as the bottom of the breaft, at the fetting on of the fhare, is too hol-low. Indeed, I do not know a better practical rule to finifh the fweep of a board, than by working the plough fome days before it is plated, as the earth will wear off thofe parts that pro-

ject

ject too much, and fill up the hollows that ought not to be, which laft circumftance fhould be attended to in plating the mould-board. not but that in fome inftances the wooden mould-board is preferable to the plated one, particularly when working in ftrong land, when there is too much moifture in it, which muft fometimes be the cafe in feed time, as at that feafon farmers cannot command their time as in breaking up or fallowing The reafon I take to be this, that the wood imbibes a due quantity of water, thus the furface of the wood being always wet, the ftickage or adhefion of the earth is not fo great as on the iron, which cannot admit the water, but the wooden mould-board wears out fo foon, and the expence of the curved board is fo great, that the inconvenience attending the iron plate muft be difpenfed with

A further great objection to the ftraight board is, that it is neceffarily too wide at heel, and confequently acts like a continued wedge I mean the common *Englifh* plough with the ftraight mould-board ; the *Scotch* one defcribed by Mr. *Dickfon*, is evidently better, as it has the wreft raifed fo as to make an angle with the plane of the horizon, from the buck of the fhare to the heel · whereas the *Englifh* wreft is parallel to the plane. To remedy the inconvenience that arifes from this form in the *Englifh* plough, they hold it over on the land-fide, otherwife, in ftrong work, they could not get it through the ground. This fubjects them to wreft-baulk the land, which is acknowledged to be a very great fault in ploughing, as part of the under furface of the land is not moved. But an intelligent plough-man will rectify this, by fetting down the fin of his fhare However, this depends on his care, occafions lofs of time, and is attended with expence in altering the irons.

Another

Another inconvenience attending this method of holding the plough on the land-fide is the increafe of friction, by fo much as the quantity of earth always fliding on the board is greater. The only advantage it feems to have beyond that of the curved-board is, that, by holding it on the land-fide, when ftriking up the laft furrow, it will have more hold of the ground, therefore not fo liable to ftrike at heel· by this means it will throw up a furrow, that the *Rotheram* will not do, when held in that direction; as the breaft of the laft, which is hollowed out, then becomes a more horizontal furface, and carries the furrow, which fhews, that the *Rotheram* fhould always be held upright, and it will then perform this laft operation quite as well as the other, provided the crumb-furrow is taken clofe to the adjoining land. On the whole, in my opinion, there are many difadvantages, and not one real advantage, attending the ftraight board. In this, I have not only my own practice to confirm me in my opinion, but alfo that of fome neighbouring farmers, who frequently borrow my ploughs to break up ground, which they cannot do with their own. This laft circumftance is no fmall proof of the preference of the curved mould-board

My plough differs fome little matter from the *Rotheram*, though I took fome hints from it. for as it was obvious that the angle at the fetting-on of the fhare was a fault, I preferred it to the *Suffolk*; which otherwife is a good little plough in light land, but has not length enough to go fteady in our ftrong land. The weight on the fhare being fo near the fulcrum at the heel, the leaft preffure on the handles or jerk of the horfe will raife it.

From the fhape of the *Rotheram*, I was led to believe, that the fegment of a circle muft be the

true

true fhape But I found it neceffary to take the
fegment of a large circle, in order to obtain an
eafy admiffion into the ground · but this carried
the mould too high on the breaft It then occurred to me, that a femi-cycloid was the proper
fhape, the bottom of which, being fo much
lefs fteep than that of a circular arc, will enter
more eafily and freely into the ground As this
kind of wedge moves the earth only on one fide,
it will act on the body of earth lifted, in proportion of its length to its thicknefs, and the
upper part, being fo much fteeper, will turn off
the mould fo much fooner than the laft-mentioned
fegment, but not fo fuddenly as the plough in
general ufe, and therefore will raife the furrow
fo much eafier, as the turning it off is flower.
I made one of the fize of the *Rotheram:* the
fweep of the breaft was defcribed by a gene-
rating circle of fixteen inches diameter, it
performed the work much better than any plough
I had ever feen, but trying it in very loofe mould,
I perceived fome earth would now and then lodge
in the throat this induced me to make another,
the fweep of which was the half of a femi-ellipfis,
whofe femi conjugate diameter was likewife fixteen inches: thus the pitch of both was exactly the
fame In the laft mentioned circumftance, this
feemed to have the preference; but as each of
them have their peculiar properties, and both
of them are preferable to any plough I have yet
feen, I fhall give a defcription of each, obferving, that if either of them is approved, it will
have the advantage of being defcribed by a certain
rule to wheelwrights, which is not the cafe with
any others, and is the reafon that they feldom
make two ploughs that go alike The firft is the
femi-cycloid, fee fig 7, plate XVII Let C E F D
be a flat board, having a ledge D F fitted to the

M m 4   bottom,

bottom, apply the wheel A B on the board to the ledge, and having fixed a pin to the edge of the wheel at the point A, move the wheel from B towards F, till it is turned half round, and then A will be at a, and the pin will have described the femi-cycloid or propofed figure A D a, which being turned upfide-down will be the true form of my plough from the point of the fhare to the throat.

The other is the half of a femi-ellipfis, of which the femi-conjugate diameter is fixteen inches, and the diftances of the focus's from the common center likewife fixteen inches, thus the figure is defcribed by a right angled triangle, whofe bafe is 32 inches, but as fome wheel-wrights may not be acquainted with the mechanical method of defcribing this figure, I fhall explain it in fig. 8, plate XVII Upon the indefinite right line A B, raife a perpendicular C D, and from the point D mark off with the compaffes fixteen inches at E, C, and F, at which points ftick in three pins and tye a ftring round them, then remove the pin at C, fix the point of the compaffes into the ftring, and defcribe the figure C G H round the two centers E F the one fourth part of the figure C G H turned upfide-down is what is required The lower part of this has as gentle an afcent as the other, and therefore enters the ground as eafily, and by rifing more fuddenly above the fhare it forms a fharper breaft, and by that means prevents any loofe mould hanging in the throat, which un-doubtedly is an advantage, efpecially when the ground is between wet and dry. But in lay ground, which is to be ploughed up for fowing, I fhould prefer the other, as it will not be fo liable to break the furrow, which fhould be carefully avoided, otherwife the grafs will be

harrowed

harrowed up and become prejudicial to the
crop Thus, as different foils will certainly
require a different form of the breaft, I fhall not
pretend to recommend either of thefe for general
ufe· what I propofe, is to give the wheelwright a
certain rule to work by, which will hold good
with every variation that may be required, either
on account of the foil, or fancy of the farmer.
This laft mechanical operation may be varied
in any manner he pleafes For example, if the
form of the breaft, fig 8, is too fteep, by extending the two centers E F to 17 inches diftance
on the tranfverfe diameter to I and K, letting
the perpendicular C D remain 16 inches, which
will be the pitch of the throat, the ftring fixed
round the triangle I C K, as explained before,
will defcribe the elliptical figure A C B, of which
the fourth part A L C is the form required, and
in this manner it may be varied by a certain
rule, which not only facilitates work, but produces an inftrument, which from its regular
form cannot caufe any obftruction in the free
paffage of the mould, which every plough I
have yet feen does, in fome part or other of the
breaft or mould-board.

These different fweeps regard only the land
fide of the plough· as to the form and fweep
of the mould-board, I confefs I have but very
lately been able to determine it by any rule that
can be laid down to a workman. My method
has been, to attend to the falling of the earth
when turned over by the breaft, and to form
the board to that curve, that it may eafily flide
over it without preffure, but, as I think I
have now difcovered a practical rule, by which a
plan of any form may be laid down on paper,
I fhall hereafter explain it, with drawings of
different

different sections of the mould-board, which I recommend for general use.

The bottom of the breast, where the buck of the share joins to the board, I make as broad as can be admitted of. This of course is very flat, which I think assists in raising the furrow, being continued in a gradual sweep to the heel of the board, which is not above half an inch wider than the fin of my share. I must here observe, that the bottom of my mould-board is an inch and an half from the bottom of the furrow, and as the upper part of the heel of the mould-board hangs over some inches, if the line of inclination was continued to the bottom of the furrow, it would not be wider than the fin of the share. In every other respect, my plough resembles the *Rotheram*, except indeed in the fin of the share, mine being much broader: the breadth of the fin of my plough, which is the size of the *Rotheram*, is full nine inches wide, and so in proportion to the size of the plough. This is contrary to the general practice, but I am convinced it is right, and speak, from experience.

My reason for trying the broad share was, that as the cohesion of the earth creates a much greater resistance than its weight does to the plough, I thought it fit to cut the whole furrow I wished to raise; whereas the narrow fin cuts only a part, and leaves the remainder to be torn up by the wrest of the plough. Some ploughmen think this last circumstance necessary in lay-land, and say, if the share cuts the whole furrow, it will slip away and be set on edge; which is certainly the fact, when the mould-board and body of the plough is badly constructed; but when the proper sweep of the board is observed, and care taken that the heel

of

of the plough is not too wide, I affert that the furrow will be turned over as flat as it is by those ploughs that only cut a part of the furrow, which laft circumftance is a confeffed fault, as a part of every furrow, fuppofe a fifth over the whole field, is left undifturbed, and is ftill of greater confequence in lay ground, which has acquired a degree of cohefion in proportion to the time it has been laid down to grafs. The objection of others, is, that in ftiff land the broad fin will fuck into the ground, or that the plough will ride upon the fin, and be thrown out of her work. I have proved the contrary to the conviction of my fervants But indeed I am very careful the fin does not hang down below the point of the fhare My rule is, that the point of the fhare, point of the fin, and heel of the land-fide, fhall all touch a level furface when the plough ftands upright, forming an arc from the point of the fhare to the heel at the bottom, and the fame on the land-fide See Plate XVII. Fig. 5 I do this becaufe the point and heel always wear the foonest, and confequently, without being hollowed, would foon become convex, after which the plough could not go fteadily For the fame reafon I am likewife careful to have the fhort fide of the buck of the fhare clear the ground by an inch, for if that ever touches the ground, it immediately throws the plough out

For the like reafon I alfo make the land-fide concave · and indeed by this form of the land-fide and bottom, I can fuppofe the friction is fomewhat diminifhed, for though friction will always be in proportion to the weight and velocity, whatever fpace the furface occupies, each part in contact bearing its fhare, and therefore as much when touching only in two points,

aa

as when touching on the whole, yet I imagine this can only hold good when the plane, on which the body is moved, is smooth and hard, but in the case of a plough moving through a body of earth, the stickage or adhesion of the earth to the plough, will be in proportion to the nature of the soil, and condition it is in as to being wet or dry, and therefore the friction be more or less, in proportion to the number of points in contact   There is also this additional reason, that the point of the share ought to tend a little into the land, because the draught of the horses is applied obliquely; especially when all the horses go in the furrow   and even when they go abreast, I have always found it necessary.   In the last case, the necessity of it appears to me to arise from the plough s not having so firm a resistance on the furrow side, which renders it liable to be thrown out of its work by the sudden jerk of a horse, and this would likewise be the case if the point of the share did not tend a little downward into the ground   In my opinion, the not ob- serving this rule is a fault in all the *Rotheram* ploughs I have seen, and the ploughman is obliged to rectify it by setting the coulter very much into land . but I think it is best, that the coulter should only just clear the land-side of the share; and I know by experience, when ploughs are made well, that is the only position they will work in   But it is impossible to lay down one general rule for the setting a coulter, either as to the vertical or horizontal angle· that must be left to the ploughman   For example. if the point of the share is not well hardened, it will in one day's work wear out of land, or out of depth · in the first case, the coulter must be set into land to keep the plough in the straight direction, as the tendency into land must coun-

teract

teract the oblique draft of the horfes · if the
point of the fhare has not depth enough, the
coulter fhould be fet backward and not too clofe
to the fhare, that the fhare may have more freedom to enter the ground if on the contrary, it
has too mu h depth, the coulter fhould be fet
forward, fometimes even before the point of the
fhare, and very low in this inftance the refiftance of the earth againft the coulter being before
the point of the fhare, it prevents its pitching
too deep this fhould likewife be done when
working in clay, for then the point will
always fuck into the ground , but when a plough
is perfectly well made, and working in ground
of moderate ftiffnefs, the coulter fhould be a
little above the point of the fhare, and juft clear
the land-fide.

The fwing-plough, when well conftructed, is a
very good inftrument but as it is liable to be
thrown out of its work by a flip of the ploughman's foot, which throws the greateft part of
his weight upon the handles, or by a jerk of
the horfes, which will elevate the point of the
fhare, it is an aukward tool to introduce into
countries where the men are not ufed to it
Therefore, where the land is dry enough to be
worked flat, which will admit of the wheel-
plough, I greatly prefer it, particularly when
neceffary to plough deep And I am of opinion
that the draught is at leaft as light, provided the
proportion of the fizes are nearly equal.

I make the form of the body of the wheel-
plough exactly the fame as that of the fwing-
plough, the only difference I make, is, that I
fet the point of the fhare more down, becaufe
now the beam becomes the moft effential lever,
which having a much fteadier fupport on the

4   frame

frame of the wheels, than it could poffibly have when hung to the traces of the horfe, the additional tendency of the plough into the ground, caufed by the dipping of the fhare, having the fteady and uniform fupport of the beam on the carriage, enables it to overcome the various obftructions in the ground, without the rifk of pitching in too deep, or of being thrown out of its work, which the fwing plough is fo liable to, when the different powers of the horfes and men lofe their equilibrium.

In this plough, the handles become a lever of the fecond kind, chiefly ufeful to lift the plough out of the ground at the ends of the lands, and in this inftance the handle and beam become one compound lever, the fulcrum being where the beam refts on the carriage If the point of the fhare be not fet deep enough, fo as to tend fufficiently into the ground, the bottom of the plough will not go on parallel to the bottom of the furrow, but will (as the farmer expreffes it) run upon her nofe. In this cafe the ploughman is obliged to throw his whole weight upon the handles, and yet this is often ineffectual; but when the point of the fhare has a fufficient tendency into the ground, the plough will go a confiderable length without holding. Here it is to be obferved, as in the foregoing inftance, that the ufe of the handles in the wheel plough is directly contrary to what it is in the fwing plough; for in the laft you raife the handles to give the point of the fhare more tendency into the ground, and prefs upon them to prize the fhare out of the ground, which fhews the neceffity of giving more depth to the point of the fhare of the wheel-plough, for, as in the fwing-plough, by raifing the handles, the inclination of the fhare

2   will

will have a greater tendency into the ground,
and that in the wheel-plough, as the beam is
supported by the carriage, the point of the share
is kept uniformly to the pitch it is set at, it is
evident that care must be taken to give it sufficient depth, if too much depth is given, that is
to be remedied by raising the beam, as will be
fully explained in its proper place. This evidently points out the utility of the carriage; and
the steady going may be accounted for, Plate
XVII. Fig 9. by the tendency of the plough
into the ground in the direction A C, being
balanced by the resistance of the carriage against
the beam (which is in the direction A B) to that
tendency; and these being equal, and in different
directions, it is plain that the progressive motion
of the plough must be in the direction A D. But
to explain this established fact by a familiar,
though trifling instance, I shall compare it to
the childrens play of shooting cherry stones, by
pressing them between their finger and thumb;
when those pressures are equal, being in different
directions, they will shoot them very straight,
otherwise they fly off obliquely· this must be
the same with the plough, for though the progressive motion of the plough is occasioned by
the draft of the horses, yet the resistance of the
earth on the share, and that of the frame against
the beam being in different directions and equal,
the progressive motion must be in a straight line
between those two powers of resistance.

Many people object to the wheel-plough,
as being heavier than the swing-plough. but
when we consider, that notwithstanding the
additional weight of the carriage, for which you
must likewise add a little more than a third part
for friction, in such a rough machine as this,

the

the whole being carried on wheels, the friction will be leffened in the ratio of the fquare of the diameter of the wheel, to the diameter of the axle. The weight of the earth upon the plough being in a great meafure fupported by the carriage, reafon plainly tells us, that the wheel-plough will be more eafily drawn than the fwing-plough, and experience has confirmed that it will. There appears alfo to be an additional advantage to the horfe,- which is, that the line of direction of the draught is not from his fhoulders to the point of the fhare, but through (or rather even with) the center of the wheel, which of courfe is not in fo oblique a direction, and confequently the advantage to the horfe will be in proportion to the length of the lever, or radius of the wheel. I do not mean, that the power of the lever has any influence or advantage in drawing the body of the plough, for that cannot be, becaufe neither B nor F in fig 10, plate XVII. have any greater progreffive velocity than the plough it-felf has; but only that its length is an advantage to the horfe, by making him draw more pa-rallel to the ground line, and makes a big wheel eafier to draw than a fmall one, that the friction in the wheel will be in proportion to the radius, and that the great wheel will furmount obftacles with more eafe than the little one

The carriage of the *Norfolk* plough feems preferable to all others, on account of its high wheels, the advantage of which I fhall endeavour to explain by fig. 10, plate XVII

Let A be the point where the power is ap-plied, that draws the wheel H C along the plane D C G, and B the center of the wheel, then D B A is the line of traction, which makes the angle of traction A D G. Now if we confider B C as a lever, whofe fulcrum, or centre of

motion

motion, is at C, the line of traction being obliquely applied to this lever at B, the drawing
power will be of no greater advantage, than if
the line of traction were applied at E to the
fhorter lever E C, to which it is perpendicular,
but if the fize of the wheel be increafed from
H C to that of I C, and the power continues to
act or pull at A, then F will be the center of
the wheel, and F A the line of traction, which
being perpendicular to the lever F C, the power
will act with the greateft force or advantage on
that lever, for drawing the wheel along the plane
D C G, both on account, of the greater length
of lever, and pulling at right angles to it. And
thus the effective power of the horfe will be as
much greater on the wheel I C, than on the
wheel H C, as the radius F C is longer than
E C. So that the higher the wheels are, the
more eafily they will be drawn, provided their
axes are equal, and below the level of the horfe's
fhoulder, when funk down by exerting himfelf
at the pull.

Though this eftablifhed fact may be fufficiently explained and underftood by many, yet by
others it may be deemed a mere *ipfe dixit*. And
as the conftruction of all wheel carriages and
rollers depends on the following propofition,
which, to the beft of my recollection, has never
been taken notice of in any book that treats on
inftruments of hufbandry, I hope it will not
appear improper, if I infert it here, with an
attempt to demonftrate it by a very familiar experiment on the fteelyards.

First, I fay, in a wheel moved along any
plane, a lever is to be found, whofe fulcrum or
center of motion is that point in the periphery
of the wheel, which is in immediate contact

with the plane, and if the line of direction of
the draught to the other end of the lever,
which is the center of the wheel, is not horizontal with the plane, it will form an angle of
traction, as in the present case, A D G, and the
power applied in the line D B A, to the long
lever C B, to which it is oblique, will be required to be as great as if it was applied to the
short lever E C, to which it is perpendicular,
in like manner, if the power was applied in the
horizon al line B K, the power required would be
as much less, than if applied in the oblique direction
D B A, as E C is shorter than C B, for in this
case the power drawing at right angles, will be
to the power drawing obliquely, as the sine
comp. of the angle of traction is to the radius,
and E C being perpendicular to B D, the hy-
pothenuse of the right angled triangle D C B,
the triangle B C E must be similar to B D C,
which is similar to A D G, because B C is parallel to A G

This I shall attempt to demonstrate by the
steelyard, that is, why the acting distance of a
power must be at right angles with the end of
the lever, and that whatever length the lever
is of, if the power is applied in an oblique line,
it will only act as a tangent to a circle, of which
the radius is at right angles with such line, but
as in the steelyards made for the use of families,
the center of motion is below the points of
suspension, and consequently will not remain
long enough in equilibrio to shew the experiment, I made one to explain this fact to my
wheeler, which has the center of motion immediately above the line, in which the points of
suspension are If the three points were exactly
in a line, equally proportionable weights would
suspend each other in any position of the beam.

I mention

mention thefe circumftances as a hirt to any one, who may chufe to try the experiment

Fig 11, plate XVII is the fteelyard I conftructed, having the beam A B 20 inches long, with the center of motion C, 4 inches from the point A, and 16 inches from B At the point A fufpend a weight W of 4 ounces, and at the point B, on the long arm C B, being four times as long as C A, hang the weight P, of one ounce, which will counterpoife the weight W, the beam will be horizontal, and the weight hang perpendicular to the beam. If you extend the beam four inches longer to D, and hang the weight P at D, it will overbalance the weight W, but if to the center C you fix the oblique arm C E, equal to C D, with the point E perpendicular to B, and hang the weight P at E, it will hang obliquely to the long arm C E, and have no more effect on the weight W, than if it hung on at B, the end of the fhort lever C B, to which it will hang perpendicular In like manner, if you hang the weight P at D, and bring the ftring over a pin at E, it will hang obliquely to both the long arms C D and C E, and have no more effect on the weight W, than if it hung on at B, to which it is perpendicular. Further, if you hang the weight P at B, and place the ftring over the pully F, the weight P, which fufpended W in equilibrio, when hanging perpendicular at B, will now, in the firft inftance, be no more effectual, than if pulling at G the end of the fhort lever C G, to which the line F B G is perpendicular, which will be as if the weight P was hung on the horizontal beam at H, as proved by the above propofition but the weight P hanging at H, not being fufficient to fufpend the weight W, the beam A C B will become a C b, to which the

line

line of direction of the power F b will be perpendicular. In this cafe, the exact proportions
of the weight will be preferved, the weight W
will hang obliquely to C a, perpendicular to K,
as P will hang obliquely to C b, perpendicular
to I, when C K will be to C I, as C A is to
C B. It is evident, to try this experiment, that the
fhort arm A C muft be made to counterpoife the
reft of the fteelyard, when no weights are hung
to either

This experiment plainly fhews, that in fig 10,
plate XVII. the power applied to the center of
the wheel H, in the direction B K, will be as
much more effectual, than when applied in the
oblique direction A B, as E O is fhorter than
B G, and therefore the power applied in the oblique direction A B D, to B C at the point B,
of no more effect than if applied to the fhort
lever E C, at the point E, to which it is perpendicular; confequently, as the power is by
fuppofition at A, and the line of traction A F
is parallel to the plane D C G, and at right angles with E C, perpendicular to the plane, it is
the moft advantageous line of direction of the
power, both on account of the application of
the power, and that the friction of the weight of the
wheel and carriage will be diminifhed, in proportion as the diameter of the wheel is to the
diameter of the axis, with this additional advantage in favour of the great wheel, that it will go
over clods and ftones, with much more eafe than
the fmall wheel, and not fink into cavities,
which would bury the fmall wheel However,
what has been proved above, is only ftrictly applicable to weights over pulhes; for, as the
power of the horfe does not folely confift in his
weight, but in the exertion of his mufcles, it
will be neceffary, that the line of traction fhould

2   incline

incline a little from his fhoulder to the ground, that he may have a firmer refiftance of the ground, to enable him to exert his mufcular ftrength.

This long digreffion from the defcription of the plough, which only was at firft intended, may be criticifed, but as a doctrine in favour of low wheels has lately found its way into the world, and as, in confequence of it, I have heard myfelf condemned by fome for the height of my wheels, and have been applied to by others for my opinion on the fubject, I thought it might not be improper to introduce it in this place, for the confideration of my brother far-mers indeed, the only apology I can make is, that I never found that this fubject was ever touched on, even in the flighteft manner, in any book that is likely to fall into their hands, otherwife it muft betray more than ftupidity, to offer to advance an explanation of a fact, that ftands felf-evident in the mind of every one the leaft converfant in mechanics

The beam of the wheel-plough feems to be as little underftood as that of the fwing-plough The reafon of its being raifed fo high in the *Norfolk* plough, may be accounted for by the height of the wheels but as I have feen the fame pitch of the beam applied to low wheels, I fhall endeavour to point out where n I think this laft method erroneous Firft, I lay down as fact, that the end of the beam, which refts on the bolfter of the carriage, muft be affected by the wheels, when they are put out of their per-pendicular pofition by clods of earth

Now, as the center of motion of the carriage is in a perpendicular from the end of the beam, between the wheels the higher the end of the beam is above the wheels, the larger the arc will be, which the end of the beam defcribes by

the

the wheels being put out of their perpendicular
position, and consequently the body of the
plough will be proportionably affected, that
is, the arc, described by the point of the share
on the horizontal plane, will be to the arc described by the end of the beam, as the length of
the bottom of the plough from point to heel, is
to the length from the end of the beam to the
heel, which is the common fulcrum. As to the
alteration on the vertical plane, it must be equal,
whether the beam is pitched high or low, only that
the ascent and descent of the point of the share will
be more gradual with high wheels, than low wheels.
Some think, that by pitching the beam so high,
the plough will go closer at heel, but the carriage acting, as a fixed perpendicular prop, will
support the beam equally steady at any height,
and if you describe a vertical arc, by the end
of the beam, the nearer it comes to a horizontal
position, the further that part, which rested on
the bolster, will go beyond the perpendicular
from the point whereon it rested, consequently,
if the frame be carried forward to that point of
the beam, the power will be applied nearer at
right angles at that point in the lever, and in
such proportion a less degree of power will be
sufficient to counteract the resistance, or in other
words, a less weight will be on the wheels
And therefore if the first application of the carriage was sufficient, a shorter beam will do, when
pitched nearer to a horizontal position, with
the additional advantage of the plough being
stronger, as the frame work is more compact.
To elucidate this more fully, I shall endeavour
to explain it by fig 12, plate XVII A B is the
high pitched beam, C the center of the wheel,
whose perpendicular frame supports the beam at
B, but as the beam or lever A B is oblique to
the

the prop C B, it acts with no greater power in supporting the weight, than the shorter beam A F, which is nearer at right angles with C F, but if the beam A D is described equal to A B and E, the center of the wheel of the carriage, which supports the beam at D, the prop E D will be nearer at right angles with the beam A D, which is equal to A B, and in that proportion the greater advantage of the lever is obtained. Thus it is evident, that in the beam A D the pressure is less on the center E, than it would be in the beam A B on the center C, consequently, if the weight is not too great at C, a shorter beam is sufficient in the direction A F

I have endeavoured to ascertain the angle which the beam ought to make with the horizontal plane, as likewise the angle which the point of the share ought to make with the same plane, but as the diversity of soil, and the different condition the same soil will be in from wetness renders it impossible to fix certain data, I found it impracticable, the only observation I have been able to make is, that when the end of the beam, that rests on the bolster, has been within ten inches of the axle of the wheels, if the point of the share tended sufficiently into the ground, the plough has gone as close at heel, as when the beam was mounted higher, and infinitely steadier, for the reasons before mentioned, therefore this must be determined by the height of the wheels, and by the different depths you wish to plough, if shallow, reason points out, that the beam need not be pitched so high, but if deep, allowance must be made for lowering the beam on the carriage The beam of my plough, which I frequently work 18 inches deep, makes an angle of 18 degrees with the horizon as to the dipping of the share, I

N n 4   fear

fear that muſt depend on the nature of the ſoil and judgement of the ploughman If the plough does not go cloſe at heel, and that this imperfection in the going of the plough is not occaſioned by the width of the heel of the mouldboard, which in that caſe will ride on the furrow, eſpecially in ſtrong land, you may depend on it, that the point of the ſhare is not ſet deep enough. Very little alteration will ſometimes produce the deſired effect, therefore it ſhould be done with caution, for if ſet too low, the beam muſt be raiſed on the bolſter of the carriage till the diagonal of the parallelogram compleated from the tendency of the ſhare, and poſition of the beam, becomes parallel to the horizon.

The only part of the wheel-plough, which now remains to be conſidered, is the chain, which faſtens the plough to the carriage In regard to the poſition of it, different countries have their different practice, they all indeed agree in this, that the end, which is made faſt to the carriage, ſhould be hooked on a little below the axle of the wheel, but the application of the other end of the chain, differs according to the cuſtom of the country, in ſome places they fix it round the near handle, immediately above or below the heel of the beam, others fix it over the beam, behind the head of the ſheath, and in ſome parts of *France* they uſe no chain, only have a wooden collar, which goes over the fore end of the beam, where it is confined by a wooden pin, which goes through the beam, and under the end of a piece of wood, which goes through the axle-tree of the wheels, to which it is likewiſe confined by a wooden pin. Now theſe three methods are as oppoſite as poſſible, yet when the plough is well conſtructed, I never could diſcover any difference ariſing from the different applica-

tion

tion of the draught, the firſt indeed evidently
ſeems beſt calculated for the ſtrength of the
plough, as the chain goes round the whole body
of it, but in this caſe, the chains are generally
laſhed up to the beam before the coulter There
are two reaſons for this, the one is, that in
ploughing deep, the chain hanging ſo low,
would prevent the mould from riſing, the other is
that, if the heel of the beam is pitched low, the
chain will incline upwards to the carriage, whereas,
I believe, it is proper that the chain ſhould have
this different direction, as it will draw the plough
into the ground, which tendency, as I have
explained before, will always have ſufficient
and ſteady reſiſtance in the carriage, againſt the
beam The *French* method is certainly bad,
nor could it produce the deſired effect, was it
not that their beam is exceſſive ſtout, not admitting of any elaſticity Cheapneſs is undoubtedly their motive, but it could not poſſibly anſwer in ſtrong work · for my own part,
I prefer the placing the chain over the beam
behind the ſheath but I uſe this precaution in my
large ploughs, I have a long link which goes
from the end of the chain on the beam round
the heel of the plough, immediately below the
heel of the beam, this confines the whole body
of the plough together, though the draught in
fact is from the top of the beam

As what I have ſaid above is in part to prove,
that the poſition of the beam cannot affect the
plough, in regard to its going cloſe at heel, I
ſhall juſt mention what I have proved to many,
which is, that unleſs a plough is narrow behind,
it cannot go cloſe at heel, but will ride on the
furrow, and that unleſs the point of the ſhare
has a ſufficient tendency into the ground, the
plough cannot go level at bottom

I have

I have already declared (what I believe will be allowed) that different soils and different operations, require different ploughs but as there are many farmers who cannot afford to have variety of ploughs, I shall venture to recommend one for general use, which seems to answer the several purposes much better than any I have yet constructed The constituent parts are put together in the manner of the *Rotheram* plough See plate XVIII fig 2 The shape of the breast, from the point of the share to the throat, is the arc of half a semi-ellipsis, whose semi-conjugate diameter is 16 inches, and the focus's at 17 inches distance from the common center See plate XVII Fig. 8. the outward sweep of which, A L C, is the above-mentioned form As to the form of the mould-board, I shall not dogmatically pronounce it the best that is, but as it is the best I have yet made, I shall venture to give the description of it, observing, that as I made it by the eye, and completed it in the field by attending to the ascent and delivery of the furrow, I took the dimensions of all the different curves, and laid them down on paper I shall describe the method by which I did it, not without hopes of its leading to a discovery of some easy practical rule for the use of workmen, who have at present no other guide but their eye, to form the sweep of a curved board, which is tedious, and consequently very expensive, and therefore I suppose the reason that the straight board is so much in use, having no other recommendation than cheapness.

Plate XVIII. represents the frame work, and dimensions of the different parts of the plough without the mould-board. A B is the beam, 6 feet long, having the under part of the two ends 14 inches from the ground line · C is the sheath,

7 inches

7 inches wide, where it is mortifed into the beam, it is 3 inches thick, and bevilled off in the breaft, from the land fide, to anfwer the curve of the mould-board the front of the fheath at C is 18 inches from A, and 16 inches perpendicular from the ground line   D is the near handle, into which the end of the beam is mortifed at A, it fhuts clofe at bottom to the hind part of the fheath, and is faftened to it by the wooden pin E, and fpikes at the bottom. F is a triangular piece of wood which fhuts on the lower part of the handle D, and is faftened to it by the pin G, and fpikes at bottom; this triangular piece makes the heel of the plough. H is the fhare, 18 inches long, from the point to the top of the buck P, having the fin Q 14 inches long, and 9 inches wide. This width is right in free land, but in ftony land it will require a point at the end, nor muft the fin be wide indeed fome lands are fo ftony as not to admit of any fin it goes on upon the end of the fheath, as in common ploughs it does on the chip, the land-fide is continued the whole length, and drops at the heel about ¼ of an inch below the triangular piece, this forms the arc at bottom, from the point of the fhare to the heel: it is faftened on by a fcrew-bolt, which goes through the triangular piece at I   The heel of the plough refts folely on the heel of the iron plate, without fuffering the wood to touch the ground; which, for the reafon given in page 540, muft diminifh the friction, but this indeed is more effectually accomplifhed by Mr. *Moore's* very ingenious thought, of placing the vertical wheel in the body of the plough, which ferves as the heel of the plough but in ftriking up the laft furrow of the land, I have experienced the advantage of the iron heel, as by its cutting into the ground it prevents the plough flipping away from her work.   K is the coulter, fixed in the

the beam with wedges 8 inches before the sheath
L is the off handle, to which the hind part of
the mould-board is fastened by the large wooden
pin M, which goes through the mould-board,
handle, and triangular piece at the heel   the
ends of both handles stand level when the plough
is upright, to render it difficult for the ploughmen to hold the plough over on the land-side.
The ends at N are 2 feet 9 inches from the
ground, and 4 feet 2 inches from the end of the
beam at A: the perpendicular from A is 6
inches behind the heel of the plough: from the
heel to the point is 3 feet. from the point of
the share to the bottom of the end of the beam
at B, is 2 feet 9 inches   O is the *Suffolk* copse
with the cat-head, as described in plate XVII. fig
1 and 2. R and S are too wooden pins which
fasten the breast of the mould-board to the
sheath.   T U two wooden pins that fasten the
tenon of the sheath into the beam.   The fram-
ing of this plough, which is the same as the *Rotheram*, appears much stronger than the common
one, and admirably well contrived to prize the
weight of earth on the share, without a possibility
of racking the tenons of the sheath and beam,
for you will observe that the handle which rests on
the triangular piece at the heel, prizes up the
lower end of the sheath on which the weight of
earth is; forcing it up to the beam, and thus,
by lifting the beam, prevents the tenon, which
is mortised into the handle, from being strained,
whereas, in the common plough they are always
pulling asunder, requiring a false coulter and
tuck to keep the beam and chip together, and
as this plough requires none, it shews how much
stronger the construction is,

Plate XIX. represents the compleat body of
the plough, the horizontal lines on the mould-
board, marked *aaaaa*, are square, with parallel
lines

the beam with wedges 8 inches before the fheath
L is the off handle, to which the hind part of
the mould-board is faftened by the large wooden
pin M, which goes through the mould-board,
handle, and triangular piece at the heel the
ends of both handles ftand level when the plough
is upright, to render it difficult for the ploughmen to hold the plough over on the land-fide
The ends at N are 2 feet 9 inches from the
ground, and 4 feet 2 inches from the end of the
beam at A: the perpendicular from A is 6
inches behind the heel of the plough from the
heel to the point is 3 feet from the point of
the fhare to the bottom of the end of the beam
at B, is 2 feet 9 inches O is the *Suffolk* copfe
with the cat-head, as defcribed in plate XVII. fig
1 and 2. R and S are too wooden pins which
faften the breaft of the mould-board to the
fheath. T U two wooden pins that faften the
tenon of the fheath into the beam. The fram-
ing of this plough, which is the fame as the *Rotheram*, appears much ftronger than the common
one, and admirably well contrived to prize the
weight of earth on the fhare, without a poffibility
of racking the tenons of the fheath and beam,
for you will obferve that the handle which refts on
the triangular piece at the heel, prizes up the
lower end of the fheath on which the weight of
earth is, forcing it up to the beam, and thus,
by lifting the beam, prevents the tenon, which
is mortifed into the handle, from being ftrained,
whereas, in the common plough they are always
pulling afunder, requiring a falfe coulter and
tuck to keep the beam and chip together; and
as this plough requires none, it fhews how much
ftronger the conftruction is,

Plate XIX. reprefents the compleat body of
the plough, the horizontal lines on the mould-
board, marked *aaaaa*, are fquare, with parallel
lines

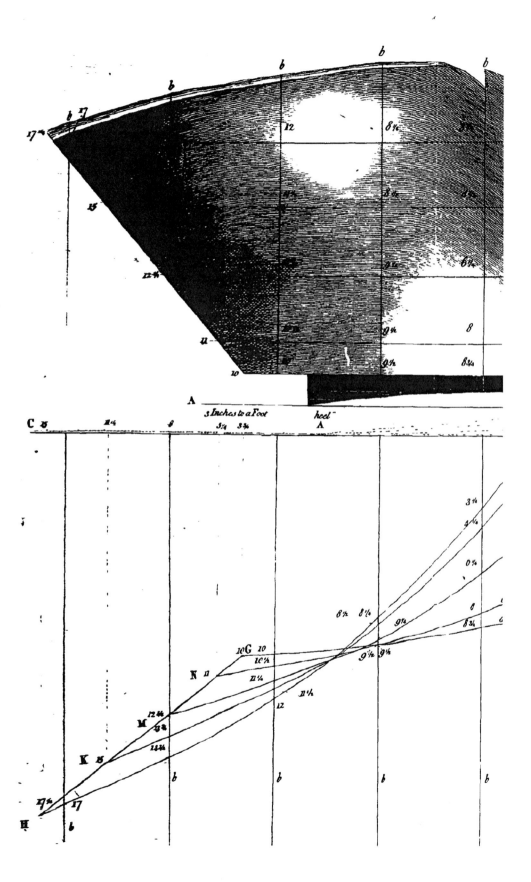

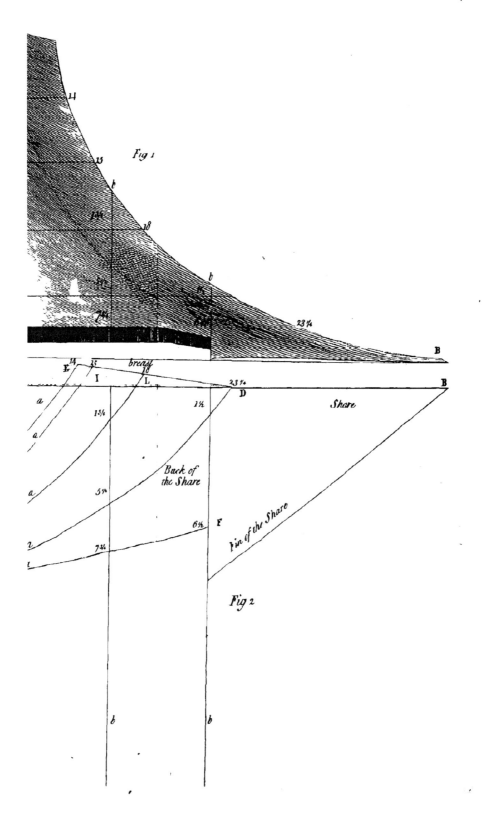

Fig 1

Fig 2

lines on the land fide of the plough, which are all 3 inches afunder, except the under one, which is only 1 ½ inch, from the fecond being 1 ½ inch clear of the bottom of the furrow. as, in this, I differ with many, fhall give my reafon, which is, that when the plough is working in land that cuts up whole furrow; if the bottom of the board, or ground-wreft, touches the furrow that is turned over, it muft prefs it in at bottom, which will naturally make it fall back again at top, or at leaft fet it on edge, and, if in loofe mould, by fqueezing in the bottom, the upper mould muft fall back into the furrow, having no bafe to fupport it my rule is, that the heel of the board fhall juft flide againft the furrow, without difplacing it from the form it fell in

The perpendicular lines *bbbbbbb* are fquare, with parallel lines on the land-fide, which are 6 inches afunder where the lines interfect, I took the dimenfions of the thicknefs with callipers, as marked on the boards which correfpond with the marks in Plate XIX. fig. 2. which reprefents the perpendicular, or bird's-eye view of the mould-board. the curved lines *aaaaa* in this figure, correfpond with the horizontal lines, and the perpendicular lines *bbbbbbb*, with the perpendiculars. where thefe lines interfect, the figures fhew the diftance from the line A B, which is fuppofed to be the land-fide of the plough: thefe correfpond with the dimenfions taken by the callipers, as marked on the upright board; they are both drawn to one fcale, of 3 inches to the foot. As it is neceffary that the breaft of the plough fhould hang over a little to the land-fide, I was obliged to raife a perpendicular board, fquare with a line drawn from the point to the heel: by this means I was enabled to fix the callipers, taking off the difference of the

thicknefs

thickneſs of the board from each meaſurement

I have been the more prolix in the deſcription of theſe figures, being unwilling to omit any circumſtance which might explain them, as, at leaſt, it is a certain and eaſy method for a wheelwright to take the exact dimenſions of any plough he is ordered to copy, and by making moulds from the curved lines in Plate XIX. fig 2. and applying them (according to the following directions) to the mould-board, when hewed out to near the ſhape, he will eaſily bring it to the required form

Let A B be a line drawn from the heel of the plough to the point of the ſhare ; extend the line from A, 15 inches to C : and at D, 23 ¼ inches diſtance from A, raiſe the line D E, which repreſents the hanging over of the breaſt of the mould-board on the land-ſide, making an angle of about 83 degrees with the plane of the horizon. Then place the mould of the lowermoſt curved line, to the angle of the buck and fin of the ſhare at F ; which is 6 ½ inches diſtance from the vertical plane of the line A B ; and 10 inches diſtance from the ſame plane at G, extending 3 ¼ inches beyond the upright ſquare of the heel A. The end of the mould at G, muſt be 1 ½ inch from the ground, but at F it will be but about an inch and a quarter, riſing gradually to the end of the buck, as repreſented in Plate XIX. You muſt then apply the uppermoſt mould at E, which is 12 inches perpendicular from the ground, and 14 inches from the perpendicular of the heel A. The mould-board muſt then be worked with the ſpoke ſhave, till the other end of the mould, when held quite horizontal, will touch at H, which is likewiſe, of courſe, 12 inches from the ground, and 17 ½ inches from C, on the vertical plane of C A B, extending 15 inches beyond the ſquare of the heel A. Theſe two curves being fitted, cut off

the

the heel of the mould-board in the line G H. You then proceed to fit the moulds I K, L M, and D N, dropping each curve 3 inches perpendicular, when the curve D N will be 3 inches from the ground, but only 1 $\frac{1}{2}$ inch from F G. This was done to take the moſt curves, where the greateſt twiſt of the board is required

With the above deſcription and drawing, my wheelwright has made exact copies of this plough, without having the original plough to work by. I therefore flatter myſelf it will be ſufficiently explanatory for the uſe of workmen —My mould-board, indeed, riſes about two inches higher, but as theſe were the only curves requiſite for turning the furrow, I thought it needleſs to inſert more lines, which the workman may do at his pleaſure; having the ſweep of the breaſt F D, and the heel of the board G H, for his direction There is likewiſe this farther advantage, that by varying the ſweep of the curved lines in Plate XIX fig 2 a workman may lay down any ſhape he thinks proper, and be certain his work will anſwer the drawing As I mentioned that this plough performed the work much better than any I had made, I muſt remark one particular circumſtance, which is, that all the curved lines nearly interſect each other in the center of the board. This was merely accidental, having formed the board entirely by eye, but may ſerve as a hint, and probably will prove, that their meeting exactly in the center, is the proper form for turning the furrow. I have reaſon to believe this was ſo; having worked the board ſome time without plates, till I found it to my mind probably it may have been worked a day or two too long, and by that means be hollowed out a little too much in the middle of the board.

I ſhall conclude, by obſerving that a plough may be made of any dimenſions, by the drawing

4

of Plate XIX. fig 2 If it is required to be fmaller, viz. of 2 feet 6 inches at the bottom, and the reft in proportion, the only alteration neceffary to be obferved is, to confider the fcale as of 3 ¾ of an inch to the foot, inftead of 3 inches if, on the contrary, it is required to be larger, viz. 4 feet long, and the whole in that proportion, the fcale muft be then confidered as being of 2 ¼ inches to the foot, inftead of 3 inches.

Ravenfbury,
Oct. 2, 1770.

On this very fenfible and truly practical effay on the conftruction of a plough, I fhall only obferve, that its utility muft be apparent to the moft fuperficial obferver. Of what confequence is it to form one perfect plough, if you have no rules by which to execute another?

The following are the particulars of this gentleman's farm.

297 Acres in all	12 Labourers
26 Grafs	3 Boys
171 Arable	37 Acres wheat
£.200 Rent	18 Oats
13 Horfes	17 Beans
6 Cows	80 Madder
300 Sheep	10 Turnips
4 Young cattle	5 Cabbages
40 Swine	13 Fallow.
1 Man	

END of the SECOND VOLUME.

Lightning Source UK Ltd.
Milton Keynes UK
177797UK00007B/103/P